Universities and the Occult Rituals of the Corporate World

Universities and the Occult Rituals of the Corporate World explores the metaphorical parallels between corporatised, market-oriented universities and aspects of the occult. In the process, the book shows that the forms of mystery, mythmaking and ritual now common in restructured institutions of higher education stem from their new power structures and procedures and the economic and socio-political factors that have generated them.

Wood argues that universities have acquired occult aspects, as the beliefs and practices underpinning present-day market-driven academic discourse and practice weave spells of corporate potency, invoking the bewildering magic of the market and the arcane mysteries of capitalism, thriving on equivocation and evasion. Making particular reference to South African universities, the book demonstrates the ways in which apparently rational features of contemporary Western and Westernised societies have acquired occult aspects. It also includes discussion of higher education institutions in other countries where neoliberal economic agendas are influential, such as the UK, the US, the eurozone states and Australia.

Providing a unique and thought-provoking look at the impact of the marketisation of higher education, this book will be essential reading for academics, researchers and postgraduate students engaged in the study of higher education, educational policy and neoliberalism. It should also be of great interest to academics in the fields of anthropology, folklore and cultural studies, as well as economics and management.

Felicity Wood is employed by the University of Fort Hare, South Africa. Her area of research interest is the way contemporary Western and Westernised societies partake of aspects of mystery, ritual and magic, especially in economic and socio-political contexts and the present-day workplace.

Routledge Research in Higher Education

Narrative, Identity, and Academic Community in Higher Education
Edited by Brian Attebery, John Gribas, Mark K. McBeth, Paul Sivitz, Kandi Turley-Ames

Learning Community Experience in Higher Education
High-Impact Practice for Student Retention
Susan Mary Paige, Amitra Wall, Joe Marren, Amy Rockwell, and Brian Dubenion

Academics Engaging with Student Writing
Working at the Higher Education Textface
Jackie Tuck

Professional Education at Historically Black Colleges and Universities
Past Trends and Outcomes
Edited by Tiffany Fontaine Boykin, Adriel A. Hilton, and Robert T. Palmer

Articulating Asia in Japanese Higher Education
Policy, Partnership and Mobility
Jeremy Breaden

Global Mobility and Higher Learning
Anatoly V. Oleksiyenko

Universities and the Occult Rituals of the Corporate World
Higher Education and Metaphorical Parallels with Myth and Magic
Felicity Wood

Developing Transformative Spaces in Higher Education
Learning to Transgress
Sue Jackson

For more information about this series, please visit: www.routledge.com/Routledge-Research-in-Higher-Education/book-series/RRHE

Universities and the Occult Rituals of the Corporate World

Higher Education and Metaphorical Parallels with Myth and Magic

Felicity Wood

LONDON AND NEW YORK

First published 2018
by Routledge
2 Park Square, Milton Park, Abingdon, Oxon OX14 4RN

and by Routledge
711 Third Avenue, New York, NY 10017

Routledge is an imprint of the Taylor & Francis Group, an informa business

© 2018 Felicity Wood

The right of Felicity Wood to be identified as author of this work has been asserted by her in accordance with sections 77 and 78 of the Copyright, Designs and Patents Act 1988.

All rights reserved. No part of this book may be reprinted or reproduced or utilised in any form or by any electronic, mechanical, or other means, now known or hereafter invented, including photocopying and recording, or in any information storage or retrieval system, without permission in writing from the publishers.

Trademark notice: Product or corporate names may be trademarks or registered trademarks, and are used only for identification and explanation without intent to infringe.

British Library Cataloguing-in-Publication Data
A catalogue record for this book is available from the British Library

Library of Congress Cataloging-in-Publication Data
A catalog record for this book has been requested

ISBN: 978-1-138-30711-7 (hbk)
ISBN: 978-1-315-14222-7 (ebk)

Typeset in Galliard
by Apex CoVantage, LLC

These metaphysics of magicians,
And necromantic books are heavenly! . . .
O what a world of profit and delight,
Of power, of honour, of omnipotence
Is promised to the studious artisan!

    Christopher Marlowe, *Dr Faustus*

Contents

Acknowledgements viii

Introduction 1
1 The magic of the market 21
2 Setting the scene 42
3 Corporate simulacra 57
4 A climate of fear 74
5 Rituals, talismans and templates 92
6 Performance and ritual 108
7 Kinship, collegiality and witchcraft 125
8 Secrecy, publicity, confusion and power 142
9 The zombies of corporate academia 153
10 Sacrifices and suffering 161
11 Smoke and mirrors and wind money 177
12 Conclusion: breaking the spell 188

Bibliography 197
Index 212

Acknowledgements

A number of points contained in this study originally appeared in *The Extraordinary Khotso: Millionaire Medicine Man of Lusikisiki* (with Michael Lewis, 2007); in a chapter in *Vernacular Worlds, Cosmopolitan Imagination*, ed. Stephanos Stephanides and Stavros Karayanni (2014a); and in articles in *Prometheus: Critical Studies in Innovation* (2010a), the *Southern African Journal for Folklore Studies* (2015b, 2013, 2010b), *Tydskrif* (2014b) and *Folklore* (2015a). Details are provided in the references.

Mathew Blatchford contributed a great deal, providing insights, information and inspiration and offering ongoing guidance.

I am grateful to Geoff Wood, who discussed this research with me, suggesting issues worth exploring and making me aware of valuable sources of information.

I owe much to my student researchers at the University of Fort Hare, Wendy Muswaka and Abbey Alao, who assisted me in my research into wealth-giving beings in southern Africa and Nigeria between 2008 to 2010. I am indebted to Sylvia Tloti, who worked with me for years as my Research Assistant, for her contribution to my research into the figure of the *mamlambo* and South African occult economies.

The National Research Foundation and the University of Fort Hare provided funding for much of the research on which this book draws.

Introduction

In today's globalised world, many professional domains have been invaded and pervaded by forms of corporate capitalism, including the sphere of higher education. In countries in which forms of market-driven capitalism hold sway, numerous universities have sought to imitate the ways of the corporate sphere. In the process, however, they have become sites of the occult. For our purposes, the term *occult* is used to denote shadowy, sometimes perilous forms of magic and mysterious, esoteric knowledge that may call to mind aspects of the supernatural. As universities have been converted into corporatised institutions under new forms of managerial governance with pseudo-executive qualities, they have become alien academic landscapes. When viewed from a metaphorical perspective, it is as if they have become characterised by forms of ritual, mythmaking and enchantment, inhabited by otherworldly presences and presided over by invisible occult forces. The beliefs and practices underpinning present-day market-oriented academic discourse and practice weave spells of corporate potency, invoking the bedazzling, hazardous magic of the market and the arcane mysteries of capitalism, thriving on equivocation and evasion all the while.[1]

In a report on current conditions in UK universities, UK academics Francis Greene, Brendan Loughridge and Tom Wilson observed that the contemporary university has changed from a "Platonic academy" to a "commercial mall" (1996). This concept can be expanded on, for many universities have mutated from institutions traditionally viewed as temples of learning initiating novices into esoteric arts into emporia peddling snake oil, in the form of dubious corporate and managerial magic purported to bestow efficiency, prosperity and accountability. In their attempts to become centres of corporate excellence, many academic institutions have become more arcane and sinister and may seem increasingly reliant on ritual, myths, mysticism and magic. Both locally and globally, current market-oriented academic discourse and procedure has come to represent a dimension of that which Peter Pels describes as "the magic of modernity . . . those enchantments that are produced by practices culturally specific to modern states, economies and societies" (2003: 5).

The term *university* is used loosely and broadly to denote present-day market-oriented institutions of higher education that have re-created themselves as pseudo-corporate enterprises, emulating the jargon, ethos and practices of the business world, while favouring neoliberal economic approaches that promote privatisation, rationalisation, consumerism, commodification and competition. The term *corporate university* also denotes institutions of this kind.[2]

The managerial hierarchies that promulgate, implement and enforce the previously mentioned changes tend to be characterised by their market-oriented ethos. Jenny Ozga, a UK academic, describes this style of managerialism as "a transmission system" enabling neoliberal economic approaches to permeate institutions of higher education (2011: 143). The term *managerialism* denotes this particular system of governance.[3] Meanwhile, when applied to contemporary contexts, *capitalism* generally signifies corporate capitalist practices that favour the previously listed neoliberal economic strategies.

The current nature of university policy and practice calls to mind aspects of the occult, as this study will show. Indeed, the changes that have taken place in higher education from the latter part of the twentieth century onwards are interconnected with the occult, generating new developments in this sphere as well. Innovation, Jean Comaroff maintains, often occurs "in situations of radical structural cleavage – such as result from conquest, proletarianization or the sudden sharpening of contradictions within the hierarchical orders" (1985: 253). The corporate restructuring of present-day higher education, combined with the imposition of internal and external market-driven managerial systems of command and control, has brought about new hierarchies and heightened existing divisions and disparities within institutions of higher education while also generating new disjunctures and contradictions. These developments have given rise to novel forms of mystery and enchantment in present-day universities, while bestowing new dimensions on long-standing aspects of the occult. This study does not deal with worldviews and cultural practices that draw on the supernatural in any conscious, deliberate way. The strange, magical qualities with which current academic processes and activities have become imbued exist in metaphorical form, and some have their sources in the farthest reaches of the imagination or the depths of the human psyche.

Various mystical, magical, ritual-like aspects of corporatised, managerially governed academic environments have certain symbolic parallels with elements of the South African supernatural. Although they do not form part of all South Africans' worldviews, they have a pervasive quality and have become part of this country's cultural, imaginative and psychic landscape. However, cosmologies that incorporate unseen, otherworldly forces and presences are by no means a peculiarly African phenomenon. As will become apparent, various traditional and modern forms of mystery and enchantment prevalent in Western societies manifest themselves, albeit if only metaphorically, in the market-oriented university context. While this casts light on certain "kindred beliefs about the world's workings" (Moore and Sanders, 2001: 10), the diverse African and Western forms of mythmaking and magic that form the focal points of the following chapters highlight the fact that occult beliefs and practices are varied, heterogeneous and mutable, shaped by – and embodying – the particular dynamics of their diverse milieus.

Certain features of various African belief systems are pertinent here. In many traditional cosmologies, aspects of which permeate various widely accepted contemporary worldviews on this continent, both the visible and the invisible form dimensions of actuality (see for instance Nyamnjoh, 2001: 29, 47). Therefore, as Achille Mbembe maintains, in terms of those epistemologies in which the seen and unseen are interconnected, it follows that an examination of the former may necessitate an exploration of the latter, while a study of the latter may enhance our understanding of the former (1997: 152–153). Certainly, aspects of the occult can cast light on the nature and effect of the forces driving corporatisation and managerialism in contemporary higher education. Thus when various corporate concepts, procedures and discourses as well as forms of authority that are prevalent in restructured, corporatised universities today are perceived as occult practices, they acquire a functionality and significance that they would otherwise lack.

This study does not attempt to undertake a comprehensive investigation of marketisation and managerialism at universities worldwide or even in the specific South African context. Instead, it isolates those features of corporatised, managerially governed universities that partake of aspects of the occult, exploring the way in which they manifest themselves in South African academia and in higher education systems in those countries where various significant parallels exist. Those procedures and discourses of the corporatised academy that have strange, invisible aspects are focused on, and the ways in which they serve as agencies for mysterious workings of power are explored. An investigation of these opaque and unseen aspects of contemporary academia will illuminate the visible: the nature and functioning of universities in their contemporary socio-economic and political contexts and the forms of power they impose, reinforce and to which they submit. In this way, the study of specific forms of magic, mythmaking and ritual can direct our gaze back to society, illuminating the socio-political, economic and cultural dynamics from which specific beliefs and practices arise, and within which they are embedded. As Pels notes, studies of the occult have the potential to draw our attention to "the practices and power relationships in which these things that we tend to call magic (or label with related terms) are caught up" (2003: 16).

Indeed, it will become apparent that the magical, mystical dimensions of current academia can be related to the new power structures and procedures that have arisen within universities and, more broadly, to the political and economic trends that have given rise to them. To varying degrees and in various respects, institutions of higher education in this country and numerous universities elsewhere have become subjugated to free-market capitalist pressures, the globalised systems of economic influence and control to which these are connected and the neoliberal economic ideologies that have informed them. Like occult forces, these political and economic dynamics may seem omnipresent, sometimes making their presence felt and directing events in mysterious, unseen ways.

The otherworldly aspects of contemporary academia are also focused on for other related reasons. Certain socio-economic and political factors and various combinations of circumstances can create a climate within which metaphorical parallels with features of the occult may not seem out of place. The conditions that can bring this about may include deep-seated changes, with new opportunities for advancement, combined with ever-increasing possibilities for decline, misfortune and calamity; widespread competitiveness and envy; an unequal distribution of power and material resources; and the uncertainties, instabilities and tensions that may stem from such phenomena. To a certain extent and to varying degrees, these conditions have come to characterise many present-day managerialised, market-driven universities. As will become apparent, these circumstances have given rise to an environment that may seem to partake of forms of ritual, mystery and magic.[4] As this suggests, the mysterious nature of the occult and the complexities of the human mind may sometimes become interconnected. Thus, in exploring the otherworldly dimensions of present-day higher education, we venture into the hidden terrain of the psyche and the imagination, examining the toll that the corporatisation and commodification of intellectual activity exact on these.

Before proceeding any further, it is worth bearing in mind that we should guard against a false nostalgia for an idealised academic past. In former days, many universities tended to be characterised by various forms of cronyism, exclusion, rivalry and malice, and all too often, university managerial structures served the interests of the ruling elite. However, the changes wrought by corporatisation and market-oriented managerialism have bestowed new disturbing dimensions on the present-day university milieu. Thus, let us concern ourselves with contemporary conditions, rather than seeking to revive that which never truly existed.

The corporate restructuring of higher education has long been the subject of much research, both in South Africa and elsewhere. As Irish academic Steve Hedley remarks, "[t]he history of any conflict is written by the victors, or so it is often said. Yet when we consider the struggles over the management of universities in recent decades, the truth may be the converse" (2010: 1). This book, however, seeks to cast a new light on the market-oriented refashioning of higher education by analysing it from a fresh perspective.

The occult aspects of present-day universities have many dimensions. First, there is faith in the magic of the market on the part of those external authorities who preside over institutions of higher education and within universities themselves. Beset as they often tend to be with financial constraints, diverse external pressures and threats to their continued survival, many institutions and those within them are often led to believe that their salvation is linked to market-oriented transformation. The forms of mythmaking, mystery and enchantment that stem from this faith in the extraordinary efficacy of the market lie at the heart of this book. Further to this, capitalism itself has mysterious, magical aspects, and these have given rise to some of the occult qualities that many restructured universities have acquired, subjugated as they are to free-market capitalist forces. The ritualistic imitations of the power relations, procedures and policies, tokens and trappings of the corporate sector and the ritual-like invocations of corporate jargon are connected to this, since these may seem to offer a means of drawing on some of the potency believed to emanate from corporate capitalism. The talismanic importance attached to templates and the interconnectedness of performance and ritual also constitute elements of such practices. Then, as a corollary, there is the magic that has been vested in the new managerial chains of command. Indeed, it is if they are equipped with a special capacity to bring about the transmutation of institutions of higher education into lower organs of the body corporate. This may stem from the notion that since present-day university managerialism often tends to be so permeated by the patterns, processes and patois of the globalised corporate world and so overlaid with its patina that it partakes of its magic and is able to work enchantments on its behalf.

The extent to which many universities have reconstructed themselves as corporate simulacra will be explored, as will the mystical, magical aspects of this process. As one feature of this, various myths underpinning the market-driven restructuring that has permeated many systems of higher education worldwide will be examined. These include the myth of the knowledge economy, the notion that commercial enterprises and institutions of higher education are essentially one and the same, and the fabulatory construct viewed as the "real world" within which restructured universities are said to be located. A related issue is worth considering. Those beliefs and practices that have been termed "cargo cults" ritually imitate distinctive Western symbols and practices, seeking to bring about the sought-after "cargo", which may sometimes take the form of Western affluence and power. Comparably, market-oriented universities emulate the ways of the corporate world in a ritual-like manner in attempts to draw closer to the potency and wealth associated with this domain.

Meanwhile, there are visitations of workers of magic, known as consultants, which tend to take place frequently and at considerable cost, on account of their association – or purported association – with the corporate sector. For this reason, consultants are often imported to offer guidance in the corporatisation of higher education. As is the case in many spiritual persuasions, in which agents of redemption offer those who seek their wisdom access to insight and enlightenment, consultants are often imported to instruct academic neophytes in the ways of corporatised academia, as are various other institutional emissaries, including Quality Assurance and Teaching and Learning Centre personnel. As we will see, however, various agents of redemption, both mystical and market-oriented, cannot always be trusted.

All the while, there is the extent to which the climate of fear prevalent at many corporatised universities has become comparable to a terror of unseen occult forces and presences in its depth and intensity. As we will see, this has heightened recourse to ritual-like activities as a form of security and guidance, a potential remedy or, at least, a panacea, among much else. As one component of this, there is the long-standing relationship between ritual and performance and the extent to which this finds expression in the mechanisms of performance management and appraisal that now loom large in the lives of many university employees. There are also the webs of mystery and secrecy that consolidate the control of the power structures, both external and internal, that hold sway over present-day universities. Although the new wave of managerialism that has swept through higher education may seem to have little in common with the supernatural, certain occult aspects of contemporary corporatised universities stem from and are reinforced by these present-day systems of command and control.

Then there are also the otherworldly forces and presences which, metaphorically speaking, might be said to have a place in the corporatised university environment. For instance, when viewed from certain symbolic perspectives, it is as if corporate academia has become the dark domain of the witch. Indeed, there are some striking metaphorical parallels between specific features of witchcraft and particular facets of the restructured university milieu. Next, the corporatised university environment has distinctive non-human inhabitants. Certain supernatural beings such as malign wealth-giving spirits and zombies might be deemed appropriate denizens of market-oriented academia. These, predator and victim, controller and controlled, cast light on aspects of many present-day institutions of higher education and on the positions of those who inhabit them. Moreover, there are the various paradoxes, equivocations and disjunctures that tend to characterise corporatised universities which, as will become apparent, have caused aspects of the occult to flourish. The ways in which market-driven restructuring and corporate managerialism have brought about contradictions, dissonance and instabilities of this kind will brought to the fore. These and various other metaphorical parallels with the occult will unfold in the following chapters. In conclusion, we will consider whether it is possible for universities and those within them to break free from the occult enchantments within which they are ensnared.

Occult economies

As we will see, the contemporary restructured universities that have taken on the procedures and practices of the corporate capitalist workplace have entered a hazardous realm, within which potentially damaging forces, both mercantile and metaphorically magical, hold sway at both seen and unseen levels. One form of modern magic that has particular bearing on the nature and functioning of corporatised, market-oriented universities is that which Jean and John Comaroff term occult economies: those practices and enterprises believed to generate wealth by shadowy, seemingly magical means (1999: 284, 279–281). In terms of the way in which they combine magic and money, occult economies constitute part of a broader phenomenon in the African supernatural, which the Comaroffs describe as the "dark magicalities of modernity" (1993: xxx). Rosalind Shaw comments on a feature of this phenomenon when she alludes to the "shadow economies" in postcolonial Sierra Leone (2001: 66). Moreover, making particular reference to the Cameroon, Peter Geschiere draws attention to the sinister aspects of this new form of moneymaking magic, describing it as "the new witchcraft of wealth" (1997: 158). The problematic aspects of the term *witchcraft* should be acknowledged. As Geschiere notes, the word carries with it a strong sense of moral condemnation. Furthermore, translating various local African terms as *witchcraft* can be reductive and misleading, since the original notions may be complex and ambiguous, possessing a diversity of meanings. Notwithstanding this, the term is utilised here, since *witchcraft* is widely used in diverse African communities, in other parts of the world and by various anthropologists (Geschiere, 1997: 12–15; see also for instance Moore and Sanders, 2001: 3).

Many occult economies are now thriving in Africa and elsewhere, fuelled by the hope that affluence might be miraculously and swiftly attainable through mysterious, extraordinarily potent agencies. This diversity of occult economies, among much else, is suggestive of the extent to which many magical beliefs and practices in Africa have become interconnected with perceptions of economic dynamics. However, as it has already been indicated, contemporary magicalities of this kind are by no means exclusive to this continent. Instead, they lie at the heart of Western and Westernised societies, surrounding that within which power is often vested and to which deep significance is often attached.

The Comaroffs apply the term *occult economies* to a range of shady wealth-generating enterprises which dabble in hazardous magic or have strange, mysterious aspects "that evoke, often parody and sometimes contort the mechanisms of the 'free' market" (1999: 286). These include the ownership of zombies; pacts with the *mamlambo*: a dangerous wealth-giving spirit; involvement in obscure, dubious ventures that promise to produce extraordinary profits almost by magic, such as pyramid schemes, chain letters and national lotteries; and the *muti* trade in human body parts (1999: 281).[5] While the Comaroffs focus on African examples of occult economies, enterprises of this kind also occur in Western societies in certain forms, as some of the preceding examples indicate. Certainly, the idea that money can be generated swiftly and almost magically by exceptional, often mysterious means is a widely cherished conviction. The Comaroffs, however, neglect to mention universities in their discussion of occult economies. Indeed, the current corporate university could be viewed as an occult economy.

Definitions and qualifications

Certain explanations and qualifications are worth noting, as the parameters of this study are set. Particular reference is made to South African universities in which market-oriented restructuring has taken place, although mention is also made of institutions elsewhere, in countries in which neoliberal economic agendas exercise a powerful sway, such as the US, the eurozone states, Australia and the UK. Indeed, as neoliberal economic approaches have become increasingly influential internationally from the 1980s onwards, many institutions of higher education in diverse parts of the world where free-market capitalist pressures are prevalent have sought to resemble business enterprises. Although both local and global dynamics affect the higher education systems in different countries in a range of ways, certain areas of commonality may occur, as forms of market-oriented capitalism extend their influence internationally, furthered by the process of globalisation. A number of important points of comparison exist globally, and to varying degrees and in various respects, present-day corporatised universities tend to have certain key features in common.

For example, while South African institutions were being remade as profit-oriented enterprises, this process was significantly shaped by international neoliberal trends. Particular countries whose systems of higher education have been substantially reconfigured in accordance with these have proved influential. Thus, South African universities looked northwards in the course of their institutional restructuring, drawing on market-driven academic models and systems of pseudo-corporate managerialism that began evolving in the UK and the US, and in Australia in the 1980s and 1990s (see for instance Webster and Mosoetsa, 2001: 7–9; Vale, 2009: 1, 4; Stewart, 2007: 135–136).

The changes in South African higher education were substantially influenced, for instance, by the restructuring of universities in the UK that took place first under the Conservative and then the New Labour governments, as a dimension of the process of the public sector "reforms".[6] There are thus some important parallels between South African universities and those in the UK, so particular attention is paid to institutions in that country.[7] For present-day South African universities, the UK experience serves not only as a looking glass but also a crystal ball of a kind. Many of the pressures experienced by South African universities have already been felt in the UK, and the current situations in higher education institutions in both these countries are comparable in some significant respects.

Another important factor that has helped determine the nature and purpose of present-day higher education in South Africa and elsewhere has been the commercialisation of higher education in the United States from the 1970s onwards. Indeed, both locally and internationally, the notion that higher education could be converted into a marketable commodity owes much to the US's example. Andrew Nash describes the way in which the restructuring of South African universities after the political transition was particularly driven by an attempt to remodel this country's system of higher education in the image of the commercialised American university (2006: 6). Colin Bundy, former vice-chancellor of the University of the Witwatersrand during this period, concurs with this in various respects (1999; cited in Webster and Mosoetsa, 2001: 7). Furthermore, UK academic Stefan Collini describes how many universities in the UK have sought to seem more like institutions in the US – "or at least some imagined version of them". This tendency, he observes, also applies to many other systems of higher education elsewhere (2012: 25).

In the course of their institutional remodelling, South African universities also turned to Australian institutions for guidance, subjugated as many of these tended to be to managerial and state control. For instance, Raimond Gaita (1998) points out that Australian universities advised South Africa's National Council for Higher Education (NCHE) and assisted in the drafting of their white paper on higher education (Bertelsen, 1998: 139; see also Louw, 2010: 2; Ramphele, 2008: 3). Moreover, drawing on her own recollections of her period as vice-chancellor of the University of Cape Town from 1994 to 2000, during the restructuring of the institution, Mamphela Ramphele commends the example set by Australian universities, observing that "education is one of Australia's fastest-growing export sectors" (2008: 203). Consequently, certain features of present-day Australian higher education illuminate some of the consequences of corporatisation and managerialism in South Africa and elsewhere.

Nonetheless, it is worth bearing in mind that the market-oriented restructuring of higher education has taken place to greater or lesser degrees and in diverse ways, depending on the extent to which various countries have subjected themselves to neoliberal economic pressures, and the ways in which their particular institutions of higher education have responded to them. This process is also shaped by the specific natures of those institutions themselves and by the perceptions of those internal and external authorities who preside over them. National and regional economic and socio-political dynamics may come into play here, as may institutional prestige and financial status and even the vagaries of senior managerial styles of governance.

Diversity, discrepancies and similarities

Consequently, both locally and internationally, corporatisation and managerialism may vary in degree and intensity on account of a variety of factors. Aspects of mystery and enchantment in institutions of higher education may vary accordingly, shaped as these are by the specific exigencies of the particular contexts within which diverse universities operate, and the variety of tensions and upheavals to which different institutions are exposed.

For example, although there are certain important parallels between aspects of higher education in diverse African states, subject as they often tend to be to many comparable pressures, the heterogeneity and multiplicity that characterise the many countries on this continent should be borne in mind. Diverse distinctions also manifest themselves in South Africa. For instance, despite the changes that have taken place after this country's political transition, marked contrasts still prevail between historically advantaged institutions (HAIs), previously termed historically white institutions (HWIs), such the University of Cape Town, the University of the Witwatersrand, Rhodes University and the University of Stellenbosch; and many of the historically disadvantaged institutions (HDIs), formerly known as historically black institutions (HBIs), including the University of Limpopo, the University of Venda and University of Fort Hare. The HAIs (some of which are highly ranked) and the HDIs still tend to be characterised by contrasts in status, infrastructural, financial and material resources.

Some similar imbalances manifest themselves elsewhere. For instance, in the UK, there are marked distinctions between the Russell Group of universities, centres of status and privilege, which receive two-thirds of the country's research funding, and various other universities relegated to subordinate positions on the national institutional hierarchy. In the USA, there is an ever-widening gap between the elite universities, such as Harvard (sometimes described as "a hedge fund with a university attached to it"), Yale, Stanford and Princeton and many other, more economically beleaguered institutions. In 2014, the endowments of these latter three universities amounted to $23.9 billion, $21.4 billion and $21 billion, respectively (Weissmann, 2015). Such distinctions are reinforced by institutional rankings and league tables. Then, both locally and internationally there are many differences not only between institutions but also internally, between various university divisions and academic disciplines, such as the Humanities and Science and Commerce. While institutions of higher education may take diverse forms, the term "university" has been applied to very different types of establishments, some of which will now be mentioned.

At one end of the spectrum there is that which tends to be termed the corporate university. This type of establishment is not to be confused with the restructured, pseudo-corporate institutions of higher education examined in this study. For our purposes, therefore, the term *corporate university* denotes this latter type of institution. On the other hand, the establishments linked to big corporations, such as McDonald's, Disney, Motorola, Telkom and Toyota, offer company-related training to employees. By this means, the company in question seeks to build or maintain organisational effectiveness and productivity, retain experienced employees and remain economically competitive. For instance, McDonald's Hamburger University offers job-specific training to McDonald's employees, while Disney University provides training for Disney personnel, in order to ensure that "every employee is properly introduced to the company and understands the importance of the brand: Disney values, Disney history and Disney traditions" (Lipp, 2013). As this statement indicates, "universities" of this kind highlight the importance of corporate loyalty and valorise the culture of the specific organisation to which they are attached. They may also strive to create the impression that the corporation in question has a long-standing history with long-established traditions. Thus, it is implied, staff members should deem it an honour to belong to the company concerned. Symbolically speaking, then, the ultimate aim of these establishments is to imprint the parent company's specific corporate brand on employees by means of vocationally focused education of this kind.

These self-styled corporate "universities" have certain key features in common with corporate institutions of higher education. In both cases, knowledge is perceived primarily in terms of financial criteria. In the Hamburger University and other similar establishments, training is provided for the monetary benefit of a particular company. Similarly, education is commodified in corporate academia, becoming a potential source of profit for universities and those who control them (and sometimes for specific employees themselves). Moreover, when envisaged as the knowledge economy, higher education is believed to enhance a country's economic well-being. Next, vocationally oriented instruction tends to be foregrounded in corporate academic curricula, as is the concept of economic competitiveness. Further to this, the notion of corporate branding has frequently taken hold in institutional discourse and culture, while much importance is attached to the concept of corporate loyalty. Subsequent chapters discuss the implications of this.

Numerous universities worldwide are state-funded public universities. On the other hand, private universities may receive funding from specific bodies, organisations or institutions, or they may be private-for-profit establishments. Some private universities may be reputable institutions funded by outside entities, such as Stanford University, one of the most highly ranked universities in the US, and Princeton, another high-status institution. On the other hand, some private-for-profit universities may be dubious operations, driven by a desire to make money, and with minimal interest in teaching and research.[8]

Nonetheless, while the diversity within present-day institutions of higher education must be acknowledged, this study does not examine the distinctions between different types of universities; neither does it seek to investigate the varying degrees of marketisation and market-oriented managerialism at institutions of higher education in South Africa and elsewhere. Instead, it focuses on those areas of commonality that illuminate its central concerns: those features of corporatisation and managerial governance in contemporary corporatised universities that partake of aspects of ritual, myth, mystery and magic. As a backdrop to this, the myths, mysticalities and enchantments within which some of the core components of contemporary capitalism are steeped are also explored.

At this point, the question may arise: why focus specifically on universities in a study of this nature? This particular exploration of the occult aspects of present-day corporatised institutions of higher education is appropriate, on account of the specific nature of universities themselves. Although higher education has evolved new otherworldly features in the last few decades, universities have long been associated with mysticism and enchantment.

The occult academy

Although many of the mysterious, magical aspects of present-day academic discourse and procedure stem from the corporate sector, universities lend themselves especially to associations with the occult on account of their specific nature. First of all, they offer a select few novices instruction in esoteric wisdom, some of which may appear obscure and arcane to outsiders. The longer the initiation into the mysteries of academia, the more possible it is that some initiates may emerge seeming like beings set apart from those around them, inhabitants of a remote, rarefied realm. Knowledge itself has had a mystical quality, for in Western cultural and intellectual life, the sense lingered over the centuries that there was almost something sacred about knowledge, venerated as Sophia, the incarnation of wisdom, and nurtured and protected in holy places, in the times when the monasteries were centres of learning in Western society, with monks as their custodians.

Traditionally, universities have had many other occult elements. For instance, they specialise in mystic hierarchies of their own, with their high priests, priestesses and holy men. There is, too, the arcane brotherhood and sisterhood of academic collegiality: once envisaged as a freemasonry of intellectual life, as separate and unique as a religious cult on account of a shared devotion to the mysteries of higher learning. This concept of collegiality has further occult dimensions, in that the influential individuals within various collegial structures could sometimes be perceived as magi of a sort, deriving their expertise and authority from mysterious agencies. In part, a status of this kind may relate to the degree to which specific individuals have access to areas of recondite wisdom, acquired through years of intensive instruction and immersion in esoteric areas of scholarship. Accordingly, certain skilled occult practitioners have drawn on the discourse of academia, as if sensing that it can be used to suggest rare and profound knowledge. For instance, Geschiere describes how Cameroonian *nganga* (workers of magic) make reference to their "professors" who instructed them in their art (2003: 166).

The mystical, unfathomable aspects of the concept of academic expertise have been distinctive features of academia from its earliest days. Small wonder, then, that present-day academics – along with other specialised practitioners, including traditional herbalists and workers of magic – still tend to emphasise the esoteric nature of their work to highlight the exceptional nature of their knowledge, accessible only to a privileged few. Later on, these points of comparison are considered in more depth. Even if only at a subliminal level, a strategy of this nature draws on the ancient belief that wisdom acquired by specially chosen individuals as a result of an intensive process of private instruction is too rare and valuable to share with outsiders. For instance, in *Sundiata*, the thirteenth-century oral epic from Mali, the *griot* (oral poet) narrating this legend makes reference to the way in which he learned his craft, concluding with these words: "I was able to see and understand what my masters were teaching me, but between their hands I took an oath to teach only what is to be taught and conceal what is to be kept concealed" (Niane: 1965: 84).

Within occult practices, as in academia and various other professional domains, the power of mystification plays an important role. This strategy has long been utilised to enhance the status of various expert practitioners in the eyes of the public, increasing the influence that they are able to wield over those around them and making it harder for their authority to be challenged. Over the centuries, for example, members of the Western medical profession have often tended to preserve a distance between themselves and their patients, divulging only limited, sometimes complicated pieces of information about the nature of their ailments, highlighting their own superior wisdom and their clients' relative ignorance in the process. Then, certain traditional herbalists, diviners and workers of magic have tended to veil much of their work in mystery in order to emphasise the rare and special nature of their knowledge.[9] This tendency has long formed a feature of academia for similar reasons. Accordingly, for instance, research findings may be encased in jargon so dense that it can become almost impossible for a non-academic outsider to penetrate them. Techniques of this nature also form a feature of the present-day corporatised university milieu, on account of the new uses to which such stratagems can be put, as we will see later on.

One of the foremost areas in which the occult mysteries of universities manifest themselves are in the time-honoured rituals of academia. Over the centuries, universities have revolved around the regular enactment of ritualistic procedures that are fundamental to their nature and function. Some of the most distinctive of these are the classic rites of passage that take the form of graduation ceremonies. Such events are steeped in pomp and protocol, requiring the donning of ceremonial regalia, followed by ritual invocations, performances and traditional songs. Then, when each of the initiates reaches the climactic moment of the ceremony, symbolic objects are formally bestowed on them, marking their passage from novice to one well versed in their chosen art. The event is presided over by the high priests of academia, with serried ranks of academic priestesses and priests in attendance, and a host of spectators seated beneath them.

Various ceremonial gatherings mark the stages of the academic year, commencing with the annual university opening ceremony. A number of other observances follow, including the quarterly Senate and Faculty Board meetings. The extent to which gatherings of this nature are characterised by ritualistic features is indicative of the special significance traditionally accorded to them. These convocations may take place in specially designated chambers often adorned with images of former high priests (symbolically speaking) and entail lengthy ceremonial proceedings which may sometimes seem to resemble ritual ordeals of a kind. At Senate meetings, as in other areas of academia, the use of Latinate terminology bestows an aura of ritual solemnity and high importance on the proceedings or the personages in question. Then, the annual or biennial academic storytelling circles, otherwise known as conferences, also have certain ritualistic features. For instance, they entail a series of presentations, often laden with professional jargon and wreathed in intellectual complexities that might seem arcane to many outsiders. At times, perhaps, it might almost seem as if conference participants are members of mysterious societies with cryptic discursive codes of their own. For conference participants, these ritualistic aspects of their gatherings may have a reassuring quality, partly on account of the regularity with which they take place and the customary patterns and procedures to which they tend to adhere. Next, the invocations of the names of the current high priests and priestesses of their discipline, accompanied by recourse to elements of their wisdom, draws on the security of the familiar and well established, thereby confirming and consolidating it. Moreover, conference presentations may also intensify the ritual-like nature of the proceedings precisely because of the way in which they may seem to lay claim to profundity while courting obscurity.

Various other rites constitute integral features of university life, but above all there are the ritual ordeals. Of all the activities that take place at universities, one particular set of procedures tends to loom larger than any other in many minds and can linger so long in the memories of those who undergo them that they can feature in their nightmares for decades thereafter. The dreaded event of examinations has ritualistic features in terms of the regularity with which it is performed, the stringent formalities to which the participants and those presiding over them are required to adhere, and also on account of the fact that this practice is a regular enactment of a long-established tradition that has struck fear into many hearts over the centuries.

As well as fulfilling certain practical functions, the dread that exams arouse represents an important part of their ritualistic nature. If a ritual instils a degree of apprehensiveness or even fear, this can ensure that the specific authorities ordaining it and the establishment to which it connected are taken seriously. Moreover, as with other, very different kinds of ritual ordeals, those who participate in examinations are put to the test in more ways than one. As in various other ritualised endurance tests, candidates are not only required to display inner resources of fortitude and forbearance, but they are also expected to carry out rigorous preparation for the trials they will undergo. These require long periods of deep concentration, while focusing intently on the task at hand. Other academic traditions that also involve ordeals of a kind, such as the viva examinations undergone by various postgraduate students, and the first lectures and conference papers delivered by members of staff newly embarked on their academic careers may be characterised by similar qualities.

However, ritual can be double-edged. Certain academic ritual-like activities, including those involving a degree of fear, such as examinations, can serve to enforce compliance and control. Indeed, the Comaroffs point out that ritual is unpredictable and ambiguous, sometimes proving liberatory and constructive while taking on reactionary qualities on other occasions (1993: xxix–xxx). This latter aspect characterises a whole new range of rituals that have come to the fore in managerially governed, corporatised universities, many of which are intended to instil acquiescence. A number of these are also designed to inspire dread. The nature of these rites and the function of the fear that they arouse will be explored further in due course.

As all these previously outlined aspects of mysticism and magic indicate, universities have long had a mystique of their own, with veiled, obscure, sometimes questionable qualities. But in today's corporatised academic climate, in which such mysteries are required to be money-spinners, the occult aspects of academia have intensified, as subsequent chapters show.

Academic limitations, institutional transformation

But in order to investigate the present, we return to the past. It is worth noting that the links between the shadowy side of the supernatural and academia are not a purely contemporary phenomenon. For instance, Christopher Marlowe's version of the story of Dr Faustus provides an example of the long-standing link between the world of the intellect and sinister occult practices. Faustus, a graduate of Wittenberg University, calls up the forces of darkness to further his own intellectual ends. As the story of Faustus reminds us, academia has long had a shady side, for universities were by no means idyllic places in the past. Ideally, academic collegiality could foster productive, supportive working relationships, yet in its less-than-ideal form, it was often characterised by cronyism, elitism, jealousy and scheming. Moreover, many temples of academic wisdom could seem like the relics of former days, clinging to various outmoded, even reactionary practices. Indeed, it could sometimes become stuffy in the ivory tower.

Prior to the process of institutional restructuring, far-reaching changes were certainly needed in numerous universities worldwide, in order to enable them to transcend their many shortcomings. For one thing various longstanding features of academia seemed ill-suited to their contemporary contexts. There was, for example, the extent to which many of the power structures in traditional institutions of higher education tended to be parochial and patriarchal. Moreover, numerous universities fostered a sense of elitism, setting institutions and those within them above and apart from the society around them. In a previous century, for instance, this state of affairs was depicted in Thomas Hardy's *Jude the Obscure* (1896). Jude Fawley, a stonemason yearning for a university education, attempts to become a student but is unable to do so on account of his working-class background. Although Hardy employed this scenario to indulge in his predilection for gloom and disaster, plunging Jude and his family into depths of extraordinary suffering (even by the standards of one of his own novels), *Jude* illustrates some of the failings of traditional universities. The novel depicts the prejudice, arrogance and exclusivity that characterised academia in Hardy's day and thereafter, and which more recent writers, including Kingsley Amis, David Lodge and Malcolm Bradbury have satirised.

In 2014, Michael Crow, president of Arizona State University, drew attention to other, related shortcomings of old-style universities: their tendency to cling to outdated, reactionary ideas and approaches. He contended that, as globalisation intensifies and globalised societies become increasingly complex, universities needed to keep pace with these changes, and therefore the restructuring of institutions of higher education was essential. Crow also maintained that universities should be innovative, constructing that which is needed in contemporary society, instead of imitating previous, outdated models and approaches that "replicate what has existed before". Such views have been echoed by many others in senior managerial positions in many institutions in diverse parts of the world. In the same year, for instance, Alwyn Louw, the president of Monash University, South Africa, stated that numerous higher learning institutions in this country and elsewhere are trapped in the past and a "massive transformation and significant paradigm shift are non-negotiable" (2014: 27). This imprecise and somewhat generalised terminology obscures more than it discloses. (Later on, it will become apparent that this tends to be a characteristic feature of senior managerial discourse.)

Nonetheless, bearing in mind the limitations of traditional academia, some of the previously cited points may seem pertinent. Certainly, to a greater or lesser extent, many of the universities of former days tended to cling to various hidebound approaches, reflected for instance, in features of their syllabi, their teaching techniques, their research priorities and their racial, gender and class-based biases. However, as subsequent chapters will indicate, many of the previously-delineated shortcomings of traditional academia have persisted in corporatised institutions of higher education, manifesting themselves in unexpected ways and taking on new forms. For instance, the nature and consequences of the sweeping changes to which both Crow and Louw allude are elided.

Crow went on to make another seemingly relevant point, maintaining that universities should "embrace their cultural, socioeconomic and physical setting". This high-sounding sentiment is reflected in some of the key documentation generated by corporatised institutions of higher education, including those in the UK, the US and South Africa. For example, university mission statements, strategic plans and sundry promotional material tend to highlight the way in which a specific institution forms part of a wider social milieu. Such documents often describe how the life of the university in question and that of the surrounding community are interconnected and that one of the institution's principal aims is to serve the needs of the society in which it is located. Thus, many corporatised universities depict social relevance and community outreach as some of their priorities, emphasising that their academic activities stem from and relate to their specific socio-cultural and economic contexts, and contribute to the greater good of the societies of which they form a part.

For example, the University of the Witwatersrand, a South African HAI, juxtaposes academic prowess and social responsibility in its mission statement, describing itself as "a gateway to research engagement and intellectual achievement in Africa", while depicting social engagement as one of its core values (2017). Likewise, the University of Cape Town, also an HAI, describes itself "as a place that is 'owned' by all its staff and students, and by the community" (2017). Such declarations form part of a broader trend. For instance, the 2015–2020 Strategic Plan of the London Metropolitan University describes how students are transformed into "effective, engaged citizens who will contribute to . . . building a better, fairer society". Similar sentiments are expressed in the University of Michigan's mission statement, which maintains that the institution develops "leaders and citizens who will challenge the present and enrich the future". Meanwhile, the mission statement of Columbia University in New York City emphasises the significance of its social context, stating that it strives to relate its teaching and research to the mighty city in which it is located, while the University of Chicago draws attention to the way in which the university forms an important part of its urban environment, playing a valuable role within it.[10]

In the previously-cited extracts and in many other university mission statements, strategic plans, promotional material and other similar documentation, institutional restructuring and social transformation seem to be interconnected. This may create the impression that numerous restructured, market-oriented universities in diverse countries are seeking to become more integrated into the societies and communities in which they are situated, thereby striving to transcend the elitism and solipsism that often tended to be perceived as cardinal features of many academic institutions in the past. However, as subsequent chapters show, the discourse, policies and procedures at many present-day institutions of higher education emanate from and reinforce ideologies and systems of influence and control that benefit the socio-economic elite rather than the societies and communities they purport to serve. It will also become apparent that certain sinister, shadowy aspects of the supernatural cast light on various destructive tendencies, imbalances and inequities in the corporatised university milieu.

Indeed, the emphasis on community involvement in many university mission statements often tends to stem from the business world, drawing on the concept of corporate social responsibility: a corporation's professed commitment to social and environmental well-being. Often, however, such altruistic sentiments amount to forms of corporate public relations and have little or no impact on the communities around them. There is always a risk that some universities' ostensible commitment to community development and social awareness may resemble this in various respects, as subsequent chapters will indicate. Moreover, the alliances between academia and state security agencies, military bodies and multinational corporations are considered later on. It will become evident that various forms of socio-cultural and scientific research, some of which might be depicted as socially relevant and developmental, focusing on specific societies and communities, including those close at hand, may have damaging effects on those societies and the individuals within them. For example, such research may further the agendas of various power players in the state, the armed forces and the corporate world who would be liable to advance their own interests at the cost of those of others. Furthermore, we will see how many corporatised universities tend to inculcate conformity and submission to those in positions of authority. Thus, the students and staff at such institutions are required to comply with, rather than challenge the status quo. In the light of this, any professions of institutional commitment to critical thinking (such as those expressed in the previously cited extract from the University of Michigan's mission statement) need to be carefully assessed.

Universities in South Africa have been hedged in by particular limitations of their own. Under the old political dispensation, they embodied much of the racial and economic stratification in South African society. All too often, they served to reinforce these divisions as well. Certainly, many South African universities have long been in need of transformation in order to bring about redress and equity, so many local academics welcomed the overhaul that began taking place in higher education from the 1990s onwards. A magic of a kind has lent force to this process of organisational change: the conviction that market-driven university restructuring would bring about an almost miraculous transformation within institutions of higher education, enabling them to transcend their elitist, conservative aspects, and that diverse benisons and benefits would follow in its wake. However, in 1998, Eve Bertelsen discussed the contradictory dynamics at work within the South African higher education milieu, warning that although universities were beginning to redress the injustices and inequities caused by apartheid, they would have to confront forces that operated in favour of a privileged elite, with an agenda that would undermine democratic, egalitarian principles (134–135).

A number of the changes that took place in South African higher education after the political transition in 1994 did have far-reaching implications for teaching and research at specific institutions and were depicted as seismic. Yet, subsequent chapters indicate that some of these alterations would ultimately tend towards the cosmetic as a result of the external forces shaping them. This would become increasingly evident when institutional emphases began shifting, and institutional gazes became directed less towards South Africa and more towards the globalised forms of economic power and control beyond it. Consequently, too, various proclaimed commitments to redress, equity and access began fulfilling the function of window dressing, partially obscuring the corporate mall beyond the glass.

Although managerial systems have changed, as have many academic environments in South Africa and elsewhere, subsequent chapters describe how new forms of manipulation, coercion, partisanship and prejudice have arisen both locally and internationally, and various degrees of power and privilege have persisted, perpetuating imbalances of the past. It is also worth noting that Crow's previously cited comments appeared on a World Bank blog. Indeed, the type of institutional restructuring that he favours operates in their interests. Moreover, Crow was formerly a CIA agent, and the morally problematic aspects of the alliance among universities, the military and state intelligence agencies are considered later on (Giroux, 2007: 20). Further to this, it has become evident that during the course of that which has often been depicted as a radical transformation process, South African universities have succumbed to neoliberal economic approaches that promise profits that come at a price. Diverse universities in other countries in which similar economic agendas are prevalent now experience comparable predicaments. The nature and implications of this subjugation to market-oriented capitalist imperatives unfold in the following chapters.

Universities have undergone a restructuring process that has altered not only their structures and procedures but also their discourses and values. Both locally and internationally, many universities are caught up in the currents of globalised neoliberalism and subjected to new economic and political coercions and constraints, while the promises and pressures of free-market capitalism hold sway as never before. For these and other reasons, universities have put themselves at the mercy of free-market capitalism, having wedded themselves to market forces in the hope that this will bring about economic and institutional security. Nowadays, universities are hawking their wares in the local and global marketplaces as part of the knowledge economy, engaged in knowledge production. However, as we will see, universities have not cast aside their esoteric, mysterious aspects. Instead, they have become more reliant on ritual, mysticism and magic than ever before. To a significant extent, this development can be related to the fact that universities have entered the marketplace, which is an occult site in certain respects.

In order to explore the reasons why a situation of this nature has come into being, let us first turn to the market itself, and the spell it seems to have cast over present-day academia. The market lures many to it, universities included, in Africa and internationally. Higher education has become drawn into the marketplace as a result of a process of coercion, seduction and entrapment, and it remains bound to the market for these reasons. The ascendancy of market forces in the university environment is reflected, for example, in the titles of numerous books and articles describing the ways in which market-oriented strategies have reshaped many universities locally, regionally and worldwide. A few such works include Howard Buchbinder's study, "The Market Oriented University" (1993), which discusses the extent to which market-driven models have come to characterise Canadian higher education, although, as Buchbinder observes, his points are applicable to universities in Europe and elsewhere (335). Guy Neave (1990) corroborates this in an article titled "On Preparing for Markets", which depicts trends in Western European higher education. Meanwhile, Mahmood Mamdani's *Scholars in the Marketplace* (2007) examines the impact of neoliberal university "reforms" in Uganda, and in a similarly titled work, *Universities in the Marketplace* (2003), Derek Bok depicts the marketisation of universities in the US. Many academics from South Africa, the UK, the US and a range of other countries discuss similar concerns (see for instance Gudeman, 1998; Olssen and Peters, 2005; Parker and Jary, 1995).

As some of the preceding points suggest, one particularly powerful factor has been shaping the current nature and direction of higher education worldwide, and one steeped especially deeply in the realms of the occult: the magic of the market.

Notes

1. Ideas and information drawn from these parts of the following sources have been developed further, combined with new material and included on pages 1–3, 6–8 and page 20 of this Introduction:

    Wood, F. 2010a. Occult Innovations in Higher Education: Corporate Magic and the Mysteries of Managerialism. *Prometheus: Critical Studies in Innovation* 28 (3): 227–228, 239–240.
    Wood, F. 2010b. Sorcery in the Academy. *Southern African Journal for Folklore Studies* 1: 1–2.
    Wood, F. 2015a. Spirits in the Marketplace: The Market as a site of the Occult in the South and West African Supernatural and in Contemporary Capitalist Cosmologies. *Folklore* 126 (3): 295–296.
    Wood, F. 2014a. Wealth-giving Mermaid Women and the Malign Magic of the Market: Contemporary Oral Accounts of the South African Mamlambo. In Stephanos Stephanides and Stavros Karayanni (eds). *Vernacular Worlds, Cosmopolitan Imagination*. Amsterdam. Brill Cross/Cultures Series: 60–61.

2. While acknowledging that *corporatisation* can have various meanings, Australian academic Margaret Thornton utilises the word to indicate "the application of business practices to public institutions to make them more like private corporations" (2004: 163). "Corporate university" denotes universities where this tendency is prevalent. It is also worth bearing in mind that this term has been applied to very different types of establishments. Numerous corporations, including McDonald's, Toyota and Disney, have set up institutions designed to provide on-the-job training to employees, which tend to be described as corporate universities. For instance, McDonald's employees may attend the Hamburger University. However, in this book *corporate university* denotes institutions of higher education that have been refashioned to resemble corporate enterprises.

3. Irish academic Steve Hedley describes several distinctive features of managerialism in contemporary market-oriented university environments. Although senior managerial staff maintain stringent control over their institutions, they and the universities over which they preside are subject to systems of managerial authority emanating from the state, the corporate world and other external bodies. For instance, the value of teaching and research is determined by means of external criteria, and the status of a managerially governed university is determined by outside reviewers. Within institutions, power is centred on those near the pinnacle of the managerial hierarchy, while individual employees and those in middle managerial positions, such as heads of departments, tend to be disempowered. For instance, the principal duties of heads of department often entail carrying out the commands issued by those above them in the institutional hierarchy, and ensuring that their departmental colleagues comply with these and other edicts (2010: 119–120).

4. A word of caution follows. The danger of reductionist, instrumentalist approaches to the complex sphere of the occult should be borne in mind, and perceptions and practices relating to this area should not be viewed purely as the products of, or expressive of tensions and instabilities. As Isak Niehaus (2001a: 10 – 11) and Peter Geschiere (1997: 281) point out in their South African– and Cameroon-based

research, inclinations towards the occult cannot be explained away in terms of their socio-political and economic contexts. Instead, they possess a significance and power of their own, as culturally shaped worldviews that have become charged with meaning, offering individuals and communities ways of apprehending and responding to the contexts they inhabit. Moreover, in its elusive, mysterious qualities, the occult can resist easy explanation and categorisation. Nonetheless, some of the factors that are said to be conducive to the growth of mystical, magical perceptions and practices are worth bearing in mind. The ways in which the changes, tensions and upheavals that have taken place in local and international institutions of higher education during the last few decades have, metaphorically speaking, brought aspects of the occult to the fore will be discussed in subsequent chapters.

5 Italics are used the first time a word from another language is mentioned. Thereafter the word is not italicised. Some of these terms have become part of South African English, since no concise, appropriate English translations exist. The Comaroffs' study has certain limitations, in that it adopts somewhat too homogenous a view of beliefs in the supernatural and socio-political dynamics in Africa. It also foregrounds the workings of economic forces, while downplaying the mystical, magical aspects of occult economies. Yet, as anthropologists such as Niehaus concede, their argument is significant, "despite the overt economism of their claims" (2001b: 203). Indeed, their article has exercised a considerable influence over subsequent ethnographic studies in this area.

6 The "modernisation" of the public sector evolved between 1979 (when Thatcher's government assumed power) and 1997, as a key element of Conservative government policy. This continued, along very much the same lines, under New Labour (see for instance Dibben and James, 2007: 1–3; Shore and Wright, 1999: 561).

7 In Desmond Ryan's discussion of what he depicts as the "Thatcher government's assault on higher education", many parallels between Thatcherite education policies and South African universities' experiences become apparent (1998: 3–32). Various local writers and researchers have drawn attention to this, including Roger Southall and Julian Cobbing (2001: 16) and Peter Vale (2009). Among much else, the theories driving the corporatisation of universities in both these countries were heavily based on the Thatcherite contention that the principal purpose of higher education was to serve the needs of the country's economy (Vale, 2009: 1, 4).

8 For instance, the Independente University and the Internacional University in Portugal were closed on these grounds in 2007 and 2009, respectively.

9 For example, a near-legendary South African *inyanga* (medicine man), Khotso Sethuntsa (1898–1972), advanced himself in his career and sought to emphasise his expertise in the otherworldly by means of mystification of this kind. As a later chapter indicates, other practitioners of magic make use of similar strategies.

10 These statements are derived from the following sources:

London Metropolitan University: Strategic Plan 2015–2020. www.londonmet.ac.uk/about/our-university/strategic-plan-2015-2020. Accessed on 19 June 2017.

University of Michigan: Mission Statement. https://president.umich.edu/about/mission. Accessed on 12 July 2017.

Columbia University in the City of New York: Mission Statement. www.columbia.edu/content/mission-statement.html. Accessed on 12 July 2017.

University of Chicago: the Office of the President. https://president.uchicago.edu. Accessed on 12 July 2017.

Vision and Mission Statement. University of the Witwatersrand. www.wits.ac.za/about-wits/governance/strategic-leadership/. Accessed on 16 May 2017.

Transformation at UCT. University of Cape Town. www.uct.ac.za/about/transformation/. Accessed on 17 June 2017.

1 The magic of the market

Whether as a specific physical place where commodities are purchased and sold, or a metaphorical construct denoting forms of global economic influence and control, the market lures many to it, with its potentially enticing wares and promises of economic profit.[1] Contemporary universities have entered the marketplace, enticed by the notion that economic prosperity will almost magically descend on institutions that submit to the control of market forces. It is worth noting, however, that universities have never been entirely exempt from the pressures of the market in one respect or another (see for instance Giroux, 2007: 111). However, now market forces are more fervently embraced than ever before.

The market university

In an article titled "Magical Market Realism", John S. Saul argues that various neoliberal economic practices that have been adopted in South Africa and elsewhere are rooted not so much in a "new realism", or economic pragmatism, as "nouveau market fetishism": faith in the magic of the market (1999: 50–51, 57). Thus, the market is conceived of as an enchanted space in which prosperity and success are located. Higher education has become caught up in this "global market utopia" (Baatjies, 2005: 26). Consequently, a belief in the near-magical efficacy of that which Buchbinder depicts as the market university (1993) has significantly influenced present-day academic policy and procedure worldwide, encouraging the marketisation of universities both locally and internationally.[2] Indeed, a widespread conviction prevails that market forces are endowed with a transformative potency, enabling institutions to become more productive, economically viable and accountable (see for instance Orr, 1997: 46; Shore and Wright, 1999: 571; Pendlebury and van der Walt, 2006: 81–183). To an extent, credence of this nature is comparable to a belief in the workings of supernatural agencies, in that both are the assurance of things unseen, not requiring any grounding in empirical fact. In these and other respects, the sense of occult potency with which the market has become imbued draws on the elusive and the intangible, stemming from a process of mythmaking and mystification. Indeed, the pre-eminence of the market and the strange, mysterious aura surrounding it owe much to the power of the imagination, and also the influence and control wielded by remote, sometimes unseen bodies and individuals whose interests contemporary market forces serve.

In present-day market-oriented universities, systems of managerial authority preside over all, and academic activity is subordinated to them. This stems from belief in another kind of magic, interconnected with confidence in the occult efficacy of the market, a faith in the transformative powers of corporate managerialism. In restructured institutions of higher education, as in many other areas of the public sphere and the corporate sector, this conviction has assumed such proportions that the notion has taken hold that progress, organisational transformation and achievement cannot be effected without the agency of managerialism.[3]

Indeed, the expansion of managerialism in universities in South Africa, the UK, the US, Australia and elsewhere is fuelled by the idea that present-day managerialism, steeped as it is in the strategies, jargon and practices of the business world, is best positioned to implement the marketisation of institutions of higher education. And so the market and managerialism have become intertwined, the former infecting the latter with some of its areas of mystery and ambivalence.

The unseen, all-pervasive aspects of corporate capitalism wield sway over the market university, for the ultimate university managers are economic and political bodies and forces, existing outside the institutional parameters but ever-present within them, in terms of the governance they exert and the extent to which they dictate policy and procedure. All the while, governmental jurisdiction over institutions of higher education in South Africa, the UK and elsewhere is increasingly determined by globalised corporate capitalism and neoliberal economic agendas. There is, for instance, the managerial role played by external funding bodies, controlled as these often tend to be by state and corporate structures. For instance, Michael Shattock draws attention to the forms of control exerted by state funding councils in the UK (2008).[4]

Next, in accordance with market-driven approaches, budget cuts, rationalisation, economic self-sufficiency, commercialisation, competitiveness, outsourcing of services to the private sector, quantitative means of assessment, and corporate managerial hegemony have all become features of the market university (see for instance Dibben and Higgins, 2004: 26, 29; Orr, 1997: 49). Thus, as universities strive to resemble business enterprises, profit-making is prioritised, and as Buchbinder observes, privatisation pervades university structures and procedures. Consequently, developments of this kind comprise one facet of the privatisation of the public domain (1993: 340).

South African researcher Liesl Orr expands on this, describing how the principal feature of the market university is the conversion of knowledge into a marketable commodity. The corporatisation of academic institutions serves to implement and further this. The implementation of quality assessments, frequently taking the form of performance indicators, entrenches the prioritisation of the calculable and quantifiable that forms a key feature of the market university (see for instance Orr, 1997: 46, 61; see also Peters, 1992: 126). The marketisation of academia is intensified by the extent to which many market-oriented universities have embraced the concept of corporate branding. As institutional identities are reconstructed in corporate capitalist terms, many universities have come to envisage themselves in terms of brands. For instance, the vice-chancellor of the University of Johannesburg once described how his institution was intent on "building a winning brand" (Rensburg, 2010: 3). Moreover, a promotional article described how this institution had "succeeded in establishing its corporate identity, having evolved into one of the most identifiable brands in the [South African] higher education landscape".[5] As will become evident later on, the corporate facades of many universities in South Africa and elsewhere may be valued more highly than institutional practice.[6]

Various universities in the US offer particularly striking instances of marketisation at work. Indeed, the consumerist nature of American society had permeated universities in the US to such an extent that, at the end of the twentieth century, Naomi Klein observed that some divisions of American academia had taken on the aspect of a shopping mall, with research chairs seemingly serving as franchises for the corporate brand names sponsoring them. For instance, there are now academic outlets for Taco Bell (the Distinguished Professor of Hotel and Restaurant Administration at Washington State University) and K-Mart (the chair of marketing at Wayne State University), among many others (2000: 101; see also Bok, 2003: 2). Developments of this kind are interconnected with the growth of that which George Ritzer (1996) depicts as the commodified, commercialised McUniversity.

Ritzer depicts McDonaldisation as the way in which the ethos and procedures of fast-food outlets such as McDonald's have permeated many social domains in the United States and worldwide, reshaping their principles and practices. Citing Max Weber (1921), Ritzer describes how purportedly rational notions, such as efficiency, predictability, calculability and a reliance on nonhuman technology, intertwined with systems of control, have come to dominate much modern Western thinking. These constitute key features of the process of rationalisation, and in many present-day Western and Westernised societies, in which so much, including knowledge, has been converted into an item for consumption, the fast-food industry has become emblematic of this (2015: 30–31). That which has been termed the McUniversity represents one dimension of these tendencies. An institution of this kind operates along essentially the same principles as a fast-food chain: producing and earning as much as possible with as little as possible (for instance with minimal expense, resources and personpower). Accordingly, the McUniversity is characterised by massification, consumerism, control systems that may take corporate, electronic and managerial forms and cost-cutting measures (involving restricting staff numbers and courses on offer while limiting infrastructural facilities). Such tendencies form core features of university restructuring and thus tend to characterise many present-day universities in varying degrees and in diverse ways. Such institutions also tend to have certain standardised qualities, conforming to fixed criteria and adhering to prescribed procedures while employing officially endorsed jargon. In this, they display some of the predictability of which Ritzer speaks. Accordingly, numerous market-oriented institutions of higher education may seem comparable to the McUniversity in various respects, as do numerous corporate "universities", such as those depicted in the opening chapter (Ritzer, 1996: 192–194).

Universities have wedded themselves to the market in other ways. For example, Klein describes how members of Nike-sponsored athletics departments or campus sports teams in the US have been attired in the company's sportswear. She cites Arizona State University, Stanford, Duke University, Penn State University and North Carolina University as a few examples of this trend. Certain North American universities, including Ottawa's Carleton University, have accorded preferential marketing opportunities to Pepsi, while other institutions, such as Kent State University and the University of British Columbia, have signed sponsorship deals with Coca-Cola. Then, Barnes and Noble has become the official bookseller at many US universities, while Taco Bell, Starbucks and Pizza Hut are featured on many university campuses (Klein, 2000: 402, 96–97, 91). Henry A. Giroux also observes that consumerism has also permeated many other public spaces at US universities (such as dining halls, open spaces and university bookshops) so that many university environments have become cluttered with the trappings of shopping malls, such as billboards, commercial logos and advertisements (2007: 105).

To varying degrees and in diverse respects, such developments would be echoed elsewhere, in universities far beyond North America. From the late 1990s onwards, various South African universities would bear the trademarks of their corporate sponsors more prominently than ever before. For instance, Jonathon Grossman describes how University of Cape Town students often enter the campus through a sports field adorned with banners advertising Old Mutual, a financial services provider. Thereafter, some students may attend a lecture in the Nedbank room (2006: 100). Moreover, many student unions in South Africa and elsewhere have mutated from communal spaces with cafeterias into conglomerates of commercial outlets. This state of affairs bears out Ritzer's observation that universities, along with other public places such as sports stadiums, hospitals, churches and museums, are being converted into sites of consumption (1999: 7, 24, 181, 189, 192).

The rise of neoliberalism that has brought the commodified, consumerist market university into being can be partly attributed to the enticing and superficially practical aspects of neoliberal notions. Neoliberalism appeals to a wide range of economic and political players, including those at the state level and in the private and public domains, by appearing to promise a means of cutting costs and generating profits at the same time. As one feature of this, it advocates reducing expenditure on the public services, higher education included, compelling them to become more commercially viable while holding forth the promise that, by this means, they can be turned into sources of economic profit and models of efficiency (see for instance Peters, 1992: 127, 138). Moreover, for various divisions of the public domain, confronted with financial constraints and uncertain, possibly even ominous future prospects, promises of this kind may seem particularly alluring. The market-oriented restructuring of higher education exerts a particular appeal in numerous countries, South Africa included, for these reasons. A local academic, Salim Vally, remarks, "In the face of mass unemployment, aligning skills to the competitive global 'new knowledge economy' is compellingly seductive and has become the obsession of [the South African] education department" (2007: 19). In these and other respects, neoliberalism fosters a belief in the magic of market forces, and the transformative power of corporatisation and commodification.

But as Vally's observation intimates, the "compellingly seductive" allure of the market can be deceptive, for the promises of economic prowess it extends can prove to be hollow. For example, many universities in South Africa and elsewhere that have placed their hopes in the market and undergone market-driven forms of restructuring are still awaiting material returns. Comparably, as an actual physical locality, the market can also be misleading and untrustworthy, a place within which it is possible for the unwary, the overly eager and those unfamiliar with the terrain to lose their wits, their wallets and their way. As various commentators, the South Korean economist Ha-Joon Chang included, have pointed out, although individuals and societies have been "told to put all [their] trust in the market", the precarious, recurrently calamitous nature of global economic patterns during the last few decades indicates that market forces cannot be relied on (2010: xiv–xv).

Spirits in the marketplace

On account of its ambiguous, illusory qualities, the market has readily lent itself to association with the supernatural in Africa. The spirit world and the marketplace both exert a perilously enticing magic, whether supernatural or mercantile, in Africa and elsewhere. Francis B. Nyamnjoh comments on one particular instance of this hazardous enchantment, comparing the occult domain of *Msa* in the Grassfields area of the Cameroon to a marketplace. Msa is inhabited by perilous, destructive beings, and is "a dangerous, mysterious and attractive world of infinite possibilities and abundance. . . . Ms is like a market, complete with traders and buyers, a bazaar where many come but where few are rewarded" (2001: 2). This may call to mind the ways in which various market-oriented bodies, corporations and institutions draw many to them. Yet, as we will see, although they may seem to offer much, ultimately they may deliver very little. As market-driven institutions, contemporary commodified, corporatised universities have also become immersed in layers of ambiguity and deception.

The deceptive, perilous aspects of the market to which Nyamnjoh alludes manifest themselves in various other ways in diverse parts of Africa. Jane Parish discusses one instance of this, describing how African spirits have become intricately involved with aspects of capitalism, maintaining that this has become a marked feature of perceptions of the supernatural on this continent (2001: 119). For instance, certain well-known and potentially hazardous wealth-giving spirits, such as the West African Mami Wata and the South African mamlambo, are said to frequent markets, busy shopping centres and other places where money is spent in the guise of expensively attired human beings, often wearing high heels and the latest fashion (Bastian, 1997: 125). As the appearance of these spirits suggests, it is as if the trappings of consumer capitalism are imbued with a special magic that can bring about the prosperity they evoke. Then, the mamlambo is sometimes scantily clad, wearing clothes that offer seductive glimpses of her curvaceous body, as enticing as the promises of economic affluence that she holds out.[7] In these and other respects, the mamlambo and the Mami Wata embody the beguiling, seductive aspects of consumer capitalism and the treacherous allure of market forces. These presences are only two of the many hazardous wealth-giving spirits that feature in a variety of present-day oral accounts of the supernatural in diverse parts of this continent. Such narratives are suggestive of the deceptive, damaging aspects of free-market capitalism, highlighting the unequal distribution of wealth it generates and the suffering it can bring about.

The connections between African spirits and the marketplace have other dimensions to them. Misty L. Bastian notes that Igbo-speaking peoples in Nigeria tend to perceive the world in terms of a marketplace, because "everyone and everything in the world passes through their markets". Convictions of this nature lend themselves to the belief that those who frequent markets are certain to encounter spirits, the inhabitants of the invisible dimension of the world (1997: 133). Ben Okri depicts a perception of this nature in his famous novel *The Famished Road*. His central character, Azaro, part human and part spirit child, wanders alone through the market and describes how humans, spirits and other supernatural beings intermingle in marketplaces as they buy and sell items (1992: 16). It is worth noting that a previous South African minister of finance, Trevor Manuel, sometimes quoted from Ben Okri, possibly because of the elusive, conveniently opaque nature of Okri's imagery. Whether or not Manuel was aware that the market took this form in Okri's work is a moot point. The Comaroffs and many other contemporary ethnographers, including Pels (2003), Parish (2001), Birgit Meyer (1998), Bastian (1997), Nyamnjoh (2001), Peter Geschiere (1997, 2003), Mark Auslander (1993), Ralph A. Austen (1993); Henrietta L. Moore and Todd Sanders discuss the occult dimensions of the marketplace, drawing attention to the way in which occult economies have been expanding as market-driven capitalism becomes increasingly potent and pervasive globally.

Notions of the market may be as mutable as views of the occult and similarly context-bound, shaped as they both are by many factors, including socioeconomic, historical and political dynamics. Roy Dilley takes cognisance of this, analysing the way in which concepts of the market are assimilated into various different societies and localities. Thereafter, such perceptions may undergo certain transmutations and adaptations in these diverse milieus (1992: 2). This is evident, for instance, in the case of one of the most successful South African entrepreneurs in the earlier part of the twentieth century, the *inyanga*, or medicine man, Khotso Sethuntsa (1898–1972). He derived much of his wealth from the charms and potions that he sold, particularly *ukuthwala*, the Xhosa term for a magical procedure for long-term wealth, widely believed to involve the ownership of the mamlambo. In the specific context within which Sethuntsa operated, in which magic was a marketable commodity, perceptions of the market incorporated areas of mystery and enchantment, as indeed they still do.

Concepts of the market may take many forms. As Arjun Appadurai has argued, perceptions of the market have political dimensions, since the value of items – and hence the demand for them – is controlled by those in positions of power (1986: 57). Further to this, Geschiere observes that notions of the market are constructed in varying ways within different milieus, thus emphasising the context-bound, mutable nature of perceptions of the market. As Geschiere also notes, that which we regard as the market is a cultural construct in various respects, since both Western and non-Western notions of the market are shaped in particular ways by their cultural contexts (1992: 160, 174). The fluidity of the concept of the market is pertinent here. The diverse ways in which market forces can be interpreted and some of the interests these interpretations can serve can be considered further.

American political analyst Thomas Frank describes how concepts of the market may be subject to manipulation and advance specific agendas, for items may not be valued according to their intrinsic worth but, rather, in terms of their status as marketable commodities. Thus, Frank contends that "[m]arkets do not determine the objective merit of things, only their price, which is to say, their merit in the eyes of capital or consumers". In consequence, he concludes that all too often such notions of value may depend on those in positions of power and control. In other words, major corporations and the very affluent tend to become the arbiters of worth, deriving part of their authority from their purported insight into market forces (2008: 88). This has implications for contemporary market-driven universities, in which ideas become valued in terms of their status as marketable commodities. Frank describes how intellectual activity can become subsumed into the service of the wealthy and powerful – becoming distorted in the process – as a result of this:

> Markets do not determine the objective merit of things, only their price, which is to say, their merit in the eyes of capital or consumers. To cast intellectual life as a "market" is to set up a standard for measuring ideas quite different from the standard of truthfulness. Here ideas are bid up or down depending on how well they please those with the funds to underwrite inquiry – which effectively means how well they please large corporations and the very wealthy.
>
> (Frank, 2008: 88)

Consequently, instead of harnessing the magical agency of the market, contemporary corporatised universities may become harnessed by the agents of the market. As Frank's observation suggests, market value may depend in part on ideas and assumptions, becoming imbued with the imaginary. We will explore the ways this has filtered through to higher education, where notions of academic worth now tend to be based on calculable, measurable forms of assessment intertwined with a faith in the magic of the market. For example, university rankings (measures of institutional merit based on achievements, performance and other capabilities) are significantly shaped by outside interests, concepts of worth that are ill-suited to a university environment, and notions of market forces. A comment made by the vice-chancellor of Melbourne University, Glyn Davis, is indicative of this: "[R]anking is a bit like a stock market. How companies are valued is a curious combination of their real performance and market confidence in them" (2013; cited in Hare, 2013).

As a result of their shifting, suggestive nature, and of the extent to which they can become bound up with the workings of the imagination, concepts of the market may take on mystical and preternatural aspects. Dilley discusses the unseen, mysterious qualities of the market, maintaining that "market transparency . . . is relative". As he points out, many people in diverse parts of the world are distanced from centres of economic power. For some of the members of such communities, the nature and operation of market forces may seem unfathomable and enigmatic (1992: 5). But even those in urban centres with insight into economic trends may not be able to fully plumb the mysteries of the market. Instead, they might perhaps sometimes be inclined to perceive it as an inscrutable force, operating in terms of enigmatic laws of its own.

Roger Dale makes a related point, drawing attention to the allusive, suggestive nature of perceptions of the market. He describes the market as a symbolic term acting "as a metaphor rather than an explicit guide for action. It is not denotative, but connotative. Thus, it must itself be 'marketed' to those who will exist in it and live with its effects" (cited in Mentor, Muschamp, Nicholls, Ozga and Pollard, 1997: 27; see also Apple, 1999: 3). In similar fashion, Dilley observes that "[a]s a displaced metaphor detached from its concrete referent, the term 'market' has become a 'pocket' whose contents are defined in relation to the uses to which it is put" (1992: 2–3). Once again, this indicates that concepts of the market are subject to manipulation and mythologising.

As the market becomes steeped in a miasma of fabrications, phantasms and figments of the imagination, so do aspects of capitalism. Various commentators, Martha Kaplan included (2003: 185), explore the extent to which capitalism is immersed in aspects of mystery and magic. There are various reasons why the occult and capitalism have become intertwined.

Capitalism and the occult

Firstly, both capitalism and the occult are forms of power and control with certain features in common. Both occult agencies and the agents of capitalism seize possession of people's bodies, productive capacities and sometimes even their existences. In Africa, the International Monetary Fund (IMF), the World Bank, the World Trade Organization (WTO), Monsanto and the Shell Corporation are typical examples of capitalist agents of this kind. Consequently, as Austen notes, both witchcraft and capitalism often tend to be regarded as the menacing "appropriation of limited reproductive resources by wealthy individuals" in many African cosmologies (1993: 92). Furthermore, globalised capitalism may appear to have certain features in common with forces of occult potency, for both may seem all-pervasive and all-controlling. Indeed, as Dave Cooper remarks, "nothing escapes commodification" (1997: 25; see also Hall, 2011: 722). Not even the emotional and spiritual lives of individuals are exempt from this, as we will see later on.

Moreover, capitalism has veiled, mysterious features, as do aspects of the occult. For instance, Moore and Sanders observe that "[i]t is no surprise to find witchcraft and anti-witchcraft practices bound up with ideas about power since witchcraft and other occult practices are themselves hidden forces in the world" (2001: 17). As a result of the invisible potency which they both appear to possess, capitalism and the otherworldly may be intermingled, each lending weight to the other. For instance, Nyamnjoh describes how this phenomenon manifests itself in the Grassfields region of the Cameroon. Citing Jean-Pierre Warnier (1993), he observes that market-based capitalism has expanded to such an extent that it has pervaded local perceptions of the supernatural, giving "a new impetus to the idioms of accumulation and dis-accumulation". Thus, contemporary accounts of occult beings and forces tend to draw on aspects of capitalism and may be steeped in capitalist imagery (2001: 46). Tendencies of this nature are a widespread phenomenon. Geschiere mentions that perceptions of sorcery in various parts of Africa have become interwoven, sometimes in an unexpected manner, with modern, often Western, procedures and items (1997: 2).[8] For instance, Parish describes how some Akan talismans in Ghana consist of credit cards on which objects of traditional significance, such as specific herbs, are plastered, giving the purchaser "the power to overcome local enemies". Moreover, "it places the wearer in an international market place" (2001: 132).

Therefore, as consumer capitalism exerts an increasingly powerful sway over African societies, new, sometimes potentially hazardous forms of magic have arisen in response. The same holds true for many societies elsewhere. As this indicates, beliefs in the occult are not so much an unchanging remnant of long-standing tradition but, rather, a group of fluid and shifting opinions, "reflecting and reinterpreting new circumstances" (Geschiere, 1997: 222). In Africa, this tendency has given birth to supernatural beings closely associated with aspects of Western capitalism, such as the South African mamlambo, while bestowing new aspects on certain long-standing beliefs. One instance of the latter tendency is the West African Mami Wata practice, which has evolved a wealth-giving dimension. Anthropologist Barbara Frank notes that the belief that individual prosperity could be gained through a hazardous pact with the spirit world, in the form of the figure of Mami Wata, became widespread after Western capitalist practices resulted in marked economic inequalities (1995: 331). In contrast, the mamlambo is a relatively recent South African supernatural presence that arose in part from economic deprivation and the lure of Western materialism.[9] (This being originated in the Eastern Cape, one of the most poverty-stricken provinces in this country.) Meanwhile, a Zimbabwean respondent remarked that more individuals were seeking assistance from wealth-giving spirits such as the *chikwambo*, because "with the harsh economic climate in our country, people do all it takes to ensure their survival" (Muswaka/Ruvimbo Masango, August 2009). In certain respects, beliefs and practices of this kind draw aspects of capitalism into "the witchcraft of wealth". Wealth-giving spirits, such as the South African mamlambo, constitute one facet of this. They promise a means, albeit a hazardous one, of acquiring some of the material benefits of the capitalist cash economy.

All the while, the pressures and enticements of free-market capitalism have become increasingly compelling, bestowing a greater force and significance on beings such as the mamlambo, the chikwambo and Mami Wata and other wealth-giving supernatural agencies. As the previously cited examples suggest, globalised capitalism has become so far-reaching, influential and pervasive in both Africa and the West that it has infiltrated the sphere of the occult, acquiring a mystical and magical, as well as a monetary, force.

Other perceptions of the supernatural have also acquired new dimensions. For example, Geschiere describes how, in contemporary rumours of *ekong*, one form of "the new witchcraft of wealth" in western parts of the Cameroon, there tends to be a close connection between the practice of ekong and the presence of Westerners, for ekong practitioners are often said to have contact with Europeans (1997: 157). Geschiere's point and the previously mentioned examples of wealth-giving magic are pertinent here. Indeed, different forms of this Western-oriented "witchcraft of wealth" manifest themselves in contemporary academia, giving rise to some of its most sinister features.

Since aspects of both the supernatural and capitalism may seem to draw upon areas of unseen potency, they can become interconnected in other respects. According to the Comaroffs, far-reaching forms of global power and influence, sometimes mysterious and damaging in their workings, may give rise to notions that malevolent forces are at work at unseen levels (1993: xxvii–xxix). Citing Warnier (1993), Francis B. Nyamnjoh observes that various studies of the re-emergence of witchcraft beliefs in the Cameroon and diverse parts of Africa have contended that the growing conviction that malign occult forces are at work can be related to the poverty, unpredictability and unease brought about by globalisation and the expansion of consumer capitalism. While Nyamnjoh emphasises that beliefs in sinister supernatural agencies cannot be explained away in terms of external socio-economic pressures, he also contends that the interrelationship between socio-economic dynamics and aspects of the occult cannot be ignored on account of the extent to which market-driven capitalism has pervaded so many societies and levels of human existence. Small wonder, then, that it has permeated perceptions of the supernatural, and that the occult has sometimes been employed to account for the upheavals and imbalances it has wrought (Nyamnjoh, 2001: 46).

Moore and Sanders contend that the expansion of globalised market-related forms of capitalism and the influences they have exerted, the changes they have brought about, the disturbances they have generated, the anxieties they have fostered, and the disparities in wealth and power they have created may sometimes help foster the growth of perceptions and practices that incline towards the occult (2001: 3). Cyprian F. Fisiy and Geschiere make a related point, linking the growth of beliefs in sinister forms of the supernatural to the expansion of neoliberal economic trends in the developing world. They maintain that the new forms of affluence stemming from free-market capitalist approaches have given rise to more rumours of witchcraft and witchcraft-related practices (2001: 243). As the market has been "liberated" from state control, a few have benefited from the opportunities offered by free-market transnational capitalism, while various forms of economic subjugation and disempowerment have arisen. These factors have helped create spaces within which aspects of the occult have flourished, some of which have permeated the sphere of higher education. As Jean Comaroff observes (1985: 253), rumours of sorcery thrive in unstable contexts, in which exceptional affluence and economic wretchedness coexist. Further to this, Meyer describes how perceptions of witchcraft have shifted during the course of African history, becoming connected to both the hazards and the possibilities of capitalism (1995: 359; see also Geschiere, 1997: 279–280). Arguably, sorcery and capitalism may lend themselves to a connection of this nature, for they both generate what may appear to be extraordinary well-being for some while plunging others into misfortune.

Accordingly, as Geschiere observes, "the mysteries of the market economy" have now been assimilated into perceptions of witchcraft. The new significance that forms of the occult have acquired in the Cameroon and other contemporary societies, including South Africa, can be viewed in relation to this. Beliefs in the workings of unseen presences and influences have intensified because convictions of this nature provide a means of explaining the seemingly unaccountable affluence acquired by some, while accounting for the sudden changes to which economic prosperity, whether individual, local or international, can be subject (1997: 221).

The relationship between capitalism and the occult is by no means a purely African phenomenon. Indeed, aspects of capitalism and perceptions of the market are steeped in aspects of mystery and magic, not only in Africa but worldwide. The myths, mysteries and enchantments surrounding contemporary Western market-based capitalism, some of which are worth touching on here, are indicative of this.

Globalised capitalism and the supernatural could be perceived as occult forces of mysterious power that move in unfathomable ways for a number of reasons. On one level, the arcane aspects of capitalist jargon might serve to reinforce perceptions of this nature among laypeople. This veiled, esoteric discourse can obscure the practices and power relations to which it alludes and the precarious, problematic nature of some of the practices it denotes. For instance, various features of stock market reports allude to certain economic states, categories or systems of authority in terminology that is suggestive of the workings of enigmatic, elusive forces. One such example is the phrase that a specific currency, such as the dollar, has "breached certain technical levels", without casting light on the nature of these levels and who ordained them. In another such instance, a particular currency, such as the South African rand, may be described as being "rangebound", suggesting that the rand has been tied in place by unknown forces for reasons that evade direct comprehension. Another such instance is the phrase "authorised financial services provider", which evokes a sense of dominion and jurisdiction, without disclosing the identity of the authorities in question or the nature of the services provided. Then, in current economic parlance, the obscure phrase "quantitative easing", denoting the printing of banknotes in times of economic crisis, is gaining ground. In part, this cryptic term has taken hold as a result of the way in which it is suggestive of amelioration and alleviation, while eliding the problematic features of the practice it denotes. It does not, for instance, indicate what form the "easing" to which it alludes will take, and at what cost it may come.

"The free market" is another enigmatic phrase, denoting the concept of freedom and the notion of marketing, without specifying the nature of that freedom, or the identities of the marketeers. This term highlights the way in which capitalism partakes of deceptive verbal magic of a kind, especially with regard to the concept of freedom. For instance, by some verbal sleight of hand, bondage to the culture of consumer capitalism is transformed into that which Bertelsen describes as "the freedom to consume" (1998: 137). Meanwhile, paradoxically, many states that permit free trade become the vassals of powerful global economies. Further to this, in terms of the concept of "free enterprise", unbridled capitalism is allowed free play. Permitted to run rampant, it becomes a force of domination and subjugation. The "free market" is laden with further contradictions, in that it imposes rules and restrictions, restricting the freedoms of those who enter its areas of control or engage with its agents. For instance, in terms of the structural adjustment programmes imposed on diverse African countries in the 1980s and 1990s by the IMF and the World Bank, countries in need of economic aid were required to submit to "free" market constraints, falling under the control of powerful global economies, surrendering their economic autonomy and subjugating themselves to forms of winner-takes-all capitalism (see for instance Nyaigotti-Chacha, 2004: 97; Sanders, 2001: 163).

Yet another example of capitalist arcana is the "hidden wealth" contained in the stock options received by executives of American corporations, purportedly as bonuses but, in actuality, as an invisible part of their salaries. These stock options are shares in the company's value, but unless these options are exercised, they do not appear to exist, and the value of other stock can remain constant. This serves in part to conceal the extent of the remuneration received by top executives; while the company itself can keep the entirety of its stock options undisclosed, thereby avoiding the tax implications.[10] Conversely, economically embattled companies can utilise this system of deception to disguise their financial situation. Shareholders, too, are kept in the dark about the actual state of their shares until such time as executives choose to exercise their options. Stock options represent a form of corporate magic, by means of which wealth may be drawn out of apparently nothing, while simultaneously vanishing from other people's possession. Similar stratagems are employed at sundry universities to keep the largesse bestowed on members of managerial staff a secret, since these employees tend to receive significant parts of their salaries in the form of perks.

The otherworldly aspects of capitalism also stem from the mysteries, magicalities and myths surrounding the item at its centre: money itself. On one level, the occult aspects of money are epitomised in the images on the US dollar bill, which depicts the mystic pyramid and the All-Seeing Eye of Freemasonic iconography (Curl, 1991: 170, 38). Marx depicts money as an abstract, mystical construction, surrounded by enchantments. Drawing on an image from mythology, he describes the extent to which, as an actual form of wealth, the value vested in money is a figment of the imagination, a "pure abstraction . . . a mere conceit. Where wealth as such seems to appear in an entirely material, tangible form, its existence is only in my head, it is a pure fantasy. Midas"(1973: 223).

Marx also draws attention to the way in which money's power resides in the symbolic qualities that are bestowed on it, as "*the general material representative of wealth*" rather than in any inherent attributes it possesses (1973: 221; see also 1973: 145, 209–212, 226). Thus, money acquires paradoxical features, as Marx describes how this item "implies the separation between the value of things and their substance" (1973: 149). In modern societies, for instance, the principal items of currency consist of pieces of paper, which derive their authority from collective fictions, in terms of which these scraps of paper become transmuted into objects of importance. Like an item in a fairy tale, money holds forth another, even more powerful promise: that it can fulfil any of the wishes of the ones who possess it. Karl-Heinz Kohl points out that money possesses a magic of this kind because it may seem as if all things can be purchased with it (2004: 86). Thus, money is laden with promises, all too often false.

More fairytale images come to the fore when the nature of money is considered. For instance, Marx describes how money transforms all the commodities with which it becomes associated. Money serves as "the universal matter in which [all commodities] must be dipped, in which they become gilded and silverplated, in order to win their independent existence as exchange values" (1973: 188). All in all, the previously quoted descriptions are suggestive of a sense that money derives its meaning, its power and its essential being from an assortment of myths, fantasies, mysteries and collective fictions. Thus, the cornerstone of the capitalist cash economy becomes a mythic construct in certain respects, heightening the magical, illusory aspects of free-market capitalism.

Other areas of capitalism are steeped in an aura of enchantment. For example, some of the foremost figures in the capitalist sphere may seem reminiscent of occult powers and principalities in certain respects. One such individual is the chairman of the Federal Reserve, who may sometimes seem to be viewed as a wizard of sorts, with the ability to utter profound pronouncements and predict the future. In particular, Alan Greenspan was viewed in this light. Joseph Stiglitz, chief economist of the World Bank until 2000, mentions that Greenspan's "words carried enormous weight, in the financial markets especially" (2004: 33).[11] Comparably, Adam Smith's and Milton Friedman's names have sometimes been invoked with reverence, as if they have taken on a stature resembling that of prophets and holy men.[12]

The inscrutable aspects of capitalism intensify its mystical qualities. Good fortune may seem to be bestowed almost at random and then withdrawn unexpectedly and inexplicably. Nyamnjoh, for example, employs the phrase "the hidden hand", which evokes economic theory; globalised neocolonial forms of economic and socio-political control, which may sometimes seem to be exercised at almost unseen levels; and invisible, unaccountable occult agencies. He contends that "in reality a hidden hand (of capital, the west, etc.) determines who among the many shall be provided for" (2001: 5–6, 35; see also Dilley, 1992: 6). The phrase "a hidden hand" is reminiscent of Adam Smith's reference to an "invisible hand". Smith makes use of this analogy in order to further his argument that economic activity can contribute to the public good. This concept has now been harnessed to contemporary free market claims that the market has a force of its own, operating for the general benefit of society. In the economic sphere, one facet of this is the neoliberal belief in the potency of a "hidden hand". This is evident in the conviction that neoliberal economic policies, such as privatisation, will result, almost magically, in marked economic improvement (see for instance Hsu, 2003: 5). Now that which Martin Parker and David Jary depict as "the engineered hidden hand" is at work in academia (1995: 322).

Yet market forces may seem to possess a strange, haphazard quality. Eric Hobsbawm alludes to the mysterious power of global economic trends, making specific reference to the "crisis decades" between the 1970s and the 1990s. In his description of this era, it is as if the global economy possesses an unseen, unknowable force of its own, eluding human control. Hobsbawm remarks that the "operations [of capitalism] had become uncontrollable. Nobody knew what to do about the vagaries of the world economy or possessed instruments for managing them" (1994: 408).

Furthermore, Hobsbawm contends that market forces may seem to have transcended human understanding and control even more with the onset of globalisation. In 1994, he observed that, after the globalisation of the economy in 1970, governments all over the world were left "at the mercy of an uncontrollable 'world market'" (411). In a description of this nature, global market dynamics may seem to resemble emanations from an unseen realm of preternatural power, as capricious and potentially perilous as supernatural presences. Small wonder, then, that present-day market-driven capitalism has sometimes become associated with the otherworldly.

Contemporary Western economic trends have furthered the growth of the occult in other related respects. As neoliberal ideologies have become more influential worldwide and globalised corporate capitalism comes to wield greater sway, the state's pre-eminent role in the public sector as principal economic provider and guardian has declined. As the hollowing out of the state continues both locally and internationally, undermining what once may have seemed relatively secure terrain, various forms of magic flow in to fill the void.

Fisiy and Geschiere reflect on this, contending that

> the defeat of the state – whether of the welfare or the authoritarian type – by the requirements of 'the market' [has left] society at the mercy of an economy that seems increasingly unpredictable and out of control. No wonder that, at the beginning of the twenty-first century, magic seems to have become a fixed corollary of modernity, not only in Africa, but also in the richer parts of the world.
> (2001: 243)

As the preceding passage suggests, the vagaries of the market and the dynamics of free-market capitalism might sometimes seem to call to mind the workings of unseen mystical phenomena, eluding complete control and comprehension. Arguably then, some of the economic forces at work in our societies today might seem to possess the potential to exert an influence over human lives as unaccountably miraculous or calamitous as the sudden intervention of magic.

Accordingly, universities have sought to draw closer to the market, surrounded as it may seem to be by an almost numinous potency. In part, the corporate makeovers upon which universities have embarked seem to stem from one aspect of this: the conviction that marketisation and managerialism are imbued with a special magic that can generate economic prosperity. In certain respects, views such as these draw on notions comparable to a belief in the efficacy of unseen occult forces and practices. In their most extreme form, views of this nature have given rise to the apotheosis of the market.

Moloch and Mammon

In present-day market-driven societies, the authority vested in the market not only transcends that once accorded to the state but, as Thabo Mbeki contended in 1998, that the market has been perceived as "a modern God, a supernatural phenomenon to whose dictates everything human must bow in a spirit of powerlessness".[13] Michael Taussig comments on the way in which globalised market forces have acquired an almost transcendent authority and influence, describing how the principal bodies that promote them, including transnational corporations and institutions such as the World Bank, the WTO and the IMF, wield such power that they appear not to be bound by the constraints that hem in other, lesser economic enterprises and organisations. Thus, as Taussig contends, they are "able to dictate the terms of misery to untold millions of people to the refrain of free competition and the sacred laws of the market" (1997: 132).[14] Taussig then draws on religious imagery to suggest the scale of this economic and socio-political hegemony, and the degree of control it exerts over the societies over which it presides, comparing it to the medieval church (1997: 132–133). Further to this, when it appears to resemble an overarching force, apparently transcending conventional checks and balances, the market becomes comparable to a sacred presence or entity.

There are diverse South African examples of the transcendent qualities that have been bestowed on the market. This is evident, for instance, in the way in which an entrepreneurial initiative at the University of the Witwatersrand known as Wits Enterprise has been depicted. In 2003, the director of Marketing and Business Development described this venture as a "channel" between "the university and the *eternal* commercial world" (my italics; cited in Pendlebury and Van Der Walt, 2006: 83). Thus, the business world is elevated to the extent that it is described as transcending earthly constraints. In other words, the university is subjugated to the imperatives of the market, which presides over it as if it were a higher force of some kind.

The market-driven ethos that universities have adopted tends to result in an unquestioning obedience to the concept of the market, combined with an ongoing, forceful proselytising, comparable to that displayed by new converts to a spiritual cult or religious fundamentalists. South African academic Peter Vale draws attention to the political aspect of this, describing how, by means of the potency of institutional jargon and procedures, the market has been decontextualised and depicted as an unquestionable part of actuality (2004: 11). A sacred figure, being or entity occupies a comparable position: placed outside any socio-political or economic framework, it occupies a position of indisputable holiness. As we are aware, this has its political uses, for religion can be invoked to underpin specific forms of political power. Comparably, when decontextualised and presented as all-powerful, incontestable and ungovernable, like an act of God or a force of nature, concepts of the market and market forces can be manipulated to further the interests of the wealthy and the influential. Indeed, this has been the case during the market-oriented restructuring of academia.

The apotheosis of the market can be viewed in relation to these forms of market-related manipulation. As an intrinsically empty concept that can be interpreted in many ways, the market has sometimes acquired a status comparable to that of a divine being. At such times, it is almost as if it has become a formless, shapeless presence, presiding over all and all-controlling. Peter Preston expands on the extent to which the inclination to view the market "as a given", existing beyond human interrogation and control, has contributed to the growth of an intellectual and political void, thus creating a climate favourable to the development of right-wing socio-political and economic ideologies. In the UK, he observes, right-wing political bodies appropriated this space, interpreting the notion of the market to suit their political agenda and deluging those around them with an "efflorescence of market-nonsense" (1992: 69), some of which has seeped into contemporary university discourse and practice.

Drawing on points made by Raymond Williams and Fredric Jameson, Bertelsen comments on the deceptive nature of market-oriented neoliberalism. She describes the extent to which certain notions of "the market" can serve as vehicles for furthering the interests of reactionary political ideologies while purporting to emanate from commonsensical practical principles. Not only does the hollowness of such notions of the market stem in part from such tendencies, but they have also been generated within an intellectual and moral vacuum. She observes that the ascendancy of neoliberal economic approaches can partly be attributed to this latter factor.

> No sooner have the rhetoricians of late capitalism proclaimed "the end of ideology" (i.e. rejected the totalising "master narratives" of the past), than they proceeded to install the neo-liberal ideology of the market as the new trans-national "commonsense".
>
> (1998: 132)

These politically and intellectually dubious views of the market have permeated the academic sphere. As Bertelsen's and Preston's observations indicate, the apotheosis of the market rests on an abyss. It has arisen within a context within which many moral, political and intellectual concerns have been stripped of significance. The fact that the market can acquire a status reminiscent of that of a deity is partially connected to the extent to which it has become an intrinsically vacuous concept that can be interpreted in many ways. The apotheosis of the market is interwoven as it is with other areas of enchantment, such as that which often lies at the heart of the magic of the market: money itself.

As we have already seen, money has sometimes been viewed as an item imbued with a mystical potency. Further to this, Guy Debord describes the invisible authority vested in money, depicting it as an agent of mysterious, almost preternatural forms of power: "[M]oney, apparently dominant, presents itself as an emissary armed with full powers who speaks in the name of an unknown force" (1983). Moreover, as Taussig observes, money is believed to perform miracles. He also remarks that "money speaks with a single voice, the common measure of all [commodities]. This alone should grant it respect bordering on the sacred" (1997: 130, 131). According to Kohl, money has long been associated with aspects of religion in Western culture. He cites examples from the ancient world, including Babylon, Greece and Rome. In this latter city, for instance, the goddess Juno was the guardian of money, and this item derives its name from the word *moneta*: the term bestowed on gold, silver and bronze bars in her temple. Moreover, Kohl observes that ancient coins depicted the gods, and nowadays this practice persists. Citing Maurice Godelier (1996), he points out that the US dollar bears the words "In God We Trust" (2004: 84, 87). Marx expands on this, suggesting that in a symbolic sense, money can acquire a status akin to that of a divine being:

> Thus, wealth (exchange value in totality as well as abstraction) exists, individualized as such, to the exclusion of all other commodities, as a singular,

tangible object, in gold and silver. Money is therefore the god among commodities. . . . From its servile role, in which it appears as mere medium of circulation, it suddenly changes to the lord and god in the world of commodities. It represents the divine existence of commodities, while they represent its earthly form.

(1973: 221)

The worship of Mammon could be borne in mind in this regard. According to the *Oxford English Dictionary*, the term originally derived from the Aramaic for "wealth", and later this became conceived of as an evil spirit personifying riches and avarice. Thus, *Mammon* came to denote a heedless, excessive devotion to money and material gain. The immoral nature of Mammon was emphasised in the Bible and in various works of Western literature, and in medieval times this figure was envisaged as a demon. Meanwhile, certain images of modern capitalist economic power call another divinity from ancient traditions to mind. Marx also depicts money as a menacing paranormal entity, drawing all material things to it and engulfing them. He begins by citing the French economist Pierre le Pesant Boisguillebert (1843), who sought economic and fiscal reforms during the reign of Louis XIV, and described money as "the hangman of all things, the moloch to whom everything must be sacrificed, the despot of commodities" (Marx, 1973: 199). The Old Testament claimed that children were sacrificed to Moloch, a Near Eastern deity. Like Mammon, this figure has taken on symbolic qualities, sometimes representing a presence or force exacting subservience and tremendous sacrifices. Marx comments further on these symbolic points of comparison:

In the period of the rising absolute monarchy with its transformation of all taxes into money taxes, money indeed appears as the moloch to whom real wealth is sacrificed. Thus it appears also in every monetary panic. From having been a servant of commerce, says Boisguillebert, money became its despot.

(1973: 199)

When related to present-day societies within which forms of market-driven capitalism wield sway, Boisguillebert's statement illuminates the extent to which not only money but also the market forces that generate it have acquired a sovereignty comparable to that accorded to an absolute monarch or a deity. Boisguillebert's comment also casts some light on the current university environment, over which monetary concerns loom largest of all. In its commodified form, knowledge has, figuratively speaking, been surrendered to that which has the capacity to deal the death blow to much that gives it significance.

Under such conditions, money, in the form of marketisation, now wields control over the nature and functioning of corporatised universities: as Moloch, devouring all that is offered to it, and as Mammon, inspiring mindless, incautious devotion. Indeed, the valorisation of that which derives from corporate capitalism, the preoccupation with profit-making and the uncritical adherence to the neoliberal ethos that characterise the contemporary corporatised university environment are comparable to the adoration of Mammon not only in their single-mindedness but also in their morally questionable, socio-politically problematic implications. The symbolic presence of these two divinities is suggestive of the extent to which certain secular, superficially rational features of modern societies derive some of their potency from the way in which they partake, even if metaphorically, of ancient areas of mystery and magic. Citing Max Weber (1968: 149), Pels comments on this tendency: "In the polytheism of values of modern society, 'many old gods rise from their graves' and 'resume their eternal struggles' in disenchanted and impersonal form" (2003: 28). In societies in which market-driven capitalism wields sway, the market is one of the foremost of these; as is the money that is often its lifeblood. Drawing substance and force from the previously mentioned all-consuming and all-absorbing antecedents, both the money and the market have been elevated to a status resembling that of a divinity.

Several questions now come to the fore. Why does market-oriented capitalism sometimes seem to wield a power of extraordinary proportions, comparable in certain respects to the potency vested in certain supernatural and spiritual agencies? Why has it become so hegemonic and socio-politically dominant that it has managed to pervade all sectors of so many societies, higher education included, and so many areas of human existence? Such questions give rise to the following chapter, which touches on some of the reasons why higher education has undergone the far-reaching changes brought about by market-driven institutional restructuring. So socio-economic and political dynamics are foregrounded in the next chapter, and those who wish to consider these may do so. Otherwise, they may omit the following section and proceed straight to the main concerns of this study: the occult dimensions of contemporary institutions of higher education that subscribe to the myths of the market and seek to emulate the ways of the corporate world.

Notes

1 Various points drawn from these sections of the following sources are incorporated into p. 21 and pp. 25–29 of this chapter:
 Wood, 2015a: 283–296.
 Wood, F. 2014a: 60–64, 68–70.
 Wood, F. 2010a: 228–232; and Wood, F. 2010b: 2–3.
 The previously cited articles explore other aspects of occult economies and free-market capitalism and different aspects of corporatised universities. The information in these studies has been revised, expanded on and linked to new concerns.
2 Howard Buchbinder outlines the various factors that brought the market university into being. These include funding cuts, developments in advanced technology, pressures emanating from the corporate sphere and the influence exerted by neoliberal economic approaches (1993: 332–333). The market university has

various distinctive features. Among much else, the need to compete for funds is highlighted; incentives based on productivity are introduced; and performance indicators, with their reliance on measurable, quantifiable data, are foregrounded as a means of assessment (see for instance Ozga, 2011: 145).
3 Numerous commentators from the diverse countries, including UK academics Rosemary Deem, Sam Hillyard and Mike Reed (2007: 4–6); Michael Shattock (2008); Deem (1998: 5, 47); Mark Olssen and Michael A. Peters (2005: 14) and Stefan Collini draw attention to this faith in the transformative powers of corporate managerialism (2012: 34).
4 In South Africa, for instance, the National Research Foundation (NRF), the country's principal research funding body, plays an influential role in shaping the nature and direction of academic research. It also promulgates and helps entrench quantifiable criteria for evaluating research.
5 UJ's Winning Brand Breeds Brand Champions. 2010. *Mail & Guardian*. 4–10 June: 41.
6 This particular concern for the institutional corporate image is evident, for instance, in the University of Stellenbosch vice-chancellor's response to the *Luister* [Luister] video (2015), which drew attention to racism on campus; and is also critiqued in the *Chartre de Désexcellence* (2014), both of which are discussed later.
7 Two postgraduate student researchers, Wendy Muswaka and Abbey Alao, conducted many interviews between 2008 and 2010 on African wealth-giving spirits, particularly the South African mamlambo and the West African Mami Wata. In a series of interviews carried out in South Africa and Nigeria, they paid special attention to oral narratives depicting the ways in which these supernatural presences are said to manifest themselves in contemporary South African and Nigerian cities. This has cast light on aspects of present-day occult economies, and their research findings are drawn upon here.
8 This phenomenon has been investigated frequently. For example, Luise White (2000) examines the way in which East and Central African vampire stories contain Western features, such as firemen, ambulances and blood transfusions, while Mark Auslander describes forms of modern magic in Ngoni witch-finding rituals in eastern Zambia (1993). See also Geschiere (1997: 10, 16, 146).
9 As the careers of leading southern African *ukuthwala* practitioners, such as the Transkei inyanga Khotso Sethuntsa indicate, the trade in ukuthwala (a procedure enabling an individual to take on the ownership of a wealth-giving mamlambo) developed under white minority rule, from the early twentieth century onwards. Moreover, belief in the mamlambo spread through southern Africa as a result of the migrant labour system, which arose as individuals lost the capacity to sustain themselves through their traditional communal lifestyle and became economically dependent on white-owned capitalist operations, such as mining and commercial farming, as Niehaus observes (2001a: 46, 56, 61).
10 Most of the key points in this paragraph derive from Joseph Stiglitz, who provides some specific examples of this secret dimension of corporate practice, noting that, by 2001, an estimated 80% of the remuneration received by corporate managers in the US consisted of options of this nature. He also states that in the same year Microsoft, Intel, Starbucks, Cisco and Yahoo! were able to boost their profits by keeping the value of their stock options undisclosed (2004: 116–117, 123–124, 166).
11 Stiglitz mentions an aspect of this, terming one book describing Greenspan's accomplishments as a "hagiography", implying that it elevated him above ordinary mortals, bestowing an infallible, all-knowing quality upon him (2004: 32).

12 The ideas in this paragraph and in other parts of this section were suggested by Mathew Blatchford.
13 This statement was made by Thabo Mbeki at the 1998 African Renaissance Conference in Johannesburg (cited in Saul, 1999: 62).
14 Various ways in which this tendency has afflicted numerous countries in Africa and elsewhere will become apparent in subsequent chapters.

2 Setting the scene

This chapter ventures into the terrain of free-market capitalism and the neoliberal economic approaches that perpetuate it, noting some of the influences these have exerted over institutions of higher education both locally and worldwide and the changes they have wrought. It does not, however, seek to provide an in-depth account of the factors that have brought about corporatisation and marketisation in many universities, nor does this study as a whole seek to do so. Instead, the key purpose of this chapter is to set the scene for what is to follow. Subsequent chapters take up the key issues at hand: the ways in which these developments have given rise to many metaphorical parallels with the occult, bestowing aspects of mystery, mythmaking, magic and ritual on present-day university environments. Then various denizens of the occult academy, both human and non-human, will enter the stage set in this chapter, and their beliefs, practices and predilections will unfold. In these subsequent sections, life, colour and detail will be added to the sketch that now follows.

A statement made in the first part of the twentieth century serves as a starting point. Derek Bok, a former president of Harvard University, describes how, as early as 1918, Thorstein Veblen objected to the way in which university administrators seemed to be "forever forcing the methods of the marketplace on a reluctant community of scholars" in a study of higher education in America. Bok observes that in Veblen's day, but even more so thereafter, it is misleading to lay the blame for this state of affairs entirely at the door of university managers. And, indeed, the reasons for the marketisation of academia in South Africa and elsewhere extend far beyond senior managerial whims (2003: 4). There are other, more far-reaching dynamics shaping the nature and functions of market-oriented universities and the policies of those who preside over them, and these are considered here. Nowadays, the internal authority structures of corporatised, managerially governed institutions of higher education are underpinned and controlled by forms of neoliberal governmentality, emanating from the state, the corporate sector and other external systems of economic and political power and control. These external managerial systems preside over the corporatisation and marketisation of academia, and they play a comparable role in other divisions of the public domain.

These dynamics have been shaped by the rise of neoliberal economic tendencies. For instance, UK academics Mark Olssen and Michael A. Peters draw attention to the influence neoliberalism wields globally, as a result of the way it has been endorsed and promulgated by powerful Western nations (2005: 314). As one dimension of this, neoliberal economic approaches promoting the privatisation of the public sector have taken hold in South Africa and elsewhere. In the UK, for instance, these trends have been shaping the nature and direction of higher education since the early 1980s while comparable changes have been taking place in South African higher education since the 1990s (see for instance Collini, 2012: 22). By 1998, South African universities had altered to such an extent that Bertelsen depicted the changes taking place in higher education and other domains of contemporary life, both in South Africa and internationally, in this way:

> As the new political-economic orthodoxy (the "Washington Consensus") driven by the multinationals, the IMF and the World Bank entrenches itself on a global scale, all aspects of social life are being commodified with remarkable speed and intensity. A new banner flies over our institutions inscribed with the triumphalist "No Alternative" of the global market system.
>
> (1998: 130)

Indeed, the last few decades have seen the ascendancy of globalised forms of economic power and control, informed by neoliberal approaches promulgated by wealthy and powerful Western governments spearheaded by the US, and presided over by transnational corporations (including Microsoft, Monsanto, McDonald's, Shell, Coca-Cola and Walmart, among a host of others) and other institutions that hold sway at national and international levels. This latter category includes the grouping that Chang describes as the "Unholy Trinity": the WTO, the World Bank and the IMF (2007: 13). These factors facilitate the dissemination of neoliberal ideologies while helping to entrench them. Thus, globalisation and neoliberalism are interconnected (Olssen and Peters, 2005: 313).[1]

Our contemporary milieu has been characterised by the relentless march of free-market capitalism and the decline of other alternatives; by the webs of influence and control which international financial networks and transnational corporations have woven around so many individuals, societies and nations; and by the forms of power that the very rich have come to wield over the lives of the majority (or the 99%, as they have sometimes been termed). In an environment of this kind, globalised capitalism may often seem to exercise a force of unprecedented proportions, drawing many areas of human activity, higher education included, under its sway.

For their part, universities are being converted into that which Bertelsen describes as "a pliant service industry for the late capitalist market system", both locally and internationally (1998: 130). As many universities in diverse nations have been redefining their nature and function in terms of market-oriented criteria, they have been placed under pressure to become more financially self-sustaining and to look beyond their traditional sources of income, such as state subsidies, for their economic survival. Directives of this kind emanate from both the state and the corporate world (Cooper, 1997: 26). This was evident, for instance, in an education white paper in the South African 1997 Government Gazette, in which the Department of Education emphasised that universities would need to raise "third-stream" funding (cited in Pendlebury and van der Walt, 2006: 81). This form of income derives from outside sources, such as industry or the business world, or by means of contracts with government bodies, for example. The white paper also expressed the oft-heard injunction that universities offer more circumscribed, specifically focused vocational courses. Demands of this kind are based on the assumption that vocationally oriented courses are more suited to the needs of the market. Other higher education systems in diverse parts of the world have had to deal with similar directives (see for instance Nakkazi, 2016; Olssen and Peters, 2005: 326, 330; Collini, 2012: 35). For instance, as some UK academics have noted, the 1987 Organisation for Economic Co-operation and Development (OECD) report contains some comparable edicts (Peters, 1992: 124; Cowen, 1996: 246 – 247).

In 2005, the South African minister of finance, Trevor Manuel, took this further, stating that "non-commercialised" public institutions were in need of that which he described as improvement. Manuel recommended that market-oriented managers be deployed to transform the institutions over which they presided into places equipped to offer more "cost-effective" "service" to their "clients" (cited in Baatjies, 2005: 1). Although Manuel was making specific reference to public health institutions, South African academic Ivor G. Baatjies observes that the terminology he employed is often applied to other areas of the public domain, higher education included (2005: 1). Similarly, Parker and Jary describe how the discourse of the business world has taken hold in higher education in the UK. While the jargon of "line managers", "customers" and "products" has been foregrounded, the language of academia has declined in significance (1995: 24–325). All in all, the pressure to imitate the corporate domain looms large in many institutions of higher education, in both the UK and beyond.[2] Just as some businesses may refashion themselves so as to appeal to a new, potentially more affluent clientele and also sometimes in the belief that good fortune may follow a change of image, so many universities have remodelled themselves for similar reasons.

In subsequent chapters, we consider some of the changes that these developments have wrought in higher education and the shadows that they have cast over present-day universities, steeping them in the mysteries of the occult.

Commodification, consumerism and higher education

As market-oriented neoliberal economic approaches gained ground and new managerial approaches informed and driven by the ethos and practices of the corporate world became more and more a feature of the restructured university environment in South Africa and elsewhere, many of those in positions of internal and external managerial authority began promoting the commodification of higher education, depicting it as a source of new economic opportunities. UK writer and academic Guy Standing describes how various areas of higher education have become commodified. As one feature of this, degrees and diplomas are becoming increasingly standardised and converted into cost-effective marketable items as online education systems take hold. For example, in the academic Walmarts otherwise known as Massive Open Online Courses (MOOCs) academic wares, often taking the form of prepackaged courses, can be disseminated en masse to vast numbers of students. Ritzer observes that eventually these disembodied sites of learning located in cyberspace may come to resemble cybermalls. In such environments, academics may come to seem ancillary and easily disposable (Standing, 2011: 68–72; Ritzer, 2015: 147–151; 1999: 24).

Thereafter, commodification extends to the students themselves: potentially profitable items augmenting the institutional income as fee-paying entities with the capacity to contribute to the institutional pass rates and ultimately the numbers of graduates. Through these quantifiable contributions, they enhance the market value and the standing (financial and otherwise) of the institutions to which they are attached (Standing, 2011: 69–72; see also Jenvey, 2013: 2). Consequently, higher education in the UK, the US, South Africa and elsewhere has become characterised by its valorisation of potentially profitable universities, departments and divisions, including those perceived as likely to reap dividends because they are promoted at state level (such as science, technology and commerce in South Africa).

The next commodification casualty is knowledge itself, often envisaged not so much as a source of potential benefit to society and the individuals within it but, rather, as a consumer product benefiting the market (Buchbinder, 1993: 335). In terms of the concept of the knowledge economy, which began coming to the fore in the 1980s, knowledge is envisaged as a marketable commodity, with the potential to enhance nations' capacities for economic growth and their abilities to compete more effectively in the international economic arena. For instance, Mamphela Ramphele, a former vice-chancellor of the University of Cape Town (thereafter appointed a managing director at the World Bank in Washington, D.C.) asserted, "We are moving into what has been described as 'the global knowledge society'. Intellectual capital will become the currency by which nations trade" (1998; cited in Bertelsen, 1998: 131). Such notions of the knowledge economy have been promoted in South Africa and elsewhere, and they form part of the superficially practical aspects of neoliberal economic approaches, in terms of which much can be put to commercial use by being offered for sale on national and international markets. Ramphele's views and other comparable notions are informed by the mythmaking surrounding the concept of the knowledge economy. The shortcomings of this body of myth will be considered later on.

Financial exigencies, economic disparities

While Ramphele's previously cited claim and other similar assertions may appear to offer a cornucopia of opportunities to institutions of higher education, the cup is empty in a significant sense. The rise of neoliberalism, with its hollowing out of the social services and its valorisation of corporatisation and privatisation, has led to leaner days for many universities, both locally and internationally. State funding for systems of higher education has become more tightly regulated by official bodies and funding cuts have become a widespread phenomenon, affecting relatively affluent and economically constrained institutions alike.[3]

Although the contemporary academic climate has become one of diminished resources, bureaucratic duties seem to have increased in direct proportion, becoming more onerous and time-consuming, while the academic workload has intensified in other respects. For example, regular audits and quality assessments and other external and internal forms of monitoring and evaluation have increased both academics' and administrators' workloads. Meanwhile, student numbers have tended to swell in many universities worldwide: a phenomenon known as massification.[4] On the other hand, academic staff numbers have often decreased, sometimes drastically. In the university context, the phrase "do more with less" seems to have become a recurrent refrain (see for instance Buchbinder, 1993: 334; Bertelsen, 1998: 140). All too often university staff may be expected to perform feats of magic, figuratively speaking, in order to accomplish this. This is not only a distinctive feature of those approaches that are sometimes termed New Public Management, or NPM, but it could also be viewed as adding a supernatural touch to the restructuring of contemporary universities.

Both locally and internationally, many universities are hedged in by numerous constraints, many of them economic, yet their security and stability and all too often their very survival have become interconnected with their capacity to be deemed financially viable and economically competitive. In general, financial issues tend to be a source of concern for the majority of universities in this continent and elsewhere, South African institutions included, so much so that a local study of the state of local higher education, published in 2006, was titled *Asinamali* [We Have No Money].

A range of African commentators have described the extent to which the economic problems with which their specific nations and many other countries on this continent are afflicted have affected the state funding available for their national education systems, especially at higher education level.[5] Yet, although numerous African universities are beset with financial hardships, various distinctions prevail. Certain universities, including various historically advantaged institutions, the South African HAIs – formerly termed HWIs – have access to alternative sources of funding in the form of endowments, private business ventures, property interests and investments. However, many other African universities, including many South African HDIs, historically disadvantaged institutions – previously termed HBIs – tend to lack financial security of this nature (Habib, Morrow and Bentley, 2008: 142). For instance, by 1999, Fort Hare and other HDIs, the Universities of Transkei, Zululand, North-West and the North had accumulated a student debt of more than R 200 million during the previous three years. Yet with the decline in state subsidies for higher education, such institutions had become increasingly reliant on student fees.[6] However, monetary issues were also a source of major concern for the elite HAIs, including the University of Cape Town and the University of the Witwatersrand. Indeed, during the last few decades, most universities in this country have come to realise that they cannot rely on state funding and student fees to meet all their financial needs. Meanwhile, the current South African economic predicament has the potential to erode sources of funding for universities even further, afflicting financially deprived rural institutions and prestigious urban universities alike.[7]

More broadly, financial concerns of various kinds loom large for numerous universities worldwide, including many of those in relatively affluent countries (although certain contextual variants do come into play). For example, Collini and various other academics from the UK describe how drastic funding cuts were imposed on UK universities under Thatcher: a strategy that continued under successive governments (Collini, 2012: 33). Furthermore, Shattock observes that it was announced that £100m would be deducted from the budget for UK universities three days after Thatcher assumed power (2008; see also Barry, Chandler and Clark, 2001: 92–93; Peters, 1992: 123). Parker and Jary also mention that academic salaries in the UK decreased by 37%, while 22% less was spent on libraries in the decade after 1980 (1995: 328, see also 322, 325).

Meanwhile, writing from the US in 2003, Bok described "the need for money" as "a chronic condition of American universities" (9). Nearly a decade later in 2011, Emanuele Saccarelli spoke of the "onslaught of budget cuts, layoffs, furloughs, and tuition hikes . . . painfully visible everywhere" in US academia (2011: 758). This long-standing, ongoing nature of universities' financial predicaments is depicted in the documentary *Starving the Beast* (2016), which describes the reduction of state support for higher education over the course of thirty-five years. Comparable conditions abound, in widespread, intensified form, as a chronic ailment afflicting diverse institutions of higher education worldwide. In Australia, for instance, Geoff Masien (2013) described how potentially disastrous funding cuts were proposed in 2013, less than six months after university budgets had been drastically reduced. Next, to varying degrees, diverse universities in economically embattled eurozone states, such as Greece, Portugal, Spain, Ireland and Italy, have felt the bite of austerity measures (see for instance Marseilles, 2013). As this indicates, certain forms of structural adjustment, including those afflicting higher education, are by no means restricted to the African continent.

Within universities, the allocation of financial resources tends to be marked by diverse discrepancies. For instance, although South African universities do receive varying degrees of economic support from the state and certain "third-stream" sources (depending on a range of factors, including institutional prestige), insufficient funding may often seem to trickle down to the academic level. Moreover, there tend to be imbalances in the financial statuses of diverse faculties and schools. For example, certain South African faculties – such as Commerce and Science and Technology – tend to have more access to internal and external funding than the Humanities. Other examples of this tendency abound. Collini (2012), for instance, notes that a disproportionate amount of external funding and internal institutional budgets is channelled towards the sciences in UK academia.[8]

Corporatised university expenditure often involves further disparities. On one hand, insufficient financial support may be directed towards important areas, such as maintenance of the institutional infrastructure, academic and otherwise. This state of affairs is compounded by the combination of massification and cost-cutting, including in the area of infrastructure, which tends to characterise the market-oriented university, resulting in overcrowding (in both lecture theatres and student residences), a lack of security and inadequate maintenance. For instance, the dilapidated state of university hostels is an ongoing cause for concern for many South African institutions, while an accommodation crisis is prevalent at various local universities. Conditions of this kind, exacerbated by the privatisation of university hostels, have triggered student protests at diverse South African institutions, including the University of Cape Town, the University of the Witwatersrand and the University of Fort Hare (see for instance Zwane and Mkwananzi, 2017: 4). Yet financial support may be lavished on high-profile occasions and activities, including university workshops in expensive, off-campus venues; costly functions attended especially by top-level management, along with the payment of the consultants who may feature in such events; and projects and enterprises purported to bestow profit or PR value or both. This tends to be a widespread practice, both locally and internationally (see for instance Ginsberg, 2011: 7, 23–24, 71; Chetty and Merrett, 2014: 111, 114).[9]

All the while, university administration has taken on a new significance, swelling to encompass and colonise more and more areas of institutional life. Yet university budgets have not expanded to accommodate this expansion in administrative activity. Instead, administrative costs often tend to absorb an ever-increasing section of institutional finances (Ginsberg, 2011: 24, 33–34). For instance, as Richard Vedder of the Centre for College Affordability and Productivity in the US, remarked, "[t]hey'll say: 'We're making moves to cut costs,' and mention something about energy-efficient light bulbs, and ignore the new assistant to the assistant to the associate vice-provost they just hired" (2014; cited in Steyn, 2016: 1).

The overriding importance attached to institutional bureaucracies is particularly evident in the disparity between managerial and academic salaries. For example, 88 senior employees at Scottish universities earned the equivalent of or even more than the first minister's salary of £140 000 in 2013.[10] In 2015, the vice-chancellor of the University of Birmingham received £416 000: almost three times more than the prime minster's salary (Chakrabortty and Weale, 2016). Moreover, certain university presidents in the US are paid a million dollars per annum or even more, and they augment their income by serving on boards of corporations. For instance, Shirley Anne Jackson, the president of Rensselaer Polytechnic Institute, reportedly earned $1.38 million per year by this means (Mills, 2012). Meanwhile, in South Africa, the *Sunday Times* described the salaries of a number of South African vice-chancellors in 2014 as "obscene", listing the names of seven vice-chancellors who had earned more than President Jacob Zuma that year.[11] Both locally and internationally, there are also stark contrasts between the salaries and perks bestowed on top management and the economic statuses of the poorer, most disempowered members of the university community, such as workers and the majority of the students. These discrepancies came to the fore in 2015 at the University of Zululand, for instance, when the vice-chancellor, Professor Xoliswa Mtose, received a lavish performance bonus shortly after the first wave of the #Fees Must Fall student protests, generated by the prospect of fee increases. Moreover, the university purchased luxury houses and furniture worth several millions of rands for Mtose and other university executives. Then, amid staff protests over low salaries, Mtose departed on a trip to the US (Govender, 2016: 5). The University of Zululand, an HDI, is located in an impoverished rural area, and many of its students come from economically deprived backgrounds.

Although diverse universities have been beset by financial concerns in the past, these have been exacerbated by the unpredictable, precarious nature of local and global economic dynamics during the last few decades. As Saccarelli notes, the current crisis in higher education is interconnected with a more far-reaching social and economic predicament (2011: 758). In 1994, Eric Hobsbawm discussed the "crisis decades" after the global economic disaster of 1973, maintaining that their history "is that of a world which has lost its bearings and slid into instability and crisis" (404). This condition continues to this day, as international economic networks have been recurrently destabilised by a series of financial calamities. For instance, Saccarelli's depiction of the financial pressures and constraints in US academia in 2011 took place in the midst of a major economic depression. Although, as US academic Carlos Alberto Torres has noted, the flawed nature of the neoliberal economic approaches underpinning market-oriented university restructuring has been highlighted by a succession of global economic crises, the marketisation of contemporary academia continues apace (2011: 177).

As a result of their various financial exigencies, many countries have become more susceptible to neoliberal economic pressures. Higher education systems in this country and elsewhere have been touched by this. However, to a certain extent, economic predicaments also serve as a pretext for the restructuring of universities in terms of neoliberal economic models. This state of affairs stems from the pervasiveness of various neoliberal ideas. These include faith in the knowledge economy, as a potential economic growth area, and the belief that universities can convert themselves into viable commercial enterprises, thus depleting less of the state's financial resources. Then, there is also the widely held notion that, should certain universities fail in this regard, they are lacking in certain significant respects.[12] Most of the circumstances that have drawn universities into the marketplace are still at work today, luring academic institutions and those who control them more and more deeply into the shadows of the occult.

Although universities tend to have been drawn into the globalised marketplace borne on a range of currents, many of which constitute part of international trends, some of these forces and pressures stem from specific contextual issues shaping particular systems of higher education at regional and local levels. The changes that have taken place in South African universities are a case in point, so some of the particularities of the South African experience are worth touching upon here. Although some of the dynamics at work within local higher education are unique to this country, it also is as if the current state of South African higher education epitomises some of the damaging and problematic consequences of setting universities adrift in the sea of globalised neoliberalism. The implications that these have had for the growth of aspects of the occult will become apparent in due course.

The South African experience

From the early 1990s onwards, South African universities began embarking on sequences of restructuring, intended to equip them for their continued journeys through changing socio-economic and political terrain. Some factors that affected the nature of the higher education system in South Africa and have shaped some of the changes that have taken place within it are worth bearing in mind. First, there is South Africa's history of racial segregation and the ways in which this has continued to influence institutions of tertiary education after the political transition in 1994. Next, this country's relative economic prosperity has enabled it to evolve into a global economic player, yet post-apartheid South African society is still characterised by a grossly unequal distribution of wealth.

Another factor worth considering is the country's diverse economic needs, post-1994.[13] Kader Asmal, then the South African minister of education, drew attention to these in 2001, concluding that "given the magnitude of our other priorities", it would not be possible to allocate substantial resources to higher education (cited in Pendlebury and van der Walt, 2006: 81). Over and above this, the new ANC-led government was confronted with various economic crises that had been generated during National Party rule, many of which were directly or indirectly engineered by apartheid or were damaging economic trends that had arisen under Nationalist governance.[14] As a result of these economic and political exigencies, neoliberal tendencies had begun emerging long before the political transition (see for instance Wood, R.J., 2014: 53).[15]

Post-1994, international dynamics also helped bring neoliberal economic imperatives to the fore. Globalised economic power structures, including transnational corporate conglomerates, and the WTO, the World Bank and the IMF, began to exert increasing influence and control worldwide, and this development did not operate entirely in South Africa's interests, particularly as a result of this country's vulnerable position as a developing nation (see for instance Wallis, 2004: 220–221). Nonetheless, South Africa's economic vulnerability was not the principal factor driving the growth of neoliberalism and the consequent commodification of academia. Instead, as South African governments, both pre- and post-1994, became drawn closer to global networks of economic power and control, they became caught up in aspects of neoliberalism, both deliberately and unwittingly. As has been indicated, this stems in part from the extent to which this approach has been promulgated by international power players and as a result of the deceptive, seemingly practical aspects of neoliberalism and the economic benefits that it is purported to provide. Moreover, the financial and sometimes organisational predicaments afflicting diverse universities in this country in various ways made them more vulnerable to forms of institutional restructuring that furthered neoliberal economic agendas.

These factors helped facilitate the market-oriented remodelling of South African institutions of higher education. For instance, the University of Fort Hare's Strategic Plan 2000 exerted a great appeal, describing how financial well-being and productivity could be brought about through institutional restructuring. By the late 1990s, the university was in a state of near-collapse, debilitated by maladministration and financial mismanagement and other problems stemming from its position as a cash-strapped HDI in a country caught up in economic predicaments of its own. Thus, it was widely hoped that if the strategic plan was successfully implemented, Fort Hare's economic and organisational woes would be eventually alleviated and that it could be transformed from a dysfunctional establishment into a fully operational university. In various respects, many other South African universities, including those in less calamitous financial straits and organisational disarray, nurtured similar hopes that a far-reaching restructuring process would bring about efficiency, accountability and financial stability.

Present-day South African universities have also been shaped by the particular nature of this country's historical legacy, which gave rise to a system of higher education characterised by various imbalances and discrepancies. This country emerged from the political transition in 1994 with thirty-six higher education institutions, twenty-one of which were universities, historically segregated in terms of race and class (Badat, 2008: 19). In general, the HDIs were located in the lower-income black residential areas, or the so-called homelands, drawing most of their student body from economically deprived African communities, thus reinforcing the Nationalist policy of separate development. The financial crises that beset institutions such as the Universities of Venda, the Transkei, Fort Hare, Zululand, the North and the North-West stemmed in part from these universities' positions as economically embattled HDIs in remote, often rural, areas. Meanwhile, HAIs were situated in relatively affluent cities and large towns, drawing the majority of their students from educationally privileged communities, and were predominantly white in terms of their staff and student composition.

Shaped and scarred by the legacy of the past, these contrasting institutions jostled with one another for secure places in the new political dispensation or shifted uneasily on the changing terrain. After the political transition, various South African universities and technical colleges were combined with one another to form new, larger institutional conglomerates, reducing the number of universities to seventeen by 2008 (Badat, 2008: 19). In many cases, HDIs and HAIs were combined to form single universities partly in an attempt to rectify some of the racial and economic stratification that South African universities embodied. For example, the University of Natal, an HAI, was combined with the University of Durban-Westville, an HDI, to form the new University of KwaZulu-Natal. However, to a certain extent the university mergers operated in the interests of the economic and educational elite. Significantly, several of the most prominent and relatively affluent HAIs, such as the University of Cape Town, the University of the Witwatersrand, the University of Stellenbosch and Rhodes University in

Grahamstown, were exempted from the mergers, thus retaining their institutional autonomy. Furthermore, the combination of prominent, relatively prosperous institutions with disadvantaged ones resulted in unequal partnerships, the majority of the HDIs entering the partnerships as the poor relations.

At present, imbalances and unequal distribution of resources remain a feature of South Africa's university landscape, as class-based distinctions between HAIs and HDIs and their positions of relative privilege and deprivation have been perpetuated. There are still marked differences between various historically disadvantaged and advantaged institutions in terms of status and access to financial, infrastructural and material resources, among much else. This tends to shape perceptions of institutional worth while influencing the extent to which specific institutions may be viewed as potential assets or liabilities. The educational elite (generally those from backgrounds with the financial wherewithal to equip them with a good education, which comes at a considerable price) tend to favour the HAIs. Such class-based distinctions often reflect the racial divisions of the past.

Racial- and class-based imbalances in higher education are by no means restricted to South Africa. For example, Goldie Blumenstyk describes how racial and economic stratification in US universities is increasing, as a result of the growing cost of a university education (2014). Collini and Sarah Amsler also discuss the ways in which many corporatised institutions of higher education in the UK tend to operate in favour of the privileged, exacerbating and perpetuating class distinctions in consequence (2012: 157; 2013: 3). Later, we consider the extent to which various institutions in South Africa and elsewhere are compelled to compete with one another, despite the disparities among them.

Subsequent chapters explore the unhealthy nature of this stress-laden competitiveness and the climate of mistrust it engenders, as well as the general atmosphere of fear and insecurity prevalent at universities in South Africa and in other countries in which certain comparable pressures towards marketisation and corporatisation are at work. Moreover, it has already become apparent that university environments in South Africa and elsewhere tend to be characterised by imbalances of power and affluence and may be destabilised by disruptions and sudden, far-reaching changes. Certainly, fears and tensions were very much a feature of South African higher education during the apartheid era, particularly at the HDIs, where forms of state-sponsored violence, intimidation and oppression could strike deep into the heart of university life. However, in present times, new instabilities and anxieties have arisen in South Africa and elsewhere.

Both locally and internationally, market-driven universities tend to labour under increasing pressures and material constraints, with the ever-present threats of funding cuts, retrenchments and closures of departments or entire institutions looming over their day-to-day activities. At the same time, to greater or lesser degrees, numerous university employees worldwide are placed under pressures of various kinds, as the spectres of quality, accountability, excellence, performance and efficiency loom over their day-to-day working lives. Moreover, many universities are now hard put to sustain their existing academic and material infrastructures or, subject as they are to sudden, unforeseen turns of fortune, fear that a fate of this nature may eventually befall them.

Various ethnographic commentators, including Cyprian F. Fisiy and Geschiere (2001: 226–243; Geschiere, 1997: 221 and 2003), Adam Ashforth (2001 and 1998), Barbara Frank (1995), Roy Dilley (1992) and the Comaroffs (1985, 1993, 1999) make points that are pertinent here. They describe the extent to which dramatic changes, deep-seated disruptions, divisions and contradictions, sudden upheavals, and precarious, stressful or economically straitened circumstances can, under certain circumstances, encourage tendencies that may call to mind occult beliefs and practices. For instance, in certain contexts such conditions may have the potential to heighten rumours that sinister supernatural agencies are at work, and they can nurture the growth of perceptions that partake of aspects of the mystical and magical. These may offer a framework for apprehending and interpreting that which may seem opaque and confusing. Moreover, the predilection to seek succour from the otherworldly may increase when everyday life seems to become a site of instability and potential menace and when earthly forms of support appear to be failing. For instance, the sociologist Dominique Desjeux (1987) is of the opinion that various witchcraft discourses may serve as attempts to "manage [the] insecurity" generated by Western modernity (cited in Geschiere, 1997: 221; see also Dilley, 1992: 6). Éric de Rosny, a Catholic priest in Doula, Cameroon, makes a similar point, maintaining that beliefs in witchcraft may seem to offer a means of making modern life more bearable by offering possible ways of apprehending and responding to it (1992; cited in Geschiere, 1997: 221). Likewise, Geschiere draws attention to the extent to which swift, dramatic changes and abrupt, unpredictable decisions and developments can encourage various individuals to turn to forms of magic, as a means of comprehending shifts and permutations of this nature and in a search for possible ways of overcoming the vicissitudes they may bring (1997: 5, 200).

Subsequent chapters explore the ways in which these tendencies manifest themselves in higher education in metaphorical form, discussing the extent to which they can be viewed in relation to the previously-delineated instabilities, upheavals, dissonances and sources of tension which have come to characterise many present-day market-driven higher education environments to varying degrees and in various respects. Although a diversity of aspects, including contextual factors and differing degrees of prestige and privilege, may affect the ways in which these occult inclinations manifest themselves in numerous countries and institutions, they make their presence felt in various ways in corporatised higher education environments worldwide.

The corporatisation of academia has been reliant on one particular form of enchantment, as the following chapter shows. It has been promoted and sustained by an ongoing process of fabulation, just as other belief systems of various kinds rely on storytelling to bring them to life and transmit them.

Notes

1 The process of globalisation encompasses the erosion of borders between states, facilitating the international movement of capital while lending weight to the increasing economic and political power wielded by transnational corporations

and international financial bodies such as South Korean economist Ha-Joon Chang's Unholy Trinity. In these and other ways, globalisation fosters the growth of neoliberalism. Globalisation and neoliberalism are interconnected in other respects. For instance, both are linked to notions of "free enterprise" and "free trade" (Chang, 2007: 13; see also Olssen and Peters, 2005: 314; Orr, 1997: 43).

2 It is worth bearing in mind that neoliberal economic practices have exercised a paradoxical effect on the forms of external governance to which present-day universities are subject. On one level, the significance of the state has been reduced in various ways, while market forces have come to wield a power resembling that formerly exercised by the state. Yet state authority has increased. In many systems of present-day higher education, for instance, the state exercises greater control over the present-day functioning of universities, requiring universities to conform to certain criteria, while imposing systems of evaluation and assessment. State funding for specific universities can be granted or withheld on the basis of this (see for instance Cooper, 1997: 27–28).

3 Many writers and researchers in the UK, South Africa and elsewhere have described how funding cuts have damaged universities in their particular countries. For example, Francis Green, Brenda Loughridge and Tom Wilson depict some examples of this in the UK (1996: 4), while Jane Duncan notes that the budgets of many South African universities began declining from the late 1990s onwards, encouraging trends towards privatisation, commercialisation and profit-generating forms of research (2007: 25). For instance, the state subsidy allocated to the University of the Witwatersrand declined by a third between 1995 and 2000 (Pendlebury and van der Walt, 2006: 18–82).

4 For example, Shattock described how higher education numbers in the UK rose by 50% between 1989 and 2004 (2008). Meanwhile, South African student numbers expanded from 420 000 in 1990 to 1.1 million in 2015. Yet as Adam Habib, vice-chancellor of the University of the Witwatersrand, remarked, state subsidies for students decreased concurrently. Consequently, tuition fees began to increase (Makoni, 2016). Further to this, James Pendlebury and Lucien van der Walt describe how student numbers swelled as never before at the University of Witwatersrand in South Africa from 2001 onwards, yet many academic posts were frozen. Moreover, while academics' workloads expanded dramatically, the pressure to generate large numbers of research outputs intensified (2006: 90–91, 88). More recently, a student protest march in France in 2015 drew attention to the deleterious effects of the combination of massification and rationalisation. In that year, for instance, student numbers had increased by 65 000, while there was said to be a shortfall of approximately 30 000 teachers and researchers (McPortland, 2015).

5 For example, Nigerians Paul Tiyambe Zeleza and Adebayo Olukoshi (2004a, 2004b: 597–598), and Isaac N. Obasi and Eric C. Eboh (2004); Mahmood Mamdani (2007) and Esther Nakkazi (2016) from Uganda; South Africans Adam Habib, Seán Morrow and Kristina Bentley (2008) and Richard Pithouse (2006); Frederick Muyia Nafukho (2004) and Dinah Mwinzi from Kenya (2004) all comment on the economic problems afflicting their various countries' universities, and those affecting higher education in the African continent at large.

6 'Corrupt Varsity Officials to Face Charges'. 1999. *Mail & Guardian* June 12. https://mg.co.za/article/1999-03-19-corrupt-varsity-officials-to-face-charges. Accessed on 12 June 2017.

7 For example, according to an annual report issued by the University of Johannesburg, the institution experienced various financial hardships in 2012, including tighter budgetary constraints and increases in utility costs, as nationwide economic hardships took their toll (Macupe and Magome, 2013). In 2013, the

deputy vice-chancellor of finance at the University of the Witwatersrand, Professor Tawana Kupe, observed that universities had to become more financially self-reliant, for other economic priorities could affect the state funding allocations for higher education. Meanwhile, the deputy vice-chancellor for finance at the University of Johannesburg, Jaco van Schoor, contended that universities would not be able to sustain themselves adequately if they relied solely on the income generated by student fees and state funding (Macupe and Magome, 2013). Indeed, the higher education budget in South Africa has not kept up with current inflation rates and ever-expanding student numbers (see for instance Gernetzky, Mashego and Hyman, 2015: 5; Speckman, 2016: 3). Local universities' financial problems are compounded by massive student debts, as the amount owed in unpaid fees continues to soar (see for instance Govender, 2015: 10).

8 This prioritisation of Science, Commerce and Technology is widespread. However, in parts of the UK, Engineering and the natural sciences have experienced various major cutbacks. This stems from various contextual factors. For example, the importance attached to certain subjects may be affected by systems of performance appraisal and other forms of assessment, and the vagaries of specific institutions. In 1996, for instance, Francis Greene, Brendan Loughridge and Tom Wilson noted that departments at Portsmouth University long perceived to possess a superior status, such as Physics, had been overtaken by departments such as Psychology. Although less highly esteemed, the latter scored more highly in the Research Assessment Exercise in 1994 (1996: 5).

9 For instance, US academic Benjamin Ginsberg observes that nearly $200 million was earmarked to extend the sporting facilities at the University of Austin, Texas, in 1998. Further to this, the administration of Ginsberg's institution, John Hopkins University, spent almost $250 million on a new software system between 2006 and 2010. Yet despite all the grandiose claims that this would vastly improve productivity, this proved to be a costly mistake that caused considerable embarrassment to those associated with it (2011: 7, 23–24, 71).

10 Fury at Salary Gap among Varsity Chiefs. *The Times* 16 April, 2013; (see also Ginsberg, 2011: 7, 71).

11 "Obscene" Pay of Varsity Heads under Scrutiny. 2015. *Sunday Times*. 8 November: 10.

12 Citing John Gray (1984: 318), Olssen and Peters remark that Darwinian notions of survival of the fittest are widely endorsed in a market-driven economy, in which the elimination of "unfit", insufficiently profit-generating organisations or enterprises is perceived as necessary and inevitable (2005: 318).

13 For one thing, as the new political dispensation sought to meet new economic demands, including the need for redress and equity, some of the money traditionally channelled into higher education was diverted to other areas. For instance, welfare spending represented the largest area of state expenditure in 1996 (Pendlebury and van der Walt, 2006: 80); while funding was required for the projects and initiatives delineated in the Reconstruction and Development Programme (RDP).

14 Many economic problems faced by the new government had arisen some time before the political transition. For example, during the 1980s there had been excessive expenditure on the military sector under P.W. Botha (initially minister of defence and thereafter head of state). South Africa's economic resources had been further depleted by the cost of implementing and maintaining separate development, and instituting and enforcing the successive regional and then national states of emergency in 1985 and between 1986 and 1990. In response to this economic predicament, neoliberal tendencies began to emerge in the late 1980s.

15 During the last few decades of National Party governance, closer links between the corporate sphere, both local and international, and the political authorities were being forged, encouraging the growth of neoliberalism (see for instance Wood, R.J., 2014: 53). Moreover, in the final years of National Party rule, moves towards privatisation were already under way with the increasing commercialisation of various state-controlled and funded bodies, such as ESKOM, the national electricity provider; SASOL, the petrochemical industry; and ISKOR, the ferrous metals industry. Other neoliberal economic strategies were also becoming evident during this time. For instance, tax cuts were imposed between 1986 and 1990 and again in 1991. (My thanks to Mathew Blatchford for providing me with information and insights.)

3 Corporate simulacra

Some of the most distinctive mythic features of present-day higher education are the forms of neoliberal folklore upon which contemporary corporatised universities depend. Like some folktales, these partake of areas of magic and fantasy. Such fables are promulgated by the principal storytellers of the marketised academy, including the divisions of Quality Assurance and Marketing and Communication and those in senior managerial positions, reliant on their storytelling skills to bewilder and bamboozle academic underlings and to ensure that their own seats of power and privilege remain secure. This fabulation also finds partial expression in university strategic plans, mission statements and policy documents, among much else. This body of myth is widely disseminated throughout the university community and frequently alluded to at university meetings.[1]

Old myths and new traditions

Numerous systems of power, including those at academic and state level, are generated and sustained by a process of mythmaking. Munro S. Edmonson observes that the "mythology of politics is in some respects its essence". He analyses the way in which the construction of a political ideology derives some of its mythic qualities from the particular mythologies upon which it is founded (1971: 232). In higher education, for instance, narratives propounding the mythos of marketisation and managerialism emanate from and are reinforced by the myths of the neoliberal ethos. Moreover, various concepts underpinning long-established features of academic discourse and procedure have mythic aspects, such as the notion of collegiality: often idealised yet all too often flawed. In his satirical work on the jargon of the corporate world, Carl Newbrook defines "collegiate" as a "fabled style of united collaboration" (2005: 55). In this respect and in certain other features of managerialised universities, one layer of myth builds on another. The current managerial myth of collegiality and the related mythologies that have arisen around the idea of team-building rests on the older notion of academic collegiality: a fable in itself in certain respects.

Those invoking narratives of this kind rely on the extent to which they may have come to seem established features of the university environment. To adapt certain points made by Harrison M. Trice and Janice M. Beyer (1984: 666), this illustrates the way in which the new managerial order seeks to appropriate certain longstanding rituals in higher education, bending them to their purposes by adapting them to suit the needs of the contemporary context. Thus, it becomes easier to import and impart some of the new policies and practices of contemporary corporate managerialism. If these are integrated into a familiar framework, initially they may be less likely to seem a departure from customary practice.

As Jeffrey C. Alexander remarks, narratives and customs, once created, eventually come to seem fixed and long-standing (2004: 537). By now, marketisation and managerialism have been features of academia for decades, so consequently, the myths on which they are reliant may seem no longer seem like disruptive intruders but, rather, like unwelcome yet familiar guests. In universities, as in other societies in which old rituals are perpetuated and re-created while new rituals are evolved, the corporate restructuring of academia is shaped and supported by a narrative framework ranging from "'time immemorial' myths to invented traditions created right on the spot" (Alexander, 2004: 530). Since fabulation of this nature can draw on both the long-established and the newly devised, this highlights the changing, innovative aspects of the mythic and the rituals that are interconnected with it (Comaroffs, 1993: xx–xxi). Yet it also illustrates the way in which both ritualistic practices and the myths surrounding them can serve to contain and control even while they usher in the new.

Those institutional storytellers that relate the fables of modernisation and transformation may delve into the store of shared meanings in order to lend weight to their narratives. Thus, they may summon up that which had resonance in days gone by, then put it to work in a new context. Marx describes tactics of this nature:

> [J]ust when they seem to be engaged in revolutionizing themselves and things . . . [they] anxiously conjure up the spirits of the past to their service and borrow from them names, battle cries and costumes in order to present the new scene of history in this time-honoured disguise and this borrowed language.
>
> (1852; see also Alexander, 2004: 530)

More than a century later, some of the principal narrators in corporatised institutions of higher education may invoke the old in order to lend weight to the new in a similar way. For instance, reference may be made to time-hallowed (although oft-disregarded) academic ideals and values, such as collegiality, the importance of teaching and the significance of original, potentially groundbreaking research; then these tend to be put to work in a new context. Research, for instance, may be subordinated to academic capitalism, and collegiality may be reduced to corporate team-building exercises and compliance with line managers. Meanwhile, teaching may be envisaged as a production line generating large numbers of graduates, human capital for workplaces governed by neoliberal economic imperatives.

Anthropologist Leo Howe describes how rituals can incorporate the "stories which [people] tell about themselves" (2000: 64). Various institutional gatherings provide an opportunity for storytelling of this kind, by means of which the myths framing corporatised university policy and procedure can be reiterated and further entrenched in the minds of the participants. Certainly, such narratives have come to form so much part of the fabric of the academic environment that they regularly come to the fore at many institutional gatherings (including departmental meetings and in academic committees). Fabulation of this kind tends to surface regularly, invited or uninvited, deliberately or inadvertently, when the business of academia is discussed, lending weight to structures of managerial authority and reinforcing perspectives and policies derived from the corporate sphere. In this way too, the fables of corporatisation and managerialism can be disseminated throughout the university community, becoming part of numerous employees' discourse and shaping their behaviour accordingly.

Beliefs in other forms of the occult can also attain a degree of credibility if they are widely disseminated and well known. For instance, in her study of vampire stories in East Africa and various other parts of the continent, Luise White describes the way in which narratives with fantastical features can acquire a quality of truth if they are widespread and familiar. She cites one respondent, who contended that one specific vampire tale was factual, saying, "It was a true story because it was known by many people and many people talked about it" (2000: 31). All too often, the corporate fabulation at restructured universities has been made to seem more convincing by this means.

Further to this, Trice and Beyer describe the role that myths, folklore and widely known stories can play in helping to forge a sense of collective purpose and meaning (1984: 654). Indeed, those performing the rites of academia may draw on some of the myths that express and reinforce their institutional ethos. Thus, they may allude to features of mission and vision statements and policy documents, and remind their audience of elements of the corporate, managerial fables framing university policy and procedure. All the while, they intone the neoliberal mantras of the market on which mythmaking of this nature is dependent.

"Real-world" mythologies

One of the principal forms of corporate folklore upon which the market-driven university is based is the tale that once upon a time, universities were otherworldly places, floating in a rarefied realm of obscure dreams and visions, all couched in esoteric jargon. But now, thanks to the miraculous workings of marketisation and managerialism, they are firmly rooted in "the real world" (a fabulatory construct in itself). In 2010, for example, the then deputy academic and research vice-chancellor of the Vaal University of Technology in South Africa narrated a tale of this nature, describing how universities such as his own had transformed themselves into "new-generation" institutions focusing "on real issues" (Louw, 2017: 2). One academic administrator in the UK who subscribed to ideas of this kind complained that academics tended "to reject the changes taking place in the real world" (cited in Deem, Hillyard and Reed, 2007: 57). Likewise, a Kenyan academic discusses the "market model" of financing Kenyan universities, maintaining that it enables institutions in his country to become more attuned "to changing social and economic *realities*" (my italics; Nafukho, 2004: 137). Collini, however, emphasises the extent to which notions of "the real world" are dependent on a process of mythmaking, regarding it as "one of the more bizarre and exotic products of the human imagination" (2012: 144). He expands on this, contending that

> wholly fictive place called "the real world" is quite unlike the actual world you and I live in. . . . [T]his invented entity called "the real world" is inhabited exclusively by hard-faced robots who devote themselves single-mindedly to the task of making money.
>
> (2012: 144–145)

Then, that which is possibly the principal invention of corporate academia underpins the preceding fabrications: the notion that recasting universities in a corporate mould is a straightforward matter because there is essentially no difference between a commercial enterprise and an institution of higher education. For example, Dr Michael Smout, a former vice-principal of Rhodes University, was of the opinion that universities "need to be more business-like" (cited in Southall and Cobbing, 2001: 16). Similar, in 1999, a previous vice-chancellor of UCT, Mamphela Ramphele, depicting herself as an innovator, stated that UCT should be "run as a business committed to balancing its books" (cited in Grossman, 2006: 94).

Both locally and internationally, many similar assertions have been made by institutional authorities, indicative of the how readily the purpose of higher education was being reduced to commercial concerns (see for instance Bertelsen, 1998: 142; Badat, 2008: 12). For instance, as Collini remarks, the Thatcher and Major governments sought to make UK universities "resemble the business-school conception of a well-run company" (2012: 34). Standing also notes that the department for business was made responsible for higher education in the UK in 2009. According to Lord Mandelson, the then business minister, this would enable universities to focus on "commercialising the fruits of their endeavour" (Standing, 2011: 68). Such assumptions underpin the corporatisation and commodification of higher education in the UK, South Africa and many other societies. All the while, however, many local and international commentators continue to draw attention to the fact that although universities are now run as if they are commercial enterprises, the differences between these two kinds of organisations has not been adequately taken into account (see for example Coldwell, 2008: 2; Bertelsen, 1998: 140–154; Collini, 2012: 153–168).

Instead, in order to maintain the illusion that universities and businesses can be envisaged as one and the same, the particular nature of universities is deliberately ignored. UK academic Jenny Ozga (2011) points out that institutions of higher education are subject to specific dynamics that determine their nature, functions and procedures. Citing Terri Seddon (1996: 34), she goes on to describe how education, with its shifting, abstract complexities, cannot easily be made to function in accordance with the "working rules" in terms of which corporations and business enterprises tend to operate (2011: 151). Nonetheless, this issue is elided, although some of the incongruities and absurdities that stem from a fallacy of this kind, reliant as they are on untranslatable concepts, are suggestive of the way in which opinions of this nature have immersed universities in a sustained process of fabulation and mythologising. For instance, when Ohio State University embarked on a partnership with Ford Motors in 1994, the university's vice-president for business predicted that this would "develop quality management in all areas of life on campus" because "the mission of this university and the corporation are not that different" (cited in Readings, 1996: 21–22).

In South Africa and many other countries, as universities have envisaged themselves as part of the commercial sector; undergoing a process of "modernisation", they have sometimes gone to extraordinary lengths to emulate the business world. For instance, Wits Enterprise, an initiative launched by the University of the Witwatersrand, described itself as a "university-owned commercial company . . . a business vehicle". The university's marketing and business development director described the initiative as a "new entrepreneurial business venture", mandated to "promote and innovatively manage increased income-generating opportunities that could follow from the effective capitalization of present and future intellectual property assets of the university and its staff" (2002; cited in Pendlebury and van der Walt, 2006: 83). As this indicates, academic endeavour is commodified to such an extent that research findings are viewed as a type of capital: "intellectual property assets", valued primarily in terms of their "income-generating" potential.

In the long run, as has often been observed, attempts to draw universities into the corporate sphere have proved damaging to the core business of universities: teaching and research.[2] The strange, paradoxical aspects that corporatised universities have acquired stem in part from this. Despite the shaky foundations on which they rest, the previously cited opinions derive some of their currency from the extent to which they function as a form of wish-fulfilment. They also owe their prevalence to the fact that they have been utilised to reinforce a further, related piece of corporate folklore: the notion that private profit is synonymous with public good. Bertelsen describes this as one of the fundamental tenets of neoliberalism, and consequently, this fallacy has come to seem commonsensical in many societies that endorse the free-market capitalist ethos. In part, the extent to which this idea has acquired an aura of widespread veracity indicates how the corporate sphere has succeeded in furthering this particular piece of fabulation (Bertelsen, 1998: 135; see also Chang, 2010: xiii).

The myth of the knowledge economy

Meanwhile, other related fables delve deeper into areas of enchantment, intimating that the corporatisation of higher education can exercise a transformative economic power over society at large. So it is as if the utopian visions of magical prosperity deriving from market forces encompass not only market-driven institutions but also the societies in which they are located. In 1985, the vice-chancellor of the University of Belfast commented on the Thatcherite educational policy that led to the corporatisation of universities, observing that "[t]here was a simplistic notion that if universities were made like businesses then something magical would happen in society" (cited in Ryan, 1998: 27). This leads us into one of the core fables of corporate academia: the myth of the knowledge economy. It is as if converting knowledge into a marketable commodity has acquired a near-magical quality as a result of the extent to which it has become depicted as a special avenue towards economic advancement on an individual, national and international scale. In 2010, the president of Harvard University remarked, "Knowledge is replacing other resources as the main driver of economic growth. . . . Higher education generates broad economic growth as well as individual success".[3] More recently, the president of Monash University in South Africa contended that the principal function of present-day institutions of higher education "is not to produce graduates and research papers, but rather deliver a sustainable, positive impact on society, industry and the global economy". Therefore, he went on to assert, "institutions have to embrace their responsibility to be partners in the social and economic development of . . . society" (Louw, 2017: 27). It is worth noting that both these university managers do not explain exactly how the economic growth to which they allude can be brought about by means of higher education, and neither do they provide evidence in support of their assertions.

Many commentators from diverse African countries have described how the notion of the knowledge economy has been depicted as a potential solution to some of the continent's economic predicaments (see for instance Nafukho, 2004a: 127; Mamdani, 2007; Moja, 2004: 23; Zeleza and Olukoshi, 2004a: 6). In South Africa, the concept of the knowledge economy has sometimes been proffered in an unsubstantiated, generalised way as a panacea for some of this country's social and economic woes (Baatjies, 2005: 26; Vally, 2007: 19). The emphasis that Ramphele places on the importance of developing and harnessing "intellectual capital", mentioned earlier on (cited in Bertelsen, 1998: 130), represents one example of this.

In various respects these and other university managerial authorities who endorse the notion of the knowledge economy echo those individuals and economic bodies in more significant positions, and to a certain extent they serve as their agents. Some of the most powerful proponents of the knowledge economy include the IMF, the World Bank, the WTO and the OECD (see for instance Olssen and Peters, 2005: 334–336; Vally, 2007: 24; Beckmann and Cooper, 2004: 2). In this and many other respects, numerous corporatised institutions of higher education often tend to further the interests of various national and international economic and political power players. The influence that the valorisation of the knowledge economy has exerted over the nature and functions of many restructured, market-oriented universities and the extent to which this notion has permeated the societies in which they are located stem from this. This feature of corporatised academia bears out Foucault's observation that "the exercise, production and accumulation of knowledge cannot be dissociated from the mechanisms of power" (1991: 165; see also Olssen and Peters, 2005: 340).

Indeed, higher education has often been bent to serve forms of economic and political power. For example, various individuals and organisations in national and international positions of authority and influence have promoted the idea of the knowledge economy, frequently in order to further their own political and ideological agendas. For example, political leaders in the UK and elsewhere have proclaimed their belief in the potentially profit-generating nature of higher education. Tony Blair, for instance, made the following comment in 2003:

> One of the most important things happening in the British economy is an increasing link between universities and business. The university sector is no longer simply a focus of educational opportunity, it is also a very, very important part of the future of the British economy.
> (cited in Beckmann and Cooper, 2004: 7)[4]

Similarly, Gordon Brown described education as one of Britain's "fastest-growing and highest value-added sectors" (2006; cited in Elliott and Atkinson, 2007: 71). This particular perception enjoys widespread currency, as is evident in the extent to which the notion of the knowledge economy has been promoted in higher education systems in diverse parts of the world, becoming an international phenomenon by the late 1990s (Chang, 2010: 179). In 2010, Chang depicted this concept as one of the key myths underpinning present-day free-market capitalism.

Notwithstanding this, some myths have a way of wearing thin, and the myth of the knowledge economy has acquired its critics as well as its proponents. For example, in 2007 the British economic commentators Larry Elliott and Dan Atkinson discussed some of the fantasies and fallacies underpinning the promotion of the knowledge economy in Tony Blair's Britain. Prior to this, in Australia, Lamont Lindstrom described how former prime minister Bob Hawke extolled the wonders of the knowledge economy in a manner that, in the eyes of some of his opponents, seemed more reliant on the workings of magic than on economic actualities. Hawke's designs for Australian higher education had much in common with those of New Labour, and he depicted his strategy as "building a clever country". Citing Tom Quirk, Tim Duncan and Richard de Latour (1990: 49), Lindstrom remarked that some of Hawke's political adversaries critiqued his plan on the grounds that such "arguments do not go beyond the first stage of simplistic assertion . . . train the population in technology and the pot of gold will follow". Thus he contended that Hawke's arguments lacked economic substance and he had resorted to verbal magic of a kind to fill the gaps in his reasoning (Lindstrom, 1993: 192–193). The same could be said for much of the other mythologising surrounding the knowledge economy that has been promulgated worldwide.

One UK commentator, whose ideas New Labour utilised as it formulated a vision of a new economy fuelled by the intellect, depicted the knowledge economy in a way that may call to mind the preternatural: "We are all in the thin air business. Our children . . . will make their livings through creativity, ingenuity and imagination" (1999; cited in Elliott and Atkinson, 2007: 77). However, when scrutinised more closely, many features of the knowledge economy may seem to melt into thin air.

First, despite the fact that knowledge has advanced over the centuries, education and national economic prowess are not always connected. For instance, Lant Pritchett, an economist who had worked for the World Bank, examined information obtained from a range of developing and wealthy countries between 1960 and 1987 and analysed further studies of this period, concluding that there was insufficient evidence to support the idea that education will give rise to economic prosperity (2001; cited in Chang, 2010: 181). Further to this, in 2010, Chang drew attention to the fact that one of the richest countries, Switzerland, had the lowest higher education rate in the wealthy world – and lower, in fact, than many far poorer countries, such as Korea, Greece and Argentina. Moreover, as Chang goes on to note, despite the fact that their economic prowess has often been attributed to education, the south-east Asian "miracle economies" had a relatively low higher education rate when they began attaining economic ascendancy. In fact, less prosperous countries such as the Philippines and Argentina had, on average, better-educated populations than economic high-fliers such as Taiwan and Korea. Then, between 1980 and 2004, at the same time as literacy rates rose from 40% to 61% in sub-Saharan Africa, their per capita income declined (Chang, 2010: 180, 185–186). Similarly, many Zimbabwean students attending South African HDIs tend to do better than many of their South African counterparts. Yet although these young Zimbabweans excel academically, this has not alleviated their country's economic woes. There are many other examples of the problems that can stem from misplaced faith in the knowledge economy, including those of Chile and Colombia. Despite the time and money both countries invested in increasing the number of student enrolments and expanding and developing higher education institutions, the quality of education declined and many university graduates' dreams of success were shattered when they found themselves unemployed (Sikhakhane, 2016: 11).

Indeed, the myth of the knowledge economy is further undermined by the problems that many graduates face when seeking employment in positions where they can put their training to good use. For example, numerous graduates in South Africa, the UK and the US find themselves employed in capacities that fall far short of their interests and expertise, as do many others worldwide (see for instance, Elliott and Atkinson, 2007: 78–79; Giroux, 2007: 109–110; Chang, 2010: 184). Worse still, as a result of current national, regional and global economic circumstances, graduate unemployment rates are high, both locally and internationally. Thus, the Chilean and Colombian graduates' predicaments are indicative of a widespread malaise. For instance, unemployed university graduates staged a protest outside my institution in 2016, drawing attention to the fact that their society seemed to have little use for their knowledge and skills. Thus, impressive higher education statistics may be of little avail if many graduates are not in a position to contribute to their countries' economic growth.

There are other reasons why there is no clear-cut correlation between education and economic development. As we know, a nation's economic well-being is affected by diverse factors, including external and internal financial and political dynamics. (Structural adjustment, we recall, was imposed on diverse African countries from the 1980s onwards, and per capita income began declining during that period.) Next, a country's economic circumstances are also dependent on the extent to which the state itself protects and facilitates domestic financial growth. Moreover, even those subjects that are believed to advance national economic prowess, such as mathematics and the sciences, will not necessarily enhance a state's productivity, for training in these subject areas may prove to have limited practical applicability in many professions (see for instance Chang, 2010: 185, 189). All in all, higher education is not necessarily connected to a country's economic advancement. Small wonder, then, that a South African writer titled an article on the fallacies underpinning the myth of the knowledge economy "Higher Education, Low Returns" (Sikhakhane, 2016: 11).

Myths, as we know, are not reliant on empirical actuality. For instance, noting how the idea of the knowledge economy has been promoted in the UK, Elliott and Atkinson examine the ways in which the illusions and delusions upon which concepts of the British knowledge economy are based have been overlooked. Thus, they conclude that "you simply come up with a different kind of reality that provides you with the sort of narrative you prefer" (2007: 76). This observation also holds true for many other countries, South Africa included, in which a belief in the near-magical efficacy of the knowledge economy is widely entertained. Consequently, notions of actuality may have to be reconfigured, in order to accommodate the idea of a knowledge economy as a significantly profit-generating financial sector.

Notwithstanding this, and despite the way in which the authority and credibility of some of its earliest proponents, such as Thatcher and Blair, have long since waned, the myth of the knowledge economy continues to exert a widespread appeal. UK academic Paul Thompson observes that its mythic features account for part of its attractiveness: the conviction that it is possible, against all odds, to triumph over economic circumstances: "Underpowered and over-hyped, [the notion of the knowledge economy] has a status of myth – an imaginary, yet heroic story" (2004; cited in Elliott and Atkinson, 2007: 78). As this suggests, the idea of the knowledge economy has taken hold in South Africa and internationally because it comes laden with promises that swift and sure ways of generating prosperity exist, just as beliefs in wealth-giving spirits and other occult economies do. Consequently, the narratives expressing these notions are widely circulated and may seem convincing for similar reasons.

The fable of the knowledge economy also draws some of its mythical aspects from the process of commodification itself. As objects become commodified, they become mystical symbols of affluence, endowed with a fetishistic significance. If a specific commodity were to be viewed objectively, from the perspective of an outsider, the reasons for the value ascribed to it might appear enigmatic, almost magical. Marx, for instance, draws on metaphysical imagery to depict the way in which commodities become endowed with an almost mystical potency (1976: 165). The worth they possess is subjective and provisional, based as it is on the way they circulate within that which Arjun Appadurai depicts as "different regimes of value in space and time" (1986: 4). In a context within which higher education has become commodified, knowledge has been converted into a marketable item, and the value ascribed to it has been inflated accordingly. Thus, the significance vested in the knowledge economy may stem in part from the extent to which it has been incorporated into what Mondher Kilani describes as "the central myth of capitalist culture – that of commodity fetishism" (1983; cited in Lindstrom, 1993: 9).

Spin doctors and simulations

In part, the incompatibilities and incongruities embodied in the myths of the knowledge economy and other forms of neoliberal fabulation now widespread in higher education in South Africa and elsewhere stem from the disparities and discrepancies generated by the very concept of corporatised, commodified institutions of teaching and learning. In a sense, the transformation process by means of which universities have been remade as corporate enterprises and knowledge has been converted into a commercial item has an almost magical aspect to it, in that it requires a transmutation of quite extraordinary dimensions, comparable to the fairytale task of spinning gold out of straw – or, in this case, steel out of straw.[5]

The word *spinning* is worth considering further, especially bearing in mind that market-oriented, corporatised universities are inhabited by a host of spin doctors, including various members of senior management and agents of the corporate world (such as diverse consultants and external assessors). They may perhaps be bent on convincing university employees (and at times, as we will see, themselves) that the corporatisation of academia is laden with benefits. They may also seek to depict the wonders of their institutional restructuring process to the outside world.

Making reference to the tales told by various spin doctors, Geschiere considers the questionable nature of the term *spinning* (2003: 175). It can relate, for instance, to the narrating of untrustworthy or improbable accounts, and thus, it is suggestive of deceit and trickery. Geschiere discusses this term further, commenting on its magical associations:

> A whole idiom has developed around ["spinning"]; hence the expressions "to spin the press" and "spinning that line" . . . . Even though the term has now acquired implications of shrewdness or even nastiness, it still evokes a kind of fairy-tale association: "spinning straw into gold" is an obvious one. Indeed, even in its political usage [as, for instance, in the term "spin

doctors"], *spinning* has retained references to fantasy and conjuring up things that are not really there.

(2003: 175)

This has bearing on aspects of corporate fabulation, and the way in which this process involves the "spinning" of various yarns, some of them with dubious features.

Another, overarching myth accounts in part for the prevalence of all these forms of market-driven mythmaking in contemporary academia. In general, the fantasy seems to prevail that by imitating corporate models, imposing managerial chains of command and invoking the jargon of the corporate world, as well as some of the mythologies that emanate from it and reinforce its ethos, a magical transformation can be wrought, by means of which universities can be transmuted into more productive, accountable and efficient institutions, working for the greater public good. This state of affairs has come to pass as a result of a faith in the near-magical potency of the corporate world, fuelled by the vague belief that the corporate sector, situated as it is in local and global marketplaces, is closest to the sources of economic profit.

Australian academic Margaret Thornton alludes to this conviction when she observes that the urge to generate profits has become a driving force in market-dominated societies. Thus, the corporation has acquired a particular significance, for it often tends to be perceived as the context within which money-making activities take place (2004: 162). A more extreme form of this perception of the corporation may possibly account in part for the alacrity and enthusiasm with which numerous universities in South Africa and elsewhere have sought to emulate the corporate sector with its managerial chains of command. The nebulous notion that economic prosperity automatically flows through corporate structures, rather like water streaming through a network of conduits, appears to permeate attitudes towards corporatisation displayed by many university managers and other members of the university community at a number of institutions. This might be one reason why, in corporate university discourse and practice, the emphasis has been on outward forms and ritual activity, rather than meaningful substance, as the following chapters show. Indeed, market-oriented institutions tend to be characterised by their ritualistic imitations of the corporate sector and their symbolic enactments of certain key qualities associated with this domain, such as excellence, quality, productivity and accountability.

Certain factors that have helped bring about this state of affairs are worth noting. When considering the various dynamics shaping local and international university restructuring, and the emulation of the ethos, practices and structures of the corporate sector that constitute a core part of this process, those strategies that have sometimes been depicted as the "modernisation" of the public sector come into play. It will become apparent that they have played a key role in immersing universities in the deceptive magicalities of the market and the dubious enchantments of the corporate world.

Cargo cults and market models

The market-oriented restructuring of universities in South Africa can partly be viewed in relation to the public sector "reforms" in the UK and to comparable changes that have taken place globally since the 1980s as neoliberal economic practices have gained ground, resulting in the expansion of marketisation, permeating even the public services. In various respects, the market-oriented restructuring of South African higher education owes much to the commercialisation and privatisation of the public services spearheaded by Thatcher and continued under New Labour.

Technically, higher education tends to be differentiated from the public sector. In this country and the UK, for example, universities tend to have more autonomy than other public services (Deem, Hillyard and Reed, 2007: 1). Nonetheless, the imposition of market-driven policies and procedures on universities under new systems of managerial governance represents one dimension of that which has been termed the "modernisation" of the public sector (see for instance Power, 1997: 42, 10).

These changes tend to be ushered in by strategies sometimes known as NPM, or New Public Management. Writing in the UK, Michael Power, once a financial auditor, depicts this as a generalised term denoting significant changes in the nature and purpose of the public domain (1997: 42–44). As Malcolm Wallis points out, countries within which public sector restructuring of this kind have taken place have undergone varied experiences (2004: 220–221).[6] However, as various researchers have noted, such changes may have certain significant features in common and tend to be presided over by similar ideological and strategic forces. Olssen and Peters, for instance, describe how the rise of neoliberalism in the 1980s and 1990s has been accompanied by the promulgating of NPM-type approaches. They also mention that these strategies emphasise the same notions, including "outputs", "outcomes" and "accountability", and concepts with mercantile qualities, such as "purchase", "ownership", "contracts" and "targets". This process is accompanied by imposing systems of monitoring and performance measurement, designed to gauge the extent to which such targets have been met and quantifiable results achieved (2005: 313, 324; see also Shattock, 2008; Deem, Hillyard and Reed, 2007: 1).

Developments of this nature are fuelled by faith in the magic of the market and accordingly the belief in the efficacy of the market university. Indeed, various writers in the UK have maintained that the concept of the market could be viewed as the cornerstone of the NPM ethos (see for instance Shattock, 2008). When discussing the market-driven restructuring of UK universities from the 1980s onwards, Chris Shore and Susan Wright allude to one distinctive facet of this: the notion that since market forces can bring about institutional transformation by providing the best systems of accountability, where these are lacking they should be introduced by means of "pseudo-market mechanisms" (1999: 571; see also Burrows, 2012: 357). Thus, in order to harness the magic of the market, academic institutions in and far beyond the UK that have been restructured in accordance with NPM-type approaches are now presided over by senior university managers masquerading as top-level corporate personnel and striving to remould institutional structures, procedures and discourses and cultures in the image of those of the corporate sector. For instance, when my university remade itself as a market-oriented establishment, it attempted to emulate certain local corporations, including Mercedes Benz in East London, the nearest large town. All the while, as universities seek to resemble commercial enterprises, consultants are often imported to facilitate changes of these nature, "float[ing] in and out to 'educate' the public sphere in the ways of corporate business" (Hall, 2011: 715).

The conviction that imitating the ways of the business world can work a special magic shapes university policy and processes to such an extent that much present-day restructured university discourse and procedure tends to revolve around ideas associated with the corporate domain such as performance, efficiency, accountability and excellence. These terms and the notions underpinning them have infiltrated the public sector in the course of the "modernisation" process and have come to haunt higher education, becoming keywords in managerial jargon and core features of university policy and praxis.

The new forms of governance that now preside over restructured universities have the primary responsibility of ensuring that ritualistic emulations of the discourse and procedure of the corporate world take place so that the magical potency that stems from these practices can be brought about. It has already become evident that corporate managerialism has become perceived as an agency equipped with a special capacity to justify, implement and enforce the changes associated with the "modernisation" process by virtue of its resemblance to systems of corporate power.

One particular set of mystical practices is worth considering here. There are certain parallels between the corporate simulacra of contemporary academia and the ritualistic imitations of Western artefacts and activities that characterise some of the assorted tendencies that have been labelled "cargo cults".[7] These and the replicas of market-driven strategies and structures now prevalent in present-day universities are underpinned by beliefs that certain types of imitation provide a means of drawing on areas of power.

Various movements and tendencies that have been depicted as "cargo cults" came particularly to the fore in Melanesia and in other parts of the South Pacific during and after World War II. To an extent, they still do so today. However, the term *cargo cult* is now contested, on account of its questionable features. For example, it is contaminated by its colonial origins, and it has been used to vaunt the achievements of the west, while denigrating Melanesian peoples (see for instance Dalton, 2004: 167; Otto, 2004: 210; Kaplan, 2004: 61). The term has further limitations, for a diversity of movements and activities with many different features and purposes have all been categorised as "cargo cults" and viewed in a similar light. However, notwithstanding the problematic nature of this term, it can cast much light on distinctive features of Western capitalist society and on certain features of the corporatisation of institutions of higher education.

Melanesian cargo practices, often incorporating distinctive Western symbols and ritualistic imitations of Western activities, tend to be carried out in the hope that they will induce the arrival of the much-desired "cargo" (Leavitt, 2004: 175).[8] Thus, cargoist cosmologies and procedures may feature symbolic replicas of Western items, structures and symbols, including airfields, warehouses, offices, flagpoles, crosses and religious vestments, official documentation, the Bible and other books used in church services, radio masts, military objects and installations. Such practices have also entailed ritual performances of activities characteristic of Westerners, including symbolic enactments of military procedures; bureaucratic, business-related or political processes; and imitations of Christian rites (see for instance Dalton, 2004: 203; Jebens, 2004: 161–162).

It is believed that such practices may bring about the arrival of the sought-after "cargo". Sometimes it is said that celestial aeroplanes will descend bearing manufactured commodities, including those regularly received by white people and, above all, money (Lindstrom, 2004: 16). Yet, the concept of cargo, which derives from the Melanesian pidgin English term *kago*, can signify far more than items of Western provenance. It has sometimes been envisaged as that which brings about socio-political transformation or religious salvation, among much else (see for instance Lindstrom, 1993: 47). Alternatively, it may hold forth the possibility of exerting a measure of control over one's circumstances in a socio-political and economic milieu that may seem to elude comprehension (Leavitt, 2004: 178–179).

In various respects, some aspects of cargo cult cosmologies and practices can be drawn upon to interrogate that which Kohl describes as the "'money-cult' issuing from the very heart of a modern capitalist society" (2004: 87). Gerrit Huizer alludes to an aspect of this, depicting the all-consuming desire for material possessions in the United States as a cargo cult of a kind (1992; cited in Jebens, 2004: 3). Doug Dalton describes how some of the "cargo" activities that ritually imitate and even parody the ways of the West illuminate the contradictions and instabilities in the Western bourgeois milieu (2004: 206). Similarly, Ton Otto maintains that "[t]he very word 'cargo cult' has provided us with a mirror in which we have failed to recognize ourselves" (1992; cited in Dalton, 2004: 199). Conceivably then, in parts of that mirror we may glimpse inclinations and notions prevalent in the contemporary university environment.

For example, Dalton observes that cargo activities may feature ritual performances of procedures characterising those in positions of dominion, which may serve as a means of partaking of, acquiring or embodying power (2004: 196–197). Similarly, university staff devise and install replicas of corporate objects and artifacts and enact corporate procedures, while intoning corporate jargon, as if they believe that the products, processes and practices emanating from this sector are vested with a special potency. Thus, to employ a concept deriving from Melanesian culture and various other cosmologies in the Pacific islands, it is as if they are imbued with *mana*, an invisible sacred force. A few of these academic imitations of the trappings and symbols of corporate power include the corporate titles of senior managerial staff (such as directors and executive deans), along with the tendency to view vice-chancellors as CEOs of newly forged corporations.

There are also the executive-style offices within which various members of senior management are housed, and the predilection for vision and mission statements recycled, for the most part, from the domains of commerce and finance. It may seem as if contemporary universities seek to attract the affluence associated with the corporate world by means of imitations of this kind. In other words, it is hoped that they will induce the arrival of the much-desired "cargo" of economic stability and security.

W. E. H. Stanner (1958–1959) alludes to the disproportionate value that participants in cargo activities attach to the cargo they seek. This can result in elaborate, even excessive rituals (cited in Tambiah, 1985: 153). Comparably, the inflated importance attached to the imitation of corporate models in the hope that they will bring about the financial prosperity and organisational efficiency associated with the corporate domain is reflected in the complicated, protracted procedures this generates. These may sometimes have a sense of unwarranted momentousness bestowed upon them by university publicity mechanisms. Among much else, the ponderous solemnity of interminable meetings, lengthy (sometimes seemingly endless) decision-making processes and the bureaucratic intricacies required for mundane administrative activities are indicative of this.

One particular form that the "cargo" can take is of special interest here. In certain cargoist movements, the sought-after cargo is knowledge, specifically those Western forms of expertise believed to provide access to money and sources of power. Viewed from this perspective, knowledge becomes perceived as valuable in terms of its potential to yield quantifiable economic benefits. The anthropologist who draws attention to this is struck by the parallels between convictions of this nature and those underpinning the present-day knowledge economy (Otto, 2004: 220, 226).

In many respects, the "cargo" that numerous corporatised institutions of higher education seek has not yet materialised. Nonetheless, it may seem that many proponents of corporatisation appear to believe that if its ritual-like imitations of the corporate domain are not yet bringing about their desired effects, if sufficiently enacted, they will begin to do so. To all appearances, they may seem convinced that they inhabit institutions that are becoming transmuted into centres of excellence, efficiency and accountability by means of the marvels of marketisation and managerialism. However, although devotees of this kind may believe that pseudo-corporate strategies and structures have generally given rise to more productive, accountable and efficient work environments in higher education, there is insufficient proof to support this, both in South Africa and internationally. To adapt a point made in 1974 by the physicist Richard P. Feynman, when he employed a "cargo cult" metaphor to highlight the shortcomings in certain distinctive perceptions and purportedly efficacious practices in modern Western societies, "they're missing something essential, because the planes don't land" (1992: 340).

Arguably, too, the devotees of the Melanesian "cargo cults" had more solid grounds for some of their convictions than the current advocates of corporatisation have for theirs. The adherents of some cargoist movements designed fake runways, having witnessed how such installations received aeroplanes bearing supplies. Aeroplanes do land on runways, but wealth does not necessarily descend on corporate institutions. In fact, economic stability may depart from a corporate enterprise just as swiftly as a plane takes off from a runway.

In itself, there is nothing wrong with attempting to make academic institutions more economically viable. Yet, as these points of contrast and comparison between aspects of market-oriented higher education and "cargo cults" indicate, some of this imitation of business-like models is fuelled by wishful thinking and thrives on illusions. For these and other reasons, problems arise when the pursuit of economic advancement and institutional security involves bedecking universities in the trappings of the corporate world, garbing them in ritual regalia which in many cases sit uneasily on them and adhering unquestioningly to a market-oriented ethos. Constant warnings are issued that if staff members or sectors of the university deviate from operating in accordance with this, institutional calamity could result, leading to retrenchments on a grand scale and the closure of parts or the whole of the entire establishment. This helps generate another distinctly occult feature of the managerialised university: its ever-present climate of fear, comparable in its all-pervasive nature to a deep-seated terror of dangerous, unpredictable supernatural forces.

Notes

1 Certain points on pp. 66–67 and p. 72 of this chapter originally appeared in Wood (2010a: 231–232 and Wood, 2014a: 68). They have since been revised and combined with new information and insights.
2 The damaging effects of reducing research and education to commercial ventures have been outlined by a range of South African academics, for example, including Eve Bertelsen (1998: 141), Ivor G. Baatjies (2005) and Nithaya Chetty (2008: 17). Moreover, a special issue of *Social Dynamics* 1997 (23) examines the corporatisation of South African universities, highlighting its shortcomings. Internationally, there are many similar critiques. For instance, Mahmood Mamdani (2007), Malcolm Saunders (2006), Martin Parker (2014), Ginsberg, Collini, Henry A. Giroux (2007) and Ryan discuss this issue in the contexts of Uganda, Australia, the UK and the US.
3 "The Role of the University in a Changing World". 2010. Speech to the Royal Irish Academy, Trinity College, Dublin.
4 Blair's statement originally appeared in *The Times Higher Education Supplement*. 5 December 2003.
5 The Comaroffs deploy part of this analogy in their discussion of occult economies, stating: "Like efforts to weave gold from straw . . . they promise to deliver almost preternatural profits" (1999: 281).
6 As Pauline Dibben, Paul Higgins and Malcolm Wallis observe, NPM-type "reforms" have been introduced for a range of reasons in various countries, and have been shaped by diverse factors, including specific political pressures and socio-economic dynamics (2004: 27; 2004: 220–221). Nonetheless, Power maintains that these various public sector "reforms" have sufficient significant features in common for it to be possible to make reference to general features of New Public Management practice in an international context (1997: 42–44). In South Africa, as Patrick Bond

notes, the NPM ethos began taking hold, along with broader neoliberal economic ideologies, from the earlier part of the 1990s onwards (2004: 194).
7 The ritual practices that Western anthropologists have termed "cargo cults" originated in the nineteenth century, in parts of the western South Pacific such as New Guinea, becoming particularly marked during and after World War II. This term has become problematic and has been critiqued in various recent anthropological studies, including Jebens (2004) and Kaplan (2004).
8 The extent to which perceptions of "cargo cults" often tend to foreground the notion of cargo has been criticised by some scholars (for instance McDowell, 1988). Nonetheless, the fact remains that this idea lies at the heart of diverse cargo cult movements and tendencies, despite their differing features and functions (Leavitt, 2004: 174).

4 A climate of fear

At present, many South African universities tend to feel that their positions are precarious ones, and their future prospects uncertain, as far as student numbers, status, sources of funding and their continued survival are concerned, as do numerous universities elsewhere. To varying degrees and in various respects, numerous universities worldwide feel insecure, even embattled, as do those within them.[1]

The sense of anxiety afflicting many university employees has been exacerbated by the way in which numerous universities have been reduced considerably, in terms of departments, courses on offer and staff numbers, both locally and internationally. In South Africa, this process commenced in the 1990s, and remains ongoing today, resulting in widespread redeployments and retrenchments, at both historically privileged institutions and disadvantaged ones. Thus, a great many present-day universities feel under threat, as do individual employees. Indeed, all too often, an "alarming preponderance of crippling fear" is prevalent, contaminating many academic environments worldwide (Giroux, 2007: 122). This chapter examines the various strands of stress and intimidation which form part of the web of fear within which many employees at present-day corporatised universities are enmeshed.

The terrors of managerialism

Conditions of this kind have been brought about by a variety of factors, one striking feature of which is the ascendancy of new forms of managerialism, both locally and worldwide. In consequence, the numbers of those in administrative, managerial positions have swelled, while academic positions have dwindled in proportion. For instance, Geoff Andrews contended that managers were one of the most swiftly expanding professional groupings in the UK (2016: 1–2).[2] Further to this, all is encased within a new complex web of bureaucracy that may sometimes seem to exist as a managerial presence in its own right, on account of the extent to which it enables forms of managerial authority, both external and internal, to pervade all areas of university life. This has had many implications for the daily working lives of academics, partly on account of the extent to which it has contributed to the growth of an institutional climate of fear.

Nowadays, many university staff members say they feel they are under surveillance, and constantly fear falling foul of management. This fear is often intensified by the way in which certain individuals in senior managerial positions may seem to have appropriated the powers more commonly associated with high priests, potentates and playground bullies: the freedom to behave as they see fit. Consequently, a sense of anxiety and insecurity has become a chronic condition in the university milieu. For instance, Webster and Mosoetsa describe how one academic stated that the new managerial system made him feel as if he was not a colleague anymore but a potentially vulnerable employee who could suddenly be deemed insubordinate. Another person said, "I feel undermined and fear for the future of the discipline". Yet another individual stated that academics "feel very insecure and feel that they are being monitored". Many staff members feared the consequences of criticising their institutional authorities and incurring managerial displeasure (2013: 12–13, 15; see also Southall and Cobbing, 2001: 21). Such sentiments tend to be widespread in restructured universities.

The extent of managerial dominion may appear all-pervasive as a result of the way it has reshaped institutional language and procedure, while foregrounding managerial imperatives (see for instance Deem and Brehony, 2005: 220). Moreover, managerial authority may sometimes seem all-encompassing on account of the hierarchies of line managers that serve as conduits for central managerial systems of control. By means of these chains of command, those at the pinnacle of institutional hierarchies exact compliance from those subordinated to them, partly by imposing targets (often dictated by external pressures) which they may be ill-equipped to meet and partly by threats, some veiled and some overt, of punitive measures should they be judged and found wanting. Ever watchful, ever conscious of being watched by means of institutional mechanisms of monitoring and surveillance, ever aware of the precariousness of their positions, and ever mindful of their institutional disciplinary codes and the punishments awaiting those who transgress them, some staff members live in such dread of incurring the displeasure of their university managements that they may seem like individuals who live in fear of arousing the wrath of unpredictable occult forces.

In their scale and unpredictability, then, and the terror they evoke, the authoritarianism and forms of intimidation in managerially governed university environments may seem comparable with menacing aspects of the occult. For instance, Nigerian academic Paul Tiyambe Zeleza alludes to the domineering tendencies prevalent in corporatised universities, highlighting the closed, autocratic nature of institutional structures of managerial jurisdiction (2004a: 52). Southall and Cobbing describe the ways in which these inclinations and qualities manifest themselves in South African universities (2001: 13). Meanwhile, Jim Barry, John Chandler and Heather Clark describe the stringent managerial control measures, bullying tactics, autocratic behaviour and other forms of managerial domination that often form features of UK academia (2001: 94). For instance, Martin Parker depicts a form of organisational restructuring at a UK business school, describing how dictatorial, intimidatory practices lent it force, bringing about consensus by means of coercion in order to ensure that all employees complied with the corporate ethos. One academic in this school said that the leadership style was characterised by "macho management posturing". If any criticisms were openly expressed, those concerned were victimised (2014: 283; 286).

In an article titled "Corrosive Leadership (Or Bullying by Another Name): A Corollary of the Corporatised Academy?" Thornton discusses the prevalence of similar tendencies at Australian universities, citing interviews with Australian academics and the findings of other Australian researchers to corroborate this. She goes on to observe that some senior managerial staff may resort to bullying tactics to compel employees to labour more intensively on behalf of their faculty, school or institution. "Authoritarian organisations" Thornton remarks, "run on the misuse of power: blame, threats and the fear of being shamed". There is a connection, as both she and Vale observe, between the autocratic nature of the managerialised university and the new forms of authoritarianism that have increasingly come to characterise the corporate sector (Thornton, 2004: 161–167, 174; Vale, 2009: 4).

In both the corporate sector and corporatised academia, authoritarian, intimidatory behaviour can take the form of deliberate role-playing. Sometimes this may be enacted by academics turned senior managers, some of whom may be unsure how their new managerial roles should be performed. Thus, they may resort to performances laden with heavy-handed authoritarianism, or they may adopt personas that may contain echoes of the classroom bully or those in positions of military command. In this way, they seek to emulate the figure of the tough-talking executive – although, when transposed to an academic context, the incongruity of such playacting may soon become apparent. American academic Charles T. Goodsell alludes to this, describing "the insecure executive who performs as martinet" (1997: 946). Although Goodsell focuses on the ritualistic aspects of public administration, his point is equally applicable to contemporary institutions of higher education that have reconstructed themselves as corporate enterprises under pseudo-executive forms of managerialism. Indeed, role-playing of various kinds pervades the contemporary market-driven university environment to such an extent that it will be considered in more depth later.

Disciplinary mechanisms and punitive measures

Managerial authority is reinforced by disciplinary measures, which can be exercised at various levels of the university hierarchy for non-compliance with managerial edicts or failure to meet prescribed targets, among much else. Many universities also include minor misdemeanours, such as sleeping at work or expressing criticism of members of senior management, in their official lists of serious offences. Thornton examines the implications of recently constructed or extensively revised university codes of conduct, frequently introduced as part of the process of institutional restructuring. Superficially, they may sometimes appear to further some commendable aims, such as employment equity and constructive workplace practices. However, as Thornton puts it, "such codes can be used as a sword, rather than a shield". They tend to be wielded as weapons of aggressive control, directed against individual employees or potentially vulnerable groupings while downplaying or eliding the problems that may arise in a market-driven work environment in which employees' rights and freedoms are eroded, while managerial control is expanded. Among much else, for example, many of the new codes of conduct may offer little or no protection against forms of bullying and intimidation, unfair dismissals, problematic promotion criteria and questionable appointments, and the awarding of contracts and tenders that may further specific parties' interests while running counter to the well-being of the institution as a whole. As Thornton observes of such disciplinary measures, "[t]heir gaze is directed downwards, never upwards" (2004: 170).

As a result of these and other factors which we will soon consider, that which Grossman describes as a general atmosphere of "fear, caution, self-censorship, passivity and demoralization" has infected numerous academic environments. Many University of Cape Town staff, he notes, suffer from this malaise, for instance (2006: 102). Moreover, Parker alludes to the atmosphere of self-loathing, dread and distrust that pervaded the UK business school to which he once belonged (2014: 287).

Additional potentially punitive strategies are at work. Olssen and Peters observe that the market now functions as a disciplinary mechanism in corporatised university environments in the UK and elsewhere. Institutions and those within them are placed under pressure to meet the perceived requirements of the market by generating a satisfactory quantity of measurable outputs and producing quantifiable evidence of productivity, efficiency and cost-effectiveness in other respects. Failure to do so has potentially disastrous consequences for individual staff members, their departments or divisions and their institution as a whole (2005: 316, 328; see also Collini, 2012: 157; Ruth, 2001: 200). Consequently, staff members may live with the hope that if their performance meets requirements, punishment will be withheld. Thus, the prospect of discipline has come to constitute an incentive of a negative kind. Moreover, as a result of the dominion now vested in senior managerial staff, and the extent to which authoritarian practices deriving from the corporate sector have permeated the institutional environment, threats of punishment carry more weight than appeals to collegiality. Accordingly, in a number of universities it may seem as if the institutional wheels are kept turning by means of intimidation and coercion. Indeed, by one means or another, individual employees tend to be frequently reminded that "they should do what they are told or face the consequences" (Hedley, 2010: 119). Conditions of this kind intensify the sense of anxiety that hovers over many institutions and their employees.

To a significant extent, this state of affairs has been brought about and compounded by forms of performance appraisal. UK academics Pauline Dibben and Paul Higgins maintain that importing systems of performance measurement from the private sector into the public services has given rise to working environments characterised by more stress and coercion (2004: 31; see also Shore and Wright, 1999: 570). Furthermore, in an article on education in the UK, Andrea Beckmann and Charlie Cooper observe that performance-related assessment and monitoring procedures can function as disciplinary mechanisms, judging, classifying and setting targets towards which institutions and employees should labour and in terms of which they are assessed (2004: 3).

These forms of appraisal tend to shape the funding allocated to a university, intensifying the pressures to which institutions and their employees are subjected, thereby heightening the institutional climate of tension and unease. For instance, Collini remarks that if insufficient numbers of students apply to a university in the UK, "they'll fail their 'targets', and their institution's funding will suffer accordingly" (2012: 157). Some of Barry, Chandler and Clark's UK respondents corroborate this, observing that this problem has been exacerbated by the extent to which targets have escalated (2001: 91).

Diverse universities worldwide are prey to similar pressures. For example, many other academics in the UK, South Africa and elsewhere describe the threats levelled against employees at their particular institutions and the forms of coercion to which they are subjected. They also note that punishment can be meted out for non-compliance with managerial instructions among much else.[3] For instance, Pendlebury and van der Walt make a point that is widely applicable when they discuss the overt and implicit connections between performance appraisals and salary levels and job security at the University of the Witwatersrand (2006: 85). Similarly, in a section of the University of Stellenbosch's website dealing with Performance Management it is stated that employees who fail to meet performance standards due to heedlessness or irresponsibility must be dealt with in terms of the University's Disciplinary Code and Procedure. Further to this, it is also noted that should an employee's performance fail to conform with officially stipulated criteria and should he or she not deliver satisfactory results within a specified period, he or she may face dismissal (University of Stellenbosch, 2010).

As Collini's and Pendlebury and van der Walt's earlier-cited comments indicate, employees, departments and institutions are subjected to threats and other intimidatory tactics relating to monetary concerns. For instance, Roger Southall and Julian Cobbing describe how staff at the East London satellite campus of Rhodes University were informed in 1997 that their institution was experiencing financial problems, but this might be remedied if certain courses, particularly in the Humanities, were terminated. However, the university management conceded that if these departments were able to devise "new and innovative" ways of increasing their student numbers within two years, then they need not fear retrenchment, at least not for the following two years, after which another review would take place. If the financial position had not been improved by the end of 1999, substantial retrenchments would result and various departments might face closure. However, two-year moratorium granted to the Humanities was subsequently revoked, and staff were retrenched (2001: 22–23). A similar threat was issued by the HEFCE (the Higher Education Funding Council for England), which set up panels of inspectors to evaluate and grade departments. According to a statement made in 1995 by the HEFCE, an "unsatisfactory department" would be granted a year to rectify its shortcomings, "after which, core funding and student places for that subject will be withdrawn" (cited in Shore and Wright,

1999: 564–565). The concept of non-viability is employed in a similar fashion. For instance, the English and Social Work Departments at my institution were informed several years ago that they had been deemed non-viable by a group of external assessors. They were therefore instructed to devise turnaround strategies to demonstrate that they could become viable. (In other words, they had to prove that they had the capacity to turn themselves around by turning a profit.)

Even highly esteemed and successful institutions, departments and schools are sometimes deemed to be underperforming. For instance, Parker mentions that the UK business school at which he once worked had an impressive international reputation and served as a major source of income for its university. Notwithstanding this, the senior university management depicted the business school as insufficiently profit-generating and market-oriented. A new dean of the school, formerly the director of a financial institution, was instated. The new dean had an autocratic managerial style, and sought to reconstruct the school, making it bear a more overt resemblance to a top-down, profit-oriented business corporation. In the process, he instituted sweeping changes, many of which had problematic features. A number of academics left the business school after the appointment of the new dean, either because they had resigned or because they had been dismissed. Those who questioned the new dean's policies tended to be bullied, threatened or disciplined. In these and other respects, he wielded control over the school by means of fear (2014: 281–292).

Imminent doom and audits

As a result of such forms of pressure and intimidation, a generalised sense of impending disaster tends to hover over many departments and universities in this country and elsewhere. Anxiety of this nature is well-founded and is periodically reinforced by warnings issued by university managerial staff and those in positions of external authority. For instance, in 1989 management consultants Jim Port and Jacqueline Burke described the dangers that universities in the UK might face if they neglected to follow a commercially-based course of action:

> In future we believe that all HEI's [Higher Education Institutions] which wish to develop and prosper will have to adopt the principles of business planning and those which fail to plan effectively will find themselves vulnerable to external forces which ultimately threaten their survival.
> (cited in Green, Loughridge and Wilson, 1996: 4–5)

In 1982, the Tory politician William Waldegrave issued a similar warning, indicative of certain central features of the philosophy underpinning what Desmond Ryan would term "the Thatcher government's attack on higher education". He declared that a "strong utilitarian wind is blowing through H E. . . . This is a chill wind for some of the less well-founded liberal arts and social science departments, and for some of the less practical science courses too" (cited in Ryan, 1998: 16–17). Standing also notes that international financial bodies, including the World Bank, have insisted that "inappropriate curricula" insufficiently geared towards the economy be discontinued (2011: 69). Similar pronouncements and demands have become features of the higher education milieu in the UK, South Africa and in many other countries, serving as threats of sorts. Accordingly, many universities and the departments within them have redefined their nature and functions in attempts to ward off disaster.

In order to effect various strategies of intimidation and control, internal or external assessors may descend on departments at certain points, subjecting them to ritual ordeals of various kinds, which tend to entail the performance of manifold bureaucratic labours, often involving the repetitive re-enactment of the same actions. On account of the frequency with which these academic ritual ordeals are performed, they have become a source of ongoing apprehension, as much may hinge on them. Sometimes these evaluators may emanate directly from the corporate world, and on other occasions they may be devotees of corporate procedures. (This latter category encompasses those who take the form of consultants.) Such assessors may seek to ascertain whether or not the department in question and the individuals therein are satisfying official requirements and delivering value for money. The consequences may range from the unpleasant to the dire, encompassing closure of a department or the retrenchment of certain employees, budget cuts or the reduction of the infrastructures to which a department has access (such as office space and lecture venues). Alternatively, and even more alarmingly, departments and individuals may be penalised for reasons that may seem to be closer to official whim than any clear-cut criteria.

One of the principal ways of generating a pervasive sense of disquiet and fear for what the future might hold is regular institutional audits, which loom over almost every aspect of the workplace. Power depicts this as "the audit explosion" (1994; 1997: 1–14). Citing H. R. Van Gunsterten (1976), he observes that current preoccupations with systems of auditing are reminiscent of the way in which an insecure ruler may attempt to consolidate his or her position by imposing intricate, all-pervasive control technologies, coupled with other restrictive measures, in order to draw attention to her or his authority (Power, 1997: 121). Collini alludes to "the all-devouring audit culture" (2012: 34), while Shore and Wright contend that "the audit phenomenon . . . has a dynamic of its own and, like Frankenstein's monster, once created, is very hard to control" (1999: 570). This image of Gothic horror is appropriate in this context, suggestive of the dread that audits can inspire (and the way they fill many staff members' minds with foreboding, just as the image of the monster haunts its creator's thoughts) and the havoc that they can wreak in the institution on which the audit team descends.

Consequently, the audit procedure resembles a ritual ordeal as a result of the dread that it evokes. Yet it differs markedly from various other trials of this nature in certain respects. Under certain circumstances, the fear occasioned by some ritual ordeals may have an empowering function, building inner resolve, but the fear instilled by the audit process and other lesser forms of internal and external evaluation may have the tendency to render those subjected to them more anxious and insecure so that they can be more easily bent to the will of those authorities that preside over these procedures.

As Power has concluded in his studies of the audit culture, regular inspections by audit teams have become a form of policing, with auditors metaphorically patrolling institutions (1997: 4–5; 1994), armed with that which Shore and Wright describe as "disciplinary mechanisms that mark a new form of coercive neo-liberal governmentality" (1999: 557). As a result, the word *audit* is routinely invoked as a warning to university staff that those who fail to comply with managerial edicts will be tested and found wanting. Thus, the university audit serves to generate a sense of fear that those being audited will fall short of the mark (the exact nature of which often tends to be shrouded in uncertainty) and face the consequences.

The all-seeing eye

All the while, employees are monitored and scrutinised as never before. Rosemary Deem, Sam Hillyard and Mike Reed depict the extent to which universities in the UK has become "subjects of and targets for" the audit culture and related forms of surveillance and assessment that now preside over the public domain (2007: 2). Thornton also remarks that the senior managerial personnel in Australia employ monitoring and auditing procedures to an unparalleled extent (2004: 164). Her point is applicable to numerous corporatised universities in South Africa and many other countries. Then, citing Power (1997), Deem, Hillyard and Reed describe how institutions have gradually become subsumed into this culture of surveillance and accountability, reluctantly accepting the control mechanisms that it has spawned (2007: 13). Such conditions have become a distinctive feature of many present-day university environments. For example, Deem, Hillyard and Reed describe how institutions, departments and individuals tend to be subjected to regular performance-based mechanisms of monitoring and evaluation at UK universities (2007: 31). As the auditing arm of the state reaches ever further into institutional life, staff members find themselves subjected to ongoing processes of regulation and self-regulation under ever-intensifying managerial control. Scrutiny of this nature is wide-ranging and pervasive, extending from public audits to self-monitoring and performance appraisals (see for instance Deem, 1998: 50; Shattock, 2008).

Cooper comments on the political roots of systems of performance appraisal, focusing particularly on the use of performance indicators. Citing Orr, he observes that these mechanisms came especially to the fore in Western Europe in the 1980s, as an instrument of the "auditing" state (1997: 38). This stems particularly from the way in which these and other performance-based methods of monitoring and evaluation generate calculable, statistical data for scrutinising institutions and the divisions, departments and employees within them and measuring the extent to which they have complied with explicit standards, met specific targets, realised measurable outcomes and generally delivered performances that satisfy official requirements. Evaluative mechanisms of this kind help reinforce systems of surveillance and governance at both state and managerial levels.

Consequently, at many institutions in diverse parts of the world, employees are monitored and controlled by means of interlocking systems of performance management and measurement. For example, Damian Ruth describes how performance appraisal techniques are employed as a form of "bureaucratic policing" at South African universities (2001: 2), while Olssen and Peters indicate that this state of affairs has also come to characterise many university environments in the UK (Olssen and Peters, 2005: 322–323). Like the long-standing ritualistic trials of academia, these performance-related mechanisms serve to impose authority and enforce acquiescence. However, like the audit procedure, these more recent forms of surveillance and scrutiny regulate and control those employees who participate in them in a more sustained and deep-seated way, thus requiring a deeper degree of submission. The university ranking system fulfils similar functions. As Amsler notes, this is an intensive but selectively based form of evaluation with far-reaching implications that categorises, classifies and then lays its conclusions bare to public scrutiny; and it is sustained by complicity and compliance (2013: 7). Such forms of surveillance may seem all-encompassing, for even those that ordain and preside over monitoring and assessment procedures are subject to scrutiny. For instance, Parker and Jary allude to the preoccupation with "validating the validators, monitoring the monitors and training the trainers" (1995: 325).

Control mechanisms of this kind have become so entrenched within so many institutions that even the discourse associated with them can acquire disquieting aspects. For instance, citing Stephen J. Ball (1998: 190–191), Beckmann and Cooper observe that the new managerial preoccupation with performance-related systems of evaluation and monitoring has given rise to "the terrors of performance and efficiency". Words like *accountability, outputs, quality* and *excellence* have come to arouse a comparable degree of apprehensiveness (2004: 2–3). In some quarters, the terminology associated with all these terms and procedures, including phrases such as "performance indicators", "key performance areas" and "the balanced scorecard", has also acquired unsettling qualities. In part, this stems from an awareness of the bureaucratic burdens that each of these procedures carries in its wake while also from fears of the possible consequences of failing to meet their stipulations.

Internal and external methods of scrutiny and control, including systems of performance management and measurement and quality assurance criteria, now pervade the working lives of employees at corporatised universities to such an extent that individuals also tend to be held responsible for monitoring themselves and facing potential penalties should they fail to do so satisfactorily. These forms of self-scrutiny have public dimensions, requiring individual staff members to put themselves on display and account for themselves in various ways. For example, in their Individual Performance Assessments (IPAs) employees may be expected to set goals for themselves, and report on the extent to which they have been able to realise these to their line managers so that their progress can be monitored. Surveillance of this nature may be taken further in various forms of self-appraisal, including Personal Development Plans, in terms of which individuals are required to embark on forms of introspection, identifying their own strengths and shortcomings, the latter sometimes euphemistically depicted as challenges. The self-evaluations that staff may be obliged to undertake may require them to draw up personal portfolios, in which they exhibit all areas of their professional lives to public scrutiny. Nowadays, numerous employees at South African universities are expected to perform duties of this kind, and similar requirements are imposed elsewhere. Such conditions breed compliance. Citing Foucault (1977), Barry, Chandler and Clark observe that these and other forms of self-scrutiny function as mechanisms "for producing docile, self-regulating bodies" (2001: 92).

These and other related requirements serve to inculcate the notion that individuals are constantly under the gaze of their institutional authorities, as if they were the inmates of a panopticon, a form of incarceration and control reliant on the principle of continuous exposure to scrutiny (Shore and Wright, 1999: 570). The authority that both the state and other external power players, including those in the corporate sector, wield over present-day universities and those within them can intensify this sense of invisible yet ever-present surveillance.

Thus, the pressure to report upwards, through tier after tier of institutional authority to the external powers who wield sway over the university as a whole, weighs heavily on an institution and on all those within it. One member of Quality Assurance at a South African university observed that "the reporting requirements have just multiplied, and everyone is bound up in them".[4] For instance, individual employees may have to report to their line managers, who in turn report to their deans, who may be expected to report to the committees in which they are involved or to those presiding over them in the institutional hierarchy. Then the process of reporting eventually extends through the upper echelons of senior management and then through chains of command extending far beyond the university to the state, and then ever upwards and onwards to even more powerful bodies, such as transnational corporate concerns or globalised structures of financial control. Hedley, for instance, describes how this has come to form an integral feature of corporatised university environments in Ireland, the UK and elsewhere (2010: 119). The audit culture and other related mechanisms of control serve to instil the impression that both individual employees and the institutions they inhabit have become more visible, transparent and assessable. This has taken place to such an extent that the sense of being under perpetual scrutiny has become one of the principal factors contributing to the current climate of fear in higher education. As in a panopticon, in which "the guards themselves must feel watched", this sense of surveillance extends through the university community to those in senior managerial positions, so that institutional authorities who become underlings when viewed in terms of more far-reaching managerial structures are both the assessors and the assessed (Shore and Wright, 1999: 569–570).

The ongoing scrutiny of staff members is interconnected with forms of centralised control. For instance, staff members' physical movements tend to be more regulated and restricted. Among much else, academic employees may be required to clock in and clock out at some universities, and compulsory attendance of meetings, such as Senate and Faculty Board, is ever more closely monitored. But on a more insidious level, forms of invisible electronic surveillance take place through university computer networks, encompassing even employees' e-mails.[5] For instance, Thornton alludes to an event that took place at an Australian university, when an academic's e-mail connection was severed as punishment for sending a message implicitly criticising university policy to other employees (2004: 172). Similarly, Parker describes how the dean of a UK business school shut down the collective e-mail forum at his school after it was used to critique one of his decisions (2014: 282, 285). Meanwhile, by means of a range of electronic control mechanisms, research data and information concerning individual employees' teaching, research, administrative and community outreach activities can be more easily captured and scrutinised. At many universities, this also applies to diverse other "immaterial doings", the minutiae of the daily round of activities, which, as UK academic Roger Burrows observes, "we now spend so much time feeding into work allocation spreadsheets" (2012: 364). Indeed, several years ago, a colleague at another South African university described how academics in her faculty were required to fill in forms accounting for every hour of their working week, detailing where they would be during each hour and what tasks they would be performing during that time. All in all, then, many present-day academic employees may feel encased in that which Parker and Jary depict as a legally sanctioned "web of corporate surveillance mechanisms" (1995: 327).

As a result of conditions of this kind, some staff members may perhaps feel that, metaphorically speaking, it is as if they, their institutions, and all individuals therein are subjected to the ever-present gaze of an invisible but all-seeing eye, monitoring and judging their every action. Employees familiar with J. R. R. Tolkien's *The Lord of the Rings* (1968) may possibly feel that they are subject to the gaze of an occult eye, as lidless and unsleeping as the ever-watchful Eye of Sauron. Certain metaphorical parallels with the all-seeing eye that constitutes a key feature of the iconography of Freemasonry may also come to mind. This image denotes Superintending Providence, knowing and seeing all, "for God is All Eyes" (Curl, 1991: 233). It is worth bearing in mind that this image of the occult, the all-seeing eye, also forms part of the iconography on the US dollar bill. Certain university employees may feel that their university management, and the external authorities to whom they are accountable are "all eyes" too. Alternatively, by a stretch of the imagination, it might almost seem as if the all-seeing eye on this item of currency has come to life and directs its gaze on the institutions now subjected to the economic forces with which it has become associated.

Geschiere's description of the supernaturally charged insight to which various practitioners lay claim, including nineteenth-century Western spiritualists and the *ngangas*, the Cameroonian workers of magic, is worth considering here. He alludes to "the 'seeing' of the nganga, with their 'second pair of eyes' . . . some sort of super-vision, but used in a context of secrecy" (2003: 177). In certain respects, this can be adapted to cast light on certain aspects of surveillance in higher education. As a result of its wide-ranging and seemingly all-pervasive aspects, it may sometimes seem as if this form of observation is endowed with almost preternatural capacities. The clandestine forms that this scrutiny can take enhance this impression.

However, there is another dimension to this. Geschiere also examines the way in which the ngangas, along with certain other skilled practitioners, such as Western "spin doctors" or publicity experts, make use of both secrecy and public display to further their interests (2003: 167–182). Comparably, in the academic context, managerial authority derives some of its power from the extent to which it exercises both blatant and covert forms of surveillance. On one hand, conspicuous and intrusive forms of internal and external monitoring – including those procedures that revolve around audits, the repeated submission of numerous reports, ongoing self-evaluations and participation in performance appraisals, among much else – feature large in many academics' working lives. Meanwhile, fears and rumours abound that subtler and more mysterious types of monitoring and scrutiny, including those of the electronic variety, may also be at work.

Corporate facades: protecting the brand

All the while, as university employees are scrutinised, disciplinary measures are often employed to stifle dissent. In 2008, Habib, Morrow and Bentley observed that various South African academics had recently departed – often at short notice – from the institutions at which they were employed (2008: 140). For instance, certain prominent individuals who publicly criticised managerial authority, such as Professor Caroline White at the then University of Natal and Dr Robert Shell from Rhodes University, were dismissed from their institutions in 2000 and 2001, respectively. A number of others, including Xolela Mangcu, formerly of the Human Sciences Research Council (HSRC), Fanie Olivier at the University of Venda, Ashwin Desai, Fazel Khan, Nithaya Chetty and John van den Berg from the University of KwaZulu-Natal were subjected to similar disciplinary action when they criticised their institutional authorities (see for instance Duncan, 2007: 9–14; Habib, Morrow and Bentley, 2008: 140; Cherry, 2014: 39; Southall and Cobbing, 2001: 2, 38; Chetty and Merrett, 2014: 142, 147–150, 179; Pithouse, 2006: xxv). During that time, threats were also levelled against academic staff at the University of South Africa (UNISA) who criticised the chairman of the University Council (Southall and Cobbing, 2001: 1–2, 21). In 2009, a report investigating academic freedom and governance at the University of KwaZulu-Natal noted that various employees "feared that speaking out on institutional matters could result in litigation against staff" (McKune, 2009: 163). As Southall and Cobbing point out, punitive action of this nature forms part of an international trend. For instance, they cite the example of Ted Steele from Wollongong University, Australia, dismissed from his institution as a disciplinary measure (2001: 29); and Parker's examples of disciplinary tactics exerted at the UK business school where he was employed also bear this out. Giroux, it is worth noting, one of the foremost critics of corporate-military control over US academia, left the United States for Canada in 2004.

In general, many academics have been silenced by the disciplinary measures that university managements are now able to exercise, or they fear that they might be punished should they draw attention to themselves. Parker, for instance, describes quarterly meetings of the UK business school where he was formerly employed, "with questions being actively discouraged and a stress on presentations from senior management, followed by an embarrassed silence or forced applause" (2014: 285). Employees' behaviour is similarly constrained in many other universities elsewhere. For instance, writing in 2014, Nithaya Chetty and Christopher Merrett described how many University of KwaZulu-National employees had succumbed to self-censorship, fearing victimisation (136, 151, 156, 169). The ways in which intimidation and disciplinary procedures are used to stifle criticism in South Africa, the UK, the US and Australia are indicative of the extent to which marketisation and corporatisation and the disciplinary measures associated with them have taken hold in diverse university environments worldwide.

As Olssen and Peters remark, notions of "market reputation" and "corporate loyalty" have become issues of much concern to institutional authorities in corporatised universities (2005: 328). Such institutions tend to be hostile to employees' criticism when it reflects unfavourably on managerial authorities or on the corporate facade of the institution itself. Next, as Jane Duncan observes, since many institutions of this kind like to envisage themselves in terms of corporate iconography, employees who publicly criticise their institutions, particularly in the media, may face disciplinary action. In fact, various South African academics that fell foul of their universities (including those mentioned earlier) have been accused of this offence. Punitive measures, Duncan maintains, have become a core component of protecting the brand (2007: 4–5, 11).

Furthermore, Shore and Wright describe how a professor at a new UK university described some of the limitations of the institution in the media. The professor was subjected to an official warning and was notified that an offence of this kind could result in dismissal (1999: 568). In 2015 in South Africa, the University of Stellenbosch authorities' response to the anti-racism Open Stellenbosch movement and the student documentary *Luister* [Listen], which describes racial prejudice in the university environment and the surrounding community, is also worth noting here. In a statement issued to all Stellenbosch University students, the university authorities claimed that the Open Stellenbosch movement's descriptions of racism on campus might harm the university's corporate image and threatened to institute disciplinary proceedings. Members of the Open Stellenbosch movement also maintained that the university seemed more interested in responding to the press than dealing with students' complaints.[6] Certainly, the media statement issued by the vice-chancellor, Professor Wim de Villers, seemed particularly concerned with refuting certain "misrepresentations" in *Luister*, rather than confronting the problems raised in the video (2015).[7] Similarly in the UK, when the prospect of university fee increases sparked off student protests in 2010, student activists in the documentary depicting these events, *Kettling of the Voices* (2015), mentioned that their institutions seemed anxious that the protests might tarnish their corporate veneers. Chetty and Merrett also observe that their institutional authorities tended not to reveal information that reflected badly upon them, only disclosing information to the press when it furthered their interests (2014: 142). Such selective strategies tend to be favoured by many other university managements. Olssen and Peters note that such tactics are a consequence of privatisation, for private sector employees are not allowed to publicly criticise their employers (2005: 327–328).

Moreover, many universities may go to extraordinarily costly lengths and embroil themselves in protracted legal proceedings in attempts to safeguard their corporate images. For instance, Chetty and Merrett describe how "a horrific pattern of costly litigation", sometimes amounting to tens of millions of rands, developed at the University of KwaZulu-Natal during their tenure at that institution (2014: 171–172, 178–179).[8] Once again, a strategy of this kind is resorted to at many institutions, even at those heavily burdened by financial concerns.

In fact, this intolerance of criticism, coupled with what can amount to near-paranoia about the possibility thereof, has now reached the point where many corporatised universities now embark on propaganda initiatives partly as a pre-emptive measure. For instance, Olssen and Peters describe how many UK universities now make use of public relations and advertising companies and consultants in attempts to ensure that their institutions are always depicted in a favourable light, despite the costs involved. The extent to which this practice has been adopted elsewhere is indicative of the extent to which the general climate of fear and insecurity prevalent in higher education today tends to infect even senior managerial staff (2005: 328). As we will see, senior managerial positions can be precarious, and the heavy-handed corporate authoritarianism that may often tend to be a feature of managerialism may stem in part from an awareness of this.

Rites of degradation

Partly in order to preserve their corporate facades, numerous corporatised universities seek to instil obedience and compliance in their employees by means of various types of intimidation and humiliation. Those practices that have been described as rites of degradation can form features of these threatening tactics (see for instance O'Day (1974). As a result of the frequency with which they may take place, the deliberate, carefully calculated ways in which they may be staged and the ceremonial way in which they may be enacted, these ritual-like activities designed to publicly humiliate certain individuals may take on ritualistic aspects. Various commentators, including Rory O'Day and Trice and Beyer (1984: 657, 659), examine the ways in which abridged versions of ritual-like processes which denigrate and debase can compose part of contemporary politics and corporate culture. Nowadays, they have filtered through to corporatised universities. In the course of these procedures, certain employees, sometimes even those in managerial positions, may be humiliated in various ways. For instance, they may be called to task and insulted in front of other staff members, whether covertly or overtly. They may also be warned that they face serious consequences that may even include demotion or retrenchment, should their performances be deemed inadequate by their institutional or organisational authorities. Thus, rites of degradation are intended to intimidate the key participant and also the spectators. Trice and Beyer also describe how consultants may play a part in events of this kind. Set apart by their seemingly objective, expert status, consultants may be called upon to produce one of the key symbols in certain rites of degradation: a report documenting the flaws and failings of specific individuals, departments or divisions (1984: 659).

It is worth noting that such rituals may come to the fore when institutional or company cultures undergo radical changes. For instance, certain rites of degradation may take place after certain companies have become absorbed into powerful international firms, or as universities remake themselves in the likeness of corporate enterprises.[9] In these cases, such rituals may be intended to compel employees to submit to the corporate culture into which their company or institution has been subsumed. More often than not, rites of degradation may be intended to emphasise that employees are duty bound to deliver that which is demanded of them (Trice and Beyer, 1984: 659). Furthermore, on account of the extent to which they may seem unfamiliar, irrational or even unfathomable, such ritual-like activities may confuse and destabilise those subjected to them, thus rendering all those involved in them, whether as victims or witnesses, more malleable.

Rites of degradation may be employed for similar reasons in other organisational environments that involve restructuring of various kinds, even at an individual level. For example, types of ritual humiliation have been utilised during military training. Certain people who underwent basic training as military conscripts in the South African Defence Force during the apartheid era have described how they were regularly subjected to a range of humiliating procedures with repetitive, sometimes apparently irrational, theatrical qualities. These rituals of degradation were intended to undermine and bewilder them, breaking down their capacities for individual self-assertion, thus making it easier to incorporate them into the military machine.[10] Meanwhile, other rituals of degradation that combine brutality and absurdity may form part of the initiation rites that may be employed at the school level, or in university or college hostels, in order to coerce newcomers to submit to the ethos of the institution of which they form a part.

It is also worth considering how certain university committee meetings may sometimes seem to serve as ceremonial sites at which various forms of verbal intimidation and humiliation are routinely played out. At some local universities, for instance, academics may be insulted and belittled for apparently groundless or insignificant reasons when they attempt to apply for promotion or research funding. (On various occasions, postgraduate students defending their dissertations or thesis proposals may be undermined in comparable fashion.) The academic rites of degradation echo some of the rituals of the school playground, self-consciously dramatic onslaughts directed against more vulnerable members of a group, designed to menace and debase. Such performances serve to vaunt the positions of those higher on the hierarchy, be it infantile or institutional, while humiliating those beneath them.

While academics have not succumbed unquestioningly to the previously outlined forms of oppression, humiliation and control, the point remains that, despite widespread academic discontent and dissatisfaction at an internal and inter-institutional level, university employees have not offered significant mass-based, sustained resistance to the worldwide corporatisation of higher education and the managerial authoritarianism that has followed in its wake.[11] In part, this is because some academics have "gone over to the dark side" (Taylor, 2003: 1), taking on senior managerial posts, or have been co-opted in other, related ways. In large part, however, it is a result of the way in which corporatisation and managerialism have given rise to a climate of fear. Grossman maintains that to a significant extent the lack of academic resistance to authoritarian, oppressive managerial measures at the University of Cape Town during the latter part of the 1990s could be ascribed to academics' perceptions that they were under threat. While this has provided fertile soil for the flourishing of that which Grossman terms "World Bank thinking", it has proved harsh terrain for the development of dissent and organisational activism (2006: 51–53, 102).

Insecurity, unpredictability and the uncanny

Other anxieties exacerbate this sense of vulnerability, including the fact that many university employees in South Africa and elsewhere occupy temporary, part-time or contractual positions more often than not. In the US, for example, the majority of the staff held tenured positions in the 1970s. At present, however, most academic appointments are for contract or part-time posts (Mills, 2012; MacGregor, 2013: 2). For instance, Tom Wilson describes how the number of UK academics on short-term contracts doubled between 1980 and 1991, while part-time posts trebled (1991: 257). Nowadays, more than half the academics at UK universities are employed on temporary contracts, many of them short-term. Some contracts may be issued for nine months, for instance, while other temporary staff may be paid by the hour. It is also worth noting that more staff occupy contract positions at the affluent Russell Group of universities than at any other institutions of higher education in the UK (Chakrabortty and Weale, 2016). Furthermore, if contracts are renewed, these may be for briefer periods. (For example, three-year contract positions may be reduced to a year, as has been the case at my university, for instance.) Small wonder, then, that French student activists' resistance to marketisation and corporatisation has been partly directed against the precarious nature of university contract positions.[12] Conditions of this kind have given rise to many protests elsewhere, including at my institution.

As a result of the preceding factors, many present-day university staff at South African universities and elsewhere tend to live in the shadow of ever-impending disasters, both real and imagined, just as there are those who believe that mysterious, malevolent supernatural forces hover over their lives, with the ability to strike suddenly and unexpectedly. Departments are closed down, sometimes swiftly or without warning; contracts are not renewed, temporary staff are discarded; long-term staff are demoted or retrenched; and members of staff, from senior management down, are often taken to task and reminded of the precariousness of their positions.

Geschiere's observation that power "is always closely related to the imaginary" (2003: 181) is worth bearing in mind. While various managerial authorities may exercise power by means of overt control and coercion, they may also rely on the workings of the imagination to entrench and enforce their dominion. In part, this is effected through instilling a climate of fear, by means of which they take residence within the imagination, asserting their authority through its agency. As a result, many university employees tend to be reduced to a state of ongoing unease, anxiety and ever-deepening dread, occasioned by recalling that which has already transpired, visualising that which might be taking place around them and, above all, by envisaging that which might come to pass. As Grossman and many other commentators indicate, this has a disempowering effect, rendering it harder for employees to resist managerial control.

This fear of the future is well-founded, for the university environment is one in which the prospect of potential catastrophe regularly comes to the fore. At times, some university employees may feel as if their institution is hurtling towards possible disaster, which might have serious implications for their departments or divisions and their own prospects of continued employment. Then, when the crisis has passed, those who emerge unscathed have barely time to recover before they become swept up in another institutional upheaval. Thereafter, perhaps after a brief lull, another potential calamity may loom. These phenomena may take a diversity of forms, ranging from financial crises to university audits to restructuring exercises at faculty or departmental level to waves of retrenchments (sometimes seemingly arbitrary, random affairs) to match and place exercises, among much else. Purportedly, this latter activity – which sometimes takes place in various South African universities, for instance – is intended to ascertain whether employees are well matched to the positions they occupy. This may require them to resubmit their curriculum vitae and degree certificates to their institutional authorities, along with additional evidence indicating their suitability for their posts. If they are deemed insufficiently qualified, experienced or inadequate, they may be placed elsewhere in the institution, or placed outside it, losing their jobs.

Consequently, an environment inhabited by mysterious, unpredictable otherworldly forces, elusive and unfathomable in everyday experience, but with the capacity to bestow good fortune or inflict suffering almost immediately, or at some indeterminate point in the future has much in common with the contemporary university milieu. As a corollary, corporatised, managerially governed university environments can take on uncanny aspects. That which might once have seemed reassuringly familiar may come to seem alien and unsettling, partly because it may seem to possess confusing or even unfathomable qualities. Further to this, routine and mundane occasions may even mutate into sites of potential menace. For example, university meetings may sometimes appear disconcerting as a result of the way in which new rules and procedures can throw various customary structures and processes into disarray. Individual and departmental encounters with members of institutional management may also become fraught with tension at times, in part because they possess the potential to give rise to unforeseen, disturbing developments. Even computer screens may possibly come to seem like windows through which the all-seeing managerial eye can scrutinise employees' activities. As this suggests, tension and anxiety can bestow uncanny aspects on mundane, commonplace features of academic workplaces. As Clifford

Geertz points out, "familiar things can give us the horrors" during times of intense stress (1973: 99).

The climate of fear that now forms a feature of many corporatised universities is connected to other developments. To legitimate the above-outlined forms of control and intimidation, and also partly as a way of seeking security and guidance in the midst of this terror, various occult practices and rituals relating to the corporate world are resorted to. However, the novel forms of ritual and enchantment that have been incorporated into higher education during the last few decades are spurious and unreliable, drawing as they do on aspects of the free-market capitalist ethos which, as we have already seen, encompasses many forms of illusion and deception.

Notes

1 Some of the ideas on pp. 75–76, 78, 80–81 of this chapter appeared in preliminary form in Wood (2010b: 3–5). They have since been developed further.
2 Andrews, Geoff. Technocrats or Intellectuals?www.signsofthetimes.org.uk/pamphlet1/techno.html, accessed on 22 March 2012.
3 For example, Power (1997: 42–43), Dibben and James (2007: 1–2), Dibben and Higgins (2004: 26, 32), Roper (2004: 124) and Webster and Mosoetsa (2001) describe how many employees at their institutions are under ongoing pressures of this nature.
4 Interview with academic from a South African university (name withheld: 2012).
5 A number of academics, including those in South Africa and the UK, draw attention to the extent to which institutional e-mail systems now enable those in senior managerial positions to monitor the daily doings of their subordinates (see for example Pithouse, 2006: xxv; Duncan, 2007: 9, 11; Burrows, 2012: 364: Chetty and Merrett, 2014: 81, 196).
6 This is depicted in the student documentary *Luister*. www.youtube.com/watch?v=SF3rTBQTQk4, accessed 1 October 2015.
7 SU Management Responds to *Luister* Video. (2015) August 22. www.sun.ac.za/english/Lists/news.DispForm.aspx?ID=2833, accessed on 13 October 2015.
8 Chetty and Merrett make specific reference to events that took place at the University of KwaZulu-Natal between 2002 and 2009.
9 For instance, certain South African executives have described how various rites of verbal degradation began taking place after their firms were merged with large American-based corporations in the 1980s (private correspondence).
10 A number of individuals who were conscripted into the apartheid-era South African Defence Force described their own experiences of rites of degradation to members of the End Conscription Campaign in the 1980s and early 1990s, for instance.
11 For example, various academics from the UK, South Africa and elsewhere note that this tendency is prevalent in many university environments in their countries, including Roger Burrows (2012: 368–369), Parker (2014: 281–286, 289), Badat (2008: 23), Duncan (2007: 16) and Habib, Morrow and Bentley (2008).
12 French students' struggle against precarious working conditions intensified during and after 2006, when the CPE (First Employment Contract) was implemented. This extended the trial period during which an employee could be dismissed without reasons being provided to two years. Julie Le Mazier, a postgraduate student at the University of Paris, observed that students' opposition to this legislation stemmed especially from their own fears about their future employment prospects (2012).

5 Rituals, talismans and templates

The new ritual practices that have become an integral part of the present-day academic environment are one distinctive feature of the corporatisation of universities. First, however, it is worth noting how readily these ritualistic features have been incorporated into higher education. They derive part of their force from the fact that ritual has long carried special weight in the university milieu, in that it has been an integral feature of the lives of universities from their earliest days, as has been emphasised at the outset.[1]

As Goodsell (1997) and Sally S. Myerhoff and Barbara G. Moore (1977) remind us, public administration tends to have ritualistic features, partly as a result of the ceremonial formality and the repetitive, sometimes stylised nature of many of its bureaucratic processes. The same could be also said for universities, and these ritual-like qualities have intensified since their restructuring, when they began taking on rituals deriving from the corporate sector and from public administration, encompassing the "repetitiously proceduralistic" qualities of the latter domain (Goodsell, 1997: 939, 956). Subsequently, these ritualistic features have become distinctively shaped by the particular exigencies of their academic context. This chapter examines the diverse forms of ritual in corporatised academia and the functions they fulfil, focusing particularly on the extent to which ritual can serve the needs of the authorities, by imparting their ideologies and inculcating conformity and compliance.

Managing insecurity: ritual and change

The new ritual-like practices of higher education have taken hold for other reasons. In part they arise in response to a widespread perception that the contemporary university milieu has altered almost beyond recognition. Indeed, the ritualisation of many contemporary academic procedures stems in part from the extent to which institutions of higher education have been destabilised and restructured in far-reaching ways and from the feelings of fear, confusion and dismay that have become features of their emotional and psychological environments. Alluding specifically to contemporary African society, the Comaroffs observe that ritual can serve as a means of asserting a degree of symbolic control over a milieu that appears to be swiftly and dramatically changing (1993: xiv; see also Geschiere, 1997: 3). This may call to mind Desjeux's contention, mentioned earlier, that certain beliefs in the occult may stem in part from the desire to "manage insecurity" in the face of instability and uncertainty. Geertz also describes the way in which rituals and the symbolic systems surrounding them provide reassurance, bestowing a sense of order in the midst of confusion, and incorporating that which might seem unfamiliar into a familiar framework (1973: 99). Thus, like beacons, they bestow light, linking those who use them to wider networks, be they mystical or social, and, like points on a compass, they offer direction, equipping those who turn to them with a sense of where they are and to where they are travelling.

Universities in this continent and other parts of the world now make use of aspects of magic and ritual for similar reasons. Cast adrift from their traditional moorings and left at the mercy of larger, more powerful outside forces, they have resorted to forms of academic-bureaucratic discourse and procedure with magical, ritualistic qualities in an attempt to regain some sense of control over a situation that appears to have slipped beyond their grasp. Indeed, many of the occult beliefs and practices in contemporary higher education that are described in the following pages fulfil this function in that they may seem to proffer a means of responding to and coping with the unstable, uncertain nature of the present-day higher education milieu. In part, they offer a way forward, providing ways of apprehending, containing or transforming it by undertaking that which becomes perceived as meaningful action. As Bronislaw Malinowski observes, belief in magic is not only an attempt to cope with the unpredictable, precarious nature of life, but it also offers a way of responding to these insecurities and uncertainties (1925; cited in Geschiere, 1997: 232). Ritual constitutes a key aspect of action of this kind.

Many commentators draw a distinction between rituals that incorporate aspects of mystery, magic and faith in the otherworldly and secular ritualistic activities and ceremonies (see for instance Bocock, 1970: 292; Moore and Myerhoff, 1997: 4; Trice and Beyer, 1984; Goodsell, 1997: 939, 944). This approach has its limitations. For instance, various writers, Taussig included, draw attention to the mystical, magical undercurrents in ceremonies and symbols of state power. Moreover, the extent to which capitalism is reliant on fantasy and myth has already been described. Indeed, it has already become apparent that the sphere of capitalist enterprise is an arcane domain, peopled by corporate and financial guru figures; presided over by unfathomable, uncontrollable forces; and characterised by a mysterious discourse that veils more than it discloses.

Accordingly, many of the ritualistic practices that have come to form a feature of corporatised higher education during the last few decades, while superficially appearing to be very much of this world, have become intertwined with aspects of mystery and enchantment, as have the convictions they embody. Moreover, they can often be best understood in terms of the workings of magic. At times, for instance, it may seem as if the notion prevails (even if only at a subliminal level) that that which is comparable to magic can be brought about provided the right conditions are created for the potency of this nature to take effect. Accordingly, various ritual-like procedures of corporate academia and the invocations and talismanic items associated with them may seem to fulfil a significant role in enabling that which has many metaphorical parallels with the magical to exercise its effect. Moreover, as new concepts, structures and procedures have been taken up by institutions of higher education, they have been incorporated into a milieu that has long been characterised by a reliance on mysticism, mythmaking and ritual. For this reason, too, corporatisation and managerialism have been integrated more readily into university environments as a result of the extent to which they are imbued with areas of mystery and unseen power. Hence, the distinction between secular and spiritual rituals becomes blurred in the academic domain, in which aspects of secular ritual, both long-standing and recent, may have certain areas of commonality with mystical beliefs and practices.

Reform rituals and rites of renewal

The otherworldly and physical actuality may become intertwined in various respects. Among much else, aspects of ritual may become harnessed to specific ideological agendas. Geertz, for instance, describes how mystical symbols and the ritualistic activities that make use of them can inform and sanction certain social norms and values, as well as the codes of conduct that perpetuate them. Moreover, Geertz and the Comaroffs depict ritual as an essential part of the process by means of which group identities can be constituted and reinforced, or recreated (Geertz, 1973: 112, 142; Comaroff, 1993: xx, xvi). Indeed, universities have long made use of ritual to establish and affirm their nature and purpose and thereafter they have sought to recast themselves in a corporate mould partially by ritual-like means. In part, they draw on ritual-like practices to reconstruct the group identity of the university community.

One such procedure that is employed to effect this is that which Goodsell terms the reform ritual. These proceedings are directed at members of the organisation, and sometimes at outsiders, such as potential clients, competitors, auditors and other external assessors (1997: 955, 951–952). University rites of this nature draw on business jargon and may employ arcane corporate imagery, such as organograms. Individuals purported to possess special insight into or expertise in institutional restructuring, such as consultants or those connected to the corporate domain, may also be imported to impart their wisdom. Initially, reform rituals may seem beneficial and reassuring, for they tend to make inspiring references to the institutional vision and mission, while alluding to the institution's strategic plan, thereby seeking to bestow a sense of purpose and direction on the proceedings. However, as Goodsell notes, since reform rituals are intended to facilitate the dismantling and reconstruction of institutions and organisations (1997: 955), the developments that may subsequently take place in the wake of ritualistic activities of this kind may prove to be variance with the constructive, visionary qualities that they may purport to possess.

Reform rituals are closely bound up with the rites of renewal that tend to characterise many organisational cultures. Procedures of this kind fulfil two very different functions simultaneously, as Trice and Beyer note. On one hand, they may seem to reassure employees that causes of collective concern are being attended to. They may also obscure significant problems or deflect attention from them by highlighting less pressing issues. Then, on the other hand, rites of renewal tend to validate and entrench the authority systems that ordain them, which do not necessarily operate in many employees' interests (1984: 661). For instance, in many university-centred rites of renewal, the cost – both literal and figurative – of market-oriented restructuring tends to be elided. Subsequent chapters will delve into the more sinister reaches of the supernatural in order to depict the price that is exacted at individual and institutional levels. According to Trice and Beyer, various oft-enacted ritualistic activities, such as team-building, can form part of certain rites of renewal (1984: 660). Not only has the term *team-building* acquired a mystical status of a kind as a result of all that has been claimed for it, but it provides yet another example of the way in which the arcane rites of the corporate world have become an integral part of current university procedure. Once upon a time, the notion of academic collegiality (problematic though it often might have been in practice) sufficed, but now the belief prevails that the rituals of team-building are needed in order to equip a group with the wherewithal to carry out its work. The ritualistic aspects of team-building activities take various different forms. For example, Trice and Beyer describe how team-building sessions can also be viewed as rites of integration, intended to develop a sense of organisational solidarity, group harmony and cohesiveness (albeit only temporary). Conferences and colloquia and internal university convocations and gatherings fulfil similar functions. Thus, whether overtly or more subtly, participants in ritual activities of this kind are encouraged (or coerced) to feel a sense of group identity at an organisational or institutional level, or within a wider professional context.

However, Trice and Beyer note that team-building can consolidate the status quo while reinforcing and justifying established authority systems and officially sanctioned norms and practices (1984: 657, 662–663). Ozga also observes that an emphasis on teamwork may serve the interests of the managerial elite by discouraging individual dissent. In these and other respects, it facilitates the manufacturing of consent (2011: 149–150). Further to this, mentioning that control can be exerted by promoting notions of conformity and group identity and thinking, Chetty and Merrett describe how the former senior managerial authorities at the University of KwaZulu-Natal sought to inculcate these ideas in order to enforce their authority during their tenure at that institution (2014: 197). It is worth bearing in mind that the ritualistic practices of team-building have often been employed for similar reasons at many institutions in South Africa and elsewhere. As contemporary academic rites are performed and their ideological content implants itself, group consensus can help prepare the ground for such ideologies to take root and grow, while fostering a sense of ideologically based group identity. At a more subliminal level, collective convictions can create the right conditions for forms of magic to take effect, be they mystical, managerial or mercantile, or a combination of all three. For instance, Levi-Strauss (1963) has explored the way in which the workings of magic depend on communal belief, as have various contemporary commentators, including Alexander (537).

Ritual and the status quo

The Comaroffs draw attention to the political aspects of ritual. Citing Bernard S. Cohn (1987), they mention the role that ritualistic, colonial pageantry and intricate, ostentatious bureaucratic ceremonies played in buttressing colonial power structures and "making imperial authority 'manifest and compelling'" (1993: xvii). The ritualistic procedures in public administration can fulfil a related function, reinforcing established conventions while helping create a culture of compliance (see for instance Goodsell, 1997: 945). The ritual-like aspects of present-day higher education fulfil a similarly reactionary role, imposing managerial, corporate authority, inculcating a culture of conformity and thereafter maintaining the status quo. Organograms fulfil this function, for instance. They have become fetishised partly since they represent a distinctive part of the ritual paraphernalia of the new corporate order, and partly on account of the way in which they can be employed as a means of control. (For instance, a colleague at another South African university described how various applications for new staff members in her faculty were turned down on the grounds that such positions did not appear in the organogram.)

These and other ritual-like features of managerially governed higher education constrain the individuals caught up in them, decreeing set codes of conduct, imposing authority systems and legitimising officially sanctioned ways of seeing. For example, various ritualistic practices in academia may familiarise participants with the norms of the globalised neoliberal world to which their institutions adhere. In a milieu of this kind, routine procedures in universities, public administration and various other workplaces have become more ritualistic as they have become more regimented, stipulating how employees should behave and also what they should think.

Of course, it should be borne in mind that the ritual-like aspects of academia also tended to serve the interests of the institutional authorities in the past. For instance, prior to university restructuring, the ritual-like academic gatherings involving those in influential academic-managerial positions (including university committee meetings, and Senate and Faculty Board meetings) could reinforce entrenched, exclusive power structures, and ideologies and practices that served the interests of those in positions of internal and external authority. They continue to do so today. The induction courses that newly appointed employees may be required to undergo at various universities in this country and elsewhere may fulfil functions of this nature, for instance. Among much else, such rites of initiation may serve to make novices aware of the systems of power that hold sway in the institutions of which they have recently become part, and the ways in which these may determine the nature and direction of their professional lives.

US academic Edward L. Schieffelin discusses the prescriptive nature of ritualistic procedures that enforce the status quo, observing that they allow no space for those who do not conform, thus compelling those who do not wish to participate in rites of this kind to abandon the group within which they take place (1985:709). Likewise, academics who do not feel able to participate in the current rituals of corporatised universities may feel driven to depart from either the institutions within which they are housed or the academic life entirely.

These and other repetitive institutional rituals may often have a laborious, time-consuming quality, serving the interests of those in positions of authority in other related respects. Paul De Frijters comments on the efficacy of this technique, describing how it is often employed as a control technology in Australian institutions of higher education and in many other universities elsewhere. He notes how many of those in top-level managerial positions may strive to keep subordinate employees busy by drawing them into a continuous series of teaching and learning programmes, university committees, evaluations, research capacity-building exercises and numerous other bureaucratic procedures (2013: 3). The enactment of such ritualistic activities necessitates the participants' obeisance to institutional and external authorities, compelling them to attend to managerial imperatives to the exclusion of much else.

Corporate magic and managerial mantras

However, in the present-day university environment, the diverse occult practices encompassing ritual, among much else, are performed for additional purposes. On one level, they are employed in academia as forms of corporate magic, in attempts to ward off the external threats with which universities are ever beset and to create the right conditions for the magic of the market to take effect. They are also intended to weave a mantle of managerialism: both protective garb and a cloak of invisibility to ensure that a specific academic institution is not singled out for unwelcome attention by representatives of the state and other external authorities and a disguise, concealing the basic fact that there are fundamental differences between an institution of higher education and a business enterprise. Moreover, aspects of the occult are utilised to impart and sustain the belief that the most effective teaching, learning and research takes place within corporatised, managerially governed universities. These occult phenomena include performance-centred ritual-like procedures, invocations and incantations; the accumulation of talismanic, fetishistic objects (most of which take electronic form); an occult hierarchy; ritual sacrifices; recourse to agents of redemption; and visitations from professional occult practitioners. Soon we will turn to some examples of these practices.

Tendencies of this nature have also arisen as a result of the extent to which the "modernisation" of the public services has altered the institutional environment. Nowadays, as already noted, university staff are placed under pressure to accomplish more and more, while systematically being deprived of the economic, infrastructural and academic wherewithal to achieve this. Accordingly, this tends to give rise to an atmosphere of ever-intensifying stress and even desperation. Under such conditions, beliefs and practices that have certain points of comparison with the features of the occult are sometimes drawn on, as if they might suddenly and almost magically offer succour to those plunged into predicaments of this kind. In certain respects, discourse and practices that call to mind aspects of ritual and magic fulfil some similar functions in the commercial sector, generated as they were by the vagaries of the market and the unpredictable mysteries of capitalism.

One form of corporate magic now widely employed in higher education is the use of words of power: expressions and incantations deriving from the globalised corporate sector. These are invoked repeatedly, as if frequent repetition will bring into being that which they denote or will summon the divinities of the market to work a transformative magic on the institution. These terms, which possess a talismanic quality and an almost voodoo-like potency,[2] include *quality, excellence, mission, premier, benchmark, strategic, top rank, world-class, flagship, team-building, auditing, performance, accountability* and even *ethics*. These words are often underpinned by mission statements and policy documents, mythic in their gap between theory and praxis, and appearance and actuality. Laden with images of pomp and potency and infused with a sense of grand purpose and direction, this high-sounding terminology has taken hold in both the academic and commercial spheres for similar reasons. This is not only on account of the forms of power, achievement and authority to which it lays claim, albeit symbolically, but also because it enables some of its users to vaunt the institutions or enterprises with which they are associated and, thereby, themselves. Thus, it appeals in part to a sense of sheer vainglory.

These previously cited terms derive some of their impact from the mantra-like fashion in which they are repeatedly intoned. Max Weber (1965: 27) depicts religious invocations as "the exercise of magical formulae" (cited in Bocock, 1970: 297) and the use of corporate power jargon in present-day higher education may seem to stem from similar, unconsciously held beliefs in the paranormal potency of certain verbal formulations. Moreover, by employing terminology such as this, with its associations of affluence and commercial prestige, its academic users partake symbolically of the magic of the corporate world. Prior to this, the above-cited words were employed to promote the brand names of transnational corporations and peddle consumer wares (Bertelsen, 1998: 142). Now they are used for similar purposes in corporatised institutions of higher education.

Jargon of this kind derives much of its force from the symbolic weight that it carries, as do the other principal corporate trappings of present-day academia. In universities, as in many other workplaces in the private sector and the public domain, the discourse that fulfils this function often exercises particular force on a symbolic level. Goodsell, for instance, makes a point that has wider relevance when he describes how some of the terminology employed in public administration embodies this:

> Budgeting, for example, portrays the notion of executive power and rationally allocated resources. Auditing points to the accountability of those handling public monies, while performance evaluation reinforces the idea of relating pay and promotion to merit.
>
> (1997: 948)

In a context of this nature, in which words speak louder than actions, that which is imbued with symbolic significance, embodying or bearing out specific notions and perceptions can bestow a certain sense of meaning, purpose and order on aspects of human experience (in this case, the university milieu). There are, for instance, the bureaucratic networks with their mysterious ramifications that constitute distinctive features of present-day restructured universities, emblematic as they are of that which is believed to bring about transparency, efficiency and cost-effectiveness. They derive special force from the extent to which they symbolise corporate chains of command.

Corporate jargon also derives part of its impact from the power of language itself, which can serve to control and command its users. In its invisible, pervasive potency, this is comparable to the workings of magic. Various types of discourse draw users into specific ideological frameworks, and once enmeshed within them, it can prove hard to break free. As Bertelsen points out, dominant or frequently used discourses serve to make the ideological practices they propound appear customary, logical and appropriate (1998: 134). The discourse now widely employed in higher education performs this role. By encasing restructured universities within a specific verbal-ideological framework, it redefines them, prescribing their nature and function. In consequence, language of this nature serves to veil the workings of power from those it dominates, obscuring ideological agendas that serve the interests of the wealthy and powerful beneath a veneer of efficiency, accountability and productivity. Shore and Wright describe how language of this kind imposes and entrenches specific notions, policies and procedures by depicting them as rational and commonsensical (1999: 559). Much of the corporate jargon now foregrounded in the university environment fulfils a function of this kind, as do the neoliberal ideologies that inform it. For example, terms like *accountability, efficiency, quality, performance* and *value for money* may appear to offer practical, constructive guidelines for enhancing institutions of higher education. However, it will become apparent that they emanate from and entrench corporatisation and commodification.

As the words of power with which corporate discourse is laden are considered, parallels with various magical beliefs and ritual practices come to the fore. *Excellence*, one of the words used most of all, can be subjected to various forms of verbal magic in that it is essentially an empty word, to be filled with whatever meanings the users seek to bestow upon it. *Quality* and *world-class* are similar terms. US academic Bill Readings remarks that "excellence has the singular advantage of being entirely meaningless, or to put it more precisely, non-referential" (1996: 22; see also Bertelsen, 1998: 143). Sometimes when particular perceptions and ideologies are hollow, various forms of magic can flow in to fill the void. This has been the case with a word like *excellence*.

Excellence derives its cachet from the fact that it has long been vested with special potency in the corporate sector. For example, Tom Peters and Robert H. Waterman's *In Search of Excellence* (2006) was highly recommended and sometimes mandatory reading for many local and international business executives, assuming a status resembling that of a sacred text in which seekers after truth are advised to immerse themselves. Many universities now aspire to excellence. The University of Syracuse, at which Readings worked, defined "The Pursuit of Excellence" as one of its goals, for instance (1996: 10). However, like the Holy Grail, excellence proves hard enough to pursue, let alone attain. So the act of striving after excellence is often depicted as an end in itself, just as almost all the knights of Camelot who embarked on the quest for the Grail had to content themselves with the knowledge that they had sought this sacred object, since only one of their number was permitted to approach it. Thereafter, it may be borne in mind, he was no longer fit for this world. It is also worth recalling that all the other knights who set off in search of the Grail failed to achieve their objective, becoming confused, overwhelmed by external forces, distracted or waylaid in the course of their quests. The quests for excellence on which institutions of higher learning embark may resemble these legendary missions in various respects.

Since excellence eludes those who aspire to it, universities tend to resort to verbal magic of a kind. *Excellence* appears to possess a special capacity to bring about that which it denotes, if repeated often enough. Indeed, reiteration can bestow a sense of truth on that which might otherwise appear far-fetched, and it can make facile assumptions and unsubstantiated allegations seem solid, objective and indisputable. According to Moore and Myerhoff, repetition is a significant feature of many rituals, since repetitive ritualistic procedures symbolically link themselves with cyclical patterns in the cosmos, evoking a sense of ongoing order and stability, thereby consolidating and legitimising ephemeral ideological notions (1977: 8). Through repetition, too, the conventions and codes underlying various ritual procedures may come to seem familiar and deep-rooted (see for instance Goodsell, 1997: 943). Repetition has become an oft-employed tactic in managerial discourse for these reasons.

Accordingly, in present-day corporatised institutions of higher education, terms like, *ethics, quality, world-class* and *excellence* are repeatedly alluded to as if they are already in existence, or as if they might be brought to pass by this means. Indeed, it is as if universities seek to bestow attributes such as excellence, quality and world-class status on themselves by means of oft-repeated ritual declarations in which they profess to be in possession of them. At times, this may serve as a form of wish-fulfilment, as if repeated reference to a far-fetched notion or narrative might bring that which it depicts into being. Thus, many institutions of higher education employ one of the principles on which magic is said to be based. Malinowski, for one, is of the opinion that "magic is an elaboration of the infant experience that a certain utterance could bring about the gratification of specific wants" (1935, cited in Pels, 2003: 11).

Practices of this kind are also prevalent in the corporate world. For instance, Kenneth Galbraith describes how Andrew W. Mellon, a prominent US banker in the 1910s and 1920s and secretary of the Treasury in the 1920s, announced the year before the 1929 Wall Street Crash that "the high tide of prosperity will continue". Galbraith then notes that similar utterances have been made by many other public figures, remarking that it is as if assertions of this nature, however improbable they may appear, are believed to possess a mystical capacity to shape the course of events:

> [T]hese are not forecasts; it is not supposed that the men who make them are privileged to look further into the future than the rest. Mr Mellon was participating in a ritual which, in our society, is thought to be of great value for influencing the course of the business cycle. By affirming solemnly that prosperity will continue, it is believed, one can help ensure that prosperity will in fact continue.
>
> (1975: 44)

In various ritual declarations in both the academic and corporate sectors, the notion of excellence is invoked because of the particular potency this term is believed to possess. Consequently, the word has been employed frequently worldwide, indiscriminately, and sometimes incongruously. For instance, Readings mentions that Cornell University Parking Services once received an award for "excellence in car parking" (1996: 24). Meanwhile, on an open day at Guantanamo Bay, designed to impress the media, the institution described itself as a site of excellence. (It did not indicate exactly what it was that it excelled in.) As a result of all the applications and misapplications to which it has been subjected, the term *excellence* is beginning to resemble cheap jam: a bland, mass-produced item that can be applied liberally to a diversity of surface areas, partially obscuring that which lies beneath it.

Nonetheless, the term *excellence* continues to be widely used for the various reasons outlined above; and also on account of the transformative magic that it appears to possess. Pithouse, for one, describes how *excellence*, like *world-class*, is used to justify corporatisation (2006: xix), transmuting it into an admirable, productive academic process.

Quality is a comparable term, laden with mystery and magic partly to compensate for the fact that, like *excellence*, it is essentially a vacuous term: a receptacle into which different meanings can be poured. As one of the principal words of power, the word *quality* is routinely uttered for purposes of ritual and enchantment, as if calling on this concept will cause it to manifest itself. Like faith, the notion of quality exists alongside hope, denoting that which it is hoped will eventually come to pass through the magical potency of words. Moreover, if the concept of quality is invoked often enough, it seems almost as if, like faith, it will come to cover a multitude of shortcomings. In today's disillusioned, dispirited academic world, we may not have much faith left, and minimal hope, so the greatest of these is quality.

Quality also tends to be frequently used partly on account of the symbolic weight with which it is laden, drawing as it does on aspects of the unseen and imaginary. Again, Marx could be borne in mind. He emphasises the mystical, cryptic aspects of value, drawing attention to the figurative aspects of this concept by depicting it as "a social hieroglyphic" (1976: 167). A hieroglyph is a symbol, and, as such, it does not exist in its own right. Similarly, the concept of value lacks independent substance and meaning. Instead, it is a social construct with symbolic features, indicative of certain ways of seeing and specific predilections in the particular social context within which value was accorded. Quality, like value, cannot be categorically defined, and the reasons why certain products of marketised universities are believed to be valuable, and thus emblematic of quality, stem from certain dominant tendencies within that specific milieu. For instance, South African academic Sioux McKenna describes the way in which *quality* and other related terms emanate from and express neoliberal ideological concerns (2011: 3). Moreover, Ian Roper remarks that, as a result of the way "quality" has been defined by Quality Assurance divisions, the concept has become closely connected "to utilitarian, market-based assumptions of what constitutes 'goodness' " (2004: 120). Accordingly, *quality* has become a term of approbation for that which helps further market-oriented agendas.

On account of these and other related features, *quality* could be described as a weasel word. McKenna depicts the deceptive, evasive features of terms such as "excellence" as weasel-words. Indeed, they have "weaseled" their way into higher education, to join the pantheon of power words in the institutional vocabulary (2011: 3). The extent to which words such as *quality* and *excellence* have established themselves reflects the way in which their potentially damaging features often tend to go undetected, just as a weasel may slip by unnoticed. Superficially, such words may seem appealing, and likewise, a weasel's appearance may belie its destructive potential. Like the creature they denote, weasel words can bite unexpectedly. In other words, they can be turned against some of their academic users.

Particularly as a result of these market-related uses to which it can be put, the notion of quality has been used to further the commodification and privatisation of the public services in the UK and elsewhere, and accordingly, it has dominated the discourse of New Public Management (Roper, 2004: 134). Nowadays, the idea of quality pervades much discourse and procedure in higher education worldwide. As a result, this concept may seem akin to a vague, amorphous and all-engulfing entity, like The Blob in a horror film.

The otherworldly aspects of the word *quality* extend further than this. The term originally had an almost mystical aspect, because, like holiness or faith, quality traditionally stood for something intrinsic and intangible that could not be interrogated, weighed or measured. However, as Southall and Cobbing have pointed out, in the current university context, quality can be quantified (2001: 16). For instance, the quality of academic work conducted by individuals, departments and institutions is assessed quantifiably. Accordingly, much significance is attached to the points on a balanced scorecard; the number of performance-related targets met; number of citations; FTE (full-time equivalent) student numbers and graduate numbers (especially postgraduates); the numerical data upon which performance indicators depend; numbers of course credits and academic outputs; numerically related journal rankings and ratings of institutions, schools, departments, and researchers; performance ratings; the scores accorded in research and teaching assessments, among much else.

Ritzer discusses the "calculability" that comprises a basic element of one of the core principles underpinning the corporatisation of higher education, rationalisation. According to Ritzer, rationalisation entails

> an emphasis on things that can be calculated, counted, quantified. It often results in an emphasis on quantity, rather than quality. This leads to a sense that quality is equal to certain usually (but not always) large quantities of things.
>
> (1999: 82)

Southall and Cobbing concur with this, concluding that, ironically, quality has come to stand for that to which it is diametrically opposed: quantity (2001: 16).

Excellence and *quality* have become two of the principal power words in contemporary higher education partly as a result of their obscure yet high-sounding nature. They are both words that intimate much, yet say very little, apart from surrounding the managerial authorities who employ them often with a mysterious aura of high importance. As these terms have been elevated, coming to preside over much university policy and procedure, their inscrutable aspects have intensified and they have become vested with a deeper magic in consequence. Words with comparable features have sometimes been used for magic of a similar kind, buttressing various authority systems by forming part of that which Kaplan depicts as "the magical technologies of pomp": the strategic use of "glorified, distinguished, ennobled, and thereby mystified words and other symbolic forms" (2003: 188–189). This mystification can drain such terminology of meaning, while also rendering it monologic and prescriptive. The language of ritual may also be characterised by similar qualities. Maurice Bloch describes the extent to which this discourse may convey minimal information, and then, as a result of its fixed, stylised nature, it closes down other communicative possibilities, while imposing set ways of seeing and doing (1974; cited in Schieffelin, 1985: 708–709). Indeed, the principal power words of corporate academia are frequently invoked by institutional authorities and those presiding over them on account of the extent to which they can be employed for purposes of this kind. Moreover, the notions of excellence and quality that they represent tend to benefit a select and compliant few, while downplaying and denigrating the many. For example, Amsler describes how the university ranking system promulgates and reinforces specific notions of value that further the interests of the privileged (2013: 6).

Corporate familiars: mission statements and templates

Like *quality*, the term *mission* has spiritual aspects to it, evoking images of a sacred quest, a venture charged with mystical significance or an enterprise of critical consequence. The word *mission* is frequently employed for this reason. Accordingly, the creation of institutional mission statements is designed to bestow a noble, hallowed quality on corporate endeavours, partly as a result of the high-minded rhetoric they employ and the lofty ideals to which they lay claim. Bertelsen outlines how *mission*, with its hallowed associations, harnesses spirituality to market forces, thereby elevating the corporations and institutions that employ this term, even if only at the level of discourse. Indeed, in terms of its special capacity to mingle the sublime and the secular, and utilise the spiritual to legitimate the pursuit of Mammon, *mission* delivers one of the principal goals of corporate endeavour: VFM, or value for money (1998: 136, 142). At the same time, these contradictions drain the term *mission* of much of its meaning. In the context of higher education, for instance, it exists primarily as a talismanic token of marketisation. Mission statements, infused with the contradictions embodied in the word *mission*, are characterised by a comparable lack of substance.

The hallowed aspects of mission statements also derive from their fetishistic function, as part of the ritual paraphernalia of the corporate sector. They are often enshrined in important places close to seats of managerial authority (such as the areas that serve as waiting rooms outside senior managerial offices), while subordinate staff members are instructed to display them, like icons, in their own departments or divisions. Like fetishes, the significance attached to mission statements derives primarily from their symbolic identity as emblems of corporate branding, while the specific messages they contain tend to be viewed as matters of secondary importance. There are, superficially, certain points of comparison between mission statements, cluttered as they are with the power words of market-oriented managerialism, and the embroidered samplers bearing religious homilies that once adorned many nineteenth-century Western homes. The latter items, decorative though they were meant to be, also served to create an impression of piety. For their part, mission statements are suggestive of a faithful adherence to corporate principles, and they do decorate dwelling places of corporate enterprise.

In order to assess quality, also to gauge whether or not an institution is entitled to lay claim to excellence, and to ascertain the extent to which an institution's academic activities are in keeping with its mission statement, the most frequently conducted ritual in corporatised higher education takes place: the completion of templates. Thus most significant academic documents, including learning guides, module descriptions, progress reports, funding applications and IPAs among much else, encase information in small electronic boxes.

Since hardly anything of substance can be performed without completing a template, these items have become fetishistic objects. William Pietz mentions that during the Enlightenment, some Western intellectuals defined fetishistic practices "as the worship of haphazardly chosen material objects believed to be endowed with purpose, intention and a direct power over the material life of both human beings and the natural world" (1998; cited in Pels, 2003: 8). Although the word *haphazard* renders the preceding definition problematic, it is nonetheless worth relating it to the corporate academic context, in which the inordinate value attached to templates may appear to be based on arbitrary criteria. The conviction that certain templates may be able to influence the course of events could also seem to be founded on an unsubstantiated, irrational faith in the importance and the efficacy of these objects.

Geertz describes the symbols on which various established religions and spiritual persuasions depend as "synoptic formulations of reality" and "templates for producing reality" as a result of the power accorded to them (1973: 95). In various respects, the templates employed in the present-day university environment fulfil both these functions. In one sense, they epitomise the nature of present-day higher education, within which everything takes place according to precise procedures and is confined and contained. Yet they may also contain versions of events which may seem to have only a tenuous connection with the empirical phenomena to which they make reference. However, as these templates and their contents are scrutinised and disseminated, and as similar versions of these documents are generated, the notions they contain may gradually take hold.

In this sense, then, templates appear to generate a "reality" that overrides physical, verifiable actualities. Mission statements could be viewed in a similar light, as vehicles for recreating actuality. They tend to be treated as if they express truths that those who inhabit the institutional environment of which they speak would do well to heed. In this, they exhibit the "deep moral seriousness" with which sacred objects are believed to be imbued (Geertz, 1973: 126). This state of affairs can have far-reaching implications, propounding one particular way of seeing and doing, while sealing off others. For instance, Sherry Ortner describes how the symbolic systems in rituals may make it hard for participants to perceive and react to a given situation in a way that runs counter to official versions of events (1978; cited in Schieffelin, 1985: 707).

Martha Kaplan and John Kelly have devised the term *state familiars* to indicate the "magical vehicles of power", such as flags and the printed word, utilised by the colonial state to impose and reinforce its dominion. According to Kaplan, these objects came to be perceived as imbued with mana by Fijian locals under colonial control. As a result of their association with colonial authority, they seemed to embody its power (Kaplan, 2003: 183–184, 188–189). The concept of "state familiars" could be adapted to the current academic context. At present, the new managerial authorities draw on "vehicles or technologies" associated with the corporate domain, with its market-oriented models of efficiency and excellence, believing that these will enable institutions of higher education to gain access to the productivity, profit and entrepreneurial capabilities associated with the business world. Thus, items such as mission statements and templates function as corporate and managerial familiars, instituting and augmenting the dominion of the market and managerial authority, just as the ceremonial trappings of state power (including flags, statues and uniforms) are used to assert governance and command deference (see for instance Goodsell, 1997: 945).

Like fetishes, templates may appear commonplace to outsiders, but to those carrying out lengthy ritual activities involving these items, they may seem fraught with meaning, sometimes obscure, but very powerful and far-reaching in its possible implications. Like talismans, too, templates have to be gathered together in large numbers to ward off the evil eye: those of external assessors and auditors.

As with the performance of a ritual, the completion of a template depends more on the enactment and form than actual substance. Provided words of power are employed (the specific terminology mandatory for parts of this ritual activity are generally stipulated in sacred texts such as policy documents) and an appropriate format is adhered to, the ritual act of filling in a template often appears to be of principal importance, while its actual content seems a matter of lesser concern. This emphasis on adhering to proper procedure is in keeping with a general tendency in ritual which, as Bloch notes, is often constrained by fixed, formulaic codes (1974; cited in Howe, 2000: 65). In fact, various ritualistic activities can become so rule-bound that they derive both their form and substance from this. John R. Searle describes stipulations of this nature as constitutive rules, which encase and also comprise the body of the ritual itself (1969; cited in Tambiah, 1985: 135). The ritual of template completion and in many of the other rites of corporate academia are characterised by regulations of this kind, in the course of which the necessity of following a precise procedure is almost obsessively reiterated.

The process of template completion has other ritual-like dimensions. For instance, the Comaroffs describe how ritual encompasses "mundane meaningful practice": apparently commonplace everyday activities that have acquired a special significance (1993: xvi). The routine bureaucratic duties that have now become some of the principal features of contemporary university life, such as the completion of templates, provide one example of this. Mundane in the extreme, their ritual-like qualities derive particularly from their monotonous aspects that crush many other areas of academic activity under their ceremonial weight, as well as from the ritualistic regularity with which such tasks have to be performed. In higher education and many other domains, the repetitive nature of ritual has an ideological function. Certain rules and practices and the power relations underlying them can be made to seem customary and incontestable as rituals reinforcing them are repeatedly carried out. In this respect, as the Comaroffs remark, "ritualization" becomes interconnected with "routinization", thereby serving the interests of the establishment (1993: xvii). Among much else, template completion serves to facilitate this.

Moreover, as Goodsell points out, the banal and tedious qualities of certain bureaucratic rituals can impose and entrench systems of command and control (1997: 957). For example, the process of routine template completion may seem so workaday and monotonous that its underlying ideological content may go undetected. Those completing templates may be required to engage with and give expression to aspects of the ideological constructs underpinning the corporatisation of higher education, in order to enact such a ritual in accordance with stipulated procedures. They may be unaware of the extent to which this ideological content may seep into their own perceptions, gradually influencing them accordingly. Many other rituals, be they secular or spiritual, exercise their authority by similar means.

The arduous nature of template completion bestows another ritual dimension upon the process. The onerous features of this activity derive in part from its time-consuming nature, the laborious detail and mental application required to fill in each of the sections according to the official stipulations, the esoteric terminology and the obscure bureaucratic minutiae that need to be summoned up in order to ensure that each section contains what is required. Just as certain religious rites can seem more meaningful if they demand a great deal from their participants, so templates may appear more significant the more difficult they are to complete. The completion of templates is a ritualistic, symbolic enactment of productivity that becomes a substitute for academic productivity itself. As institutional bureaucracy intensifies its stranglehold on the university environment, academics lose the time and the space to think and thus to develop their teaching and research.[3] In the light of this, the prominence accorded to template completion casts doubt on one of the principal myths of managerialism: that the new bureaucratic structures of corporate academia will result in a more productive working environment. Many members of staff become skilled at filling in templates, to the cost of much else.

Notes

1 Various points from Wood (2010a: 232–234) and Wood (2010b: 5–8) have been revised, expanded on and incorporated into pp. 92–93 and 96–107 of this chapter. These previously cited studies investigate other aspects of the occult academy.
2 This phrase is adapted from Ryan, who observes that "in the general rhetoric of the market used by the Thatcher government, the incantation 'manufacturing industry' bore almost voodoo power" (1998: 16).
3 Citing psychologist Eric Santner, Peter Stewart comments that "Kafka's fictional accounts of the terror of unavoidable bureaucratic entrapment" provide another, comparable image of this state of affairs (2007: 3).

6 Performance and ritual

At this point, we turn from templates to that which they often enshrine: the mystical tenets of performance measurement and management, with which staff are expected to comply. All too often, staff are expected to complete templates to display evidence of satisfactory performance. Indeed, one reason why templates have been foregrounded in current university procedure has much to do with that which Stephen J. Ball, citing Lyotard (1984), depicts as the "terror" of performativity (2000: 1). Templates may sometimes seem to embody a feature of this, for they often serve as a means of monitoring and regulating employees (see for for instance Ozga, 2011: 147, Olssen and Peters, 2005: 319–320). Accordingly, systems of performance appraisal have become potent control mechanisms in the corporatised university milieu, and this section considers the ways in which the performance-centred rites of present-day higher education serve as a means of imposing and entrenching the status quo. The interconnectedness of performance and ritual has bearing on this, casting light on the nature and functions of the ritual-like features of the corporatised university milieu.[1]

Current institutional landscapes tend to be cluttered by systems of monitoring and appraisal associated with systems of performance management and measurement, methods of control that derive from the corporate world, particularly from US-based corporate practice. The concept of performance has come to constitute a core feature of market-driven academia as a result of the fixation with performance that many universities have acquired in their desire to emulate corporate models. Moreover, this has much to do with the extent to which the audit culture has taken hold in diverse systems of higher education. Shore and Wright contend that the term "performance" is one of the key words associated with the audit culture, along with terms like "transparency", "accountability" and "quality", and that all these concepts are nurtured and expanded by the audit system (1999: 566).

Performance now lies near the heart of much corporate university procedure, intensifying its ritual-like aspects. The extent to which systems of performance measurement and management loom large in many present-day university environments is symptomatic of this.[2] The pre-eminence accorded to performance-related procedures is evident in the extent to which concepts such as key performance areas, performance indicators, performance outcomes, performance objectives, IPAs, performance ratings, performance attributes and other performance-related activities and notions tend to feature prominently in much institutional discourse, while shaping and directing the day-to-day working lives of many university employees in various significant respects. These practices have become some of the foremost ritualistic features of the market-oriented, managerially governed university landscape as a result of the regularity with which they take place, the ceremonial way they are staged, the symbolic significance attached to them as well as the ritual solemnity surrounding them and the amount of time and effort expended in order to perform them in a manner acceptable to the authorities ordaining them, be they internal or external.

Drawing on Lyotard's critique of the ways in which the concept of performativity, the "optimizing [of] the system's performance-efficiency" (1984: xxiv), has been foregrounded in various social structures, UK academics Robert Cowen (1996: 247–249) and Rosemary Deem (1998: 53) describe how concepts of viable academic labour have become bound up with notions of quantifiable, visible performativity. The preoccupation with performance in present-day academia is emblematic of the extent to which the neoliberal ethos, which places emphasis on that which is fixed, verifiable and quantifiable at the cost of much else, has permeated higher education. Various features of institutional performance management and measurement systems embody this, making regular reference to organisational and faculty scorecards, performance indicators and performance attributes, targets and measures of success in achieving these objectives, among much else. Thus, more often than not, individual and collective performance tends to be subjected to numerically based forms of ranking, rating and assessment. However, solid, measurable, seemingly straightforward systems of this nature, based on actual achievements (or the lack thereof) and capacity to conform to stipulated criteria (or the failure to do so) are allusive and ephemeral in various respects. Ironically, the focus on solid, tangible evidence of performance has often tended to be the very factor shifting this concept away from factual, empirical terrain and into the sphere of symbolism and ceremony. Paradoxically, some of the most symbolic, ritualistic features of university life now revolve around the concept of performance.

Ritual and the power of performance

The relationship between ritual and performance has many facets to it, which hearken back to ancient forms of ritual while also illuminating ritualistic features of the contemporary workplace and the functions they fulfil. We may recall, for instance, that some of the earliest dramatic performances in Western society took on ritual form. Ancient and Classical Greek drama, for instance, has its origins in the annual festival of Dionysus, and the rites associated with this event took on an increasingly theatrical quality over the time, culminating in the development of Greek drama.

In contemporary times, this link between drama and ritual continues to play itself out, albeit in changed form. Certainly, ritualistic activities enacted in diverse workplaces, including the corporate sector, higher education, public administration and other sections of the public domain that have been restructured in corporate mode, have various theatrical aspects. These may, for instance, incorporate stylised, self-consciously staged performances, involving role-playing of various kinds, as a number of commentators, including Shore and Wright, Goodsell and Trice and Beyer, observe. Indeed, many present-day universities and a range of employees within them draw on the dramatic not only to bestow significance and substance on institutional policies and procedures but for their very survival as well. For example, enactments of many performance-related ritualistic activities tend to form key components of many of the individual and collective institutional presentations self-consciously staged for a diversity of audiences, which may incorporate teams of potentially critical reviewers who could not only shorten the run of the production but close down the theatre itself.

As a result of these ritual-like aspects they have acquired and the importance attached to them, various systems of monitoring and evaluation have acquired theatrical aspects, as has the audit culture that frames them. For example, performances that have been carefully planned and sometimes rehearsed in advance may take place during forms of external and internal evaluation, such as performance measurement procedures, quality assessments and institutional audits.

Power, for example, highlights the performative, ceremonial features of the audit process, contending that "[a]t worst, auditing tends to become an organisational ritual, a dramaturgical performance" (1997: 141). This theatrical aspect can sometimes manifest itself in the role-playing that may take place during the course of an audit, with some of the participants adopting the roles of potentially all-seeing auditors. Meanwhile, those actors who appear before them, sometimes in the roles of petitioners, promoters, spin doctors or supplicants, may be concerned above all to deliver a satisfactory performance. These carefully staged productions, Power maintains, have intensified over the years, giving rise to "increasingly formalized rituals of accounting and verification" (1997: 138). Shore and Wright concur with this, describing how performances that have been carefully planned and rehearsed in advance tend to take place during procedures such as audits. Thus, they conclude that "[t]he audit visits enhance 'performance', but in a different sense to that intended by the government's discourse" (1999: 567). Marc Abélès maintains that there are parallels between "modern political rituals" and traditional rites that have been the subject of anthropological study (1988: 391). Shore and Wright expand on this, observing that the university audit calls to mind aspects of older ritual procedures while, in Abélès's words, "invent[ing] an altogether new costume for itself" (Abélès, 1988: 398–399; Shore and Wright, 1999: 567).

Some of the reasons why this state of affairs has arisen and why performance has become foregrounded in contemporary higher education and in many other present-day workplaces can be best understood when we consider the role that performance plays as a moving force within ritual. Indeed, much can hinge on performance and it can achieve that which cannot be realised by any other means.

Certainly, performance lies at the heart of many ritual activities, possessing a special capacity to breathe life into them and to bestow a significant quality upon the beliefs and practices with they are associated. As Schieffelin observes, enacting communal rituals can bestow a sense of actuality and immediacy upon the abstract and the conceptual, so that their symbolic content may seem meaningful and compelling (1985: 707–708). For instance, as will become evident, when the ritual-like procedures of corportised academia are enacted, they embody certain aspects of the ideological perspectives that brought them into being and lend weight to them.

Expressive rituals and symbolic enactments

As a result of the symbolic force that is vested in it, the concept of performance has become meaningful in itself, while actual performances can sometimes serve as a means to power. For example, various features of Melanesian "cargo cult" practices involving physical performance are believed to offer a means of accessing or embodying power (Dalton, 2004: 196–197). Members of the Tuka movement in Fiji, for instance, incorporated symbols of colonial authority into their ritualised activities for these reasons (Kaplan, 2003: 184, 188). By means of ritualistic performances involving such items, participants partook of the potency with which they were associated. In comparable fashion, various ritual-like performances in restructured universities modelled on those in the corporate sector, including the "rituals of verification" involved in the audit process (Power, 1997), the enactments of corporate procedures and the invocations of corporate jargon, are believed to draw close to sources of power, through enacting, incorporating or calling on that which possesses or is associated with areas of potency. In various respects, then, they invoke that which is believed to possess *mana*. When viewed from this perspective, the imitative, emblematic features of such performances may be envisaged as mirrors within which certain qualities that are valorised in neoliberal economic agendas and in the audit culture that helps enforce them are reflected, in order to bring into being that which they reflect.

Consequently, going through the motions becomes not so much an imitation of accountability, productivity, efficiency, excellence or quality as an embodiment of that feature, or as evidence that such an attribute exists, even if only at a hypothetical, conceptual level. For instance, participating in protracted and tedious meetings at which very little or nothing at all is achieved emulates productive professional labour, thus creating the impression of productivity. Moreover, the notion now seems to prevail that the longer members of staff are seen carrying out university-related work, all too often of a bureaucratic nature, the more productive they will be. For example, generating numerous templates crammed with verbiage mimics constructive work while giving the appearance of effectiveness and accountability. Then participating in external and internal forms of monitoring and evaluation involving the manufacturing and the enactment of that which signifies efficiency and accountability, including the production of myriad paper trails testifying to these things, tends to fulfil a similar function.

Procedures of this kind have antecedents in public administration. Goodsell depicts the construction of paper trails as a key symbolic activity within this sector. Even if that to which paper trails allude does not exist in any significant form, these are emblematic of attempts to conform to official requirements. Thus, the production of paper trails represents that which has been termed an expressive ritual: a public performance enacting key social norms (1997: 951, 955). In present-day higher education, ritual performances of this nature embody some of the concepts and principles around which institutional identity is constructed, in accordance with which employees are expected to mould themselves. Expressive rituals are concerned with outward display and tend to be enacted with an audience in mind. Accordingly, the creation of a paper trail is one such ritual performance that exists primarily for the benefit of particular spectators.

Various commentators also describe how paper trails have come to serve as tokens of efficiency, accountability, quality and so on rather than as evidence of these attributes themselves. Shore and Wright, for instance, describe how paper trails play a significant symbolic role in higher education in the UK and elsewhere. They note that this comes to the fore during the audit procedure, during which a proliferation of paper trails are displayed for public scrutiny in almost ritual-like fashion (1999: 570). Further to this, making reference to the work of Bruce G. Charlton and Peter Andras (2002: 14), Taylor contends that the British regime of Quality Assurance Auditing does not so much enhance the quality of teaching, but establishes that auditable paper trails exist (2003: 3). Indeed, paper trails appear to fulfil similar symbolic functions in diverse parts of the world, South Africa included.

Comparably, the symbolic significance with which enactments of performance monitoring and appraisal procedures can be vested may sometimes seem to far outweigh the meaningfulness of their actual content. Indeed, all too often, as Ruth remarks, "the procedure rules, rather than the process itself" (2001: 213). Ball corroborates this, making specific reference to education in the UK (2000: 6 – 7, 13), as do many other academics from diverse parts of the world. For example, the concern with providing proof of performance during the rites of performance measurement and management may evoke symbolic enactments from various individuals, departments or institutions, who may feel driven to display, inscribe, enact or utter that which is emblematic of performance. This may take place, for instance, when employees are required to draw up individual Personal Development Plans and IPAs or similar performance-related documentation. For those at senior managerial level, the documents generated by these activities may be required primarily for symbolic purposes, as tokens of staff commitment to the ideas of performance, accountability and productivity and to the notions of quality and excellence. As such, these are expressive ritualistic activities that may tend to exercise their effect primarily at a conceptual level. Power argues that providing evidence of auditable performance may fulfil a function of this nature, for instance (1997: 121). In these and other respects, then, many of the ritual performances of academia may become an end in themselves.

Power relations and control mechanisms

Partly as a result of the frequency with which they are enacted, symbolic performances centred around notions such as quality, accountability, productivity, efficiency and excellence have become such a standardised part of present-day university discourse and procedure that they have come to resemble conventionalised ritual behaviour. As Tambiah remarks, such conduct "psychically distances" actors from the actuality of that which they enact, gradually draining it of meaning (1985: 132). As they follow well-trodden one-way tracks that lead into cul-de-sacs, these standardised ritualistic performances come to resemble displays of conformity. Citing Suzanne Langer (1951), Tambiah remarks that such enactments can consist of little more than tokens of compliance with officially sanctioned codes of conduct. Whether inscribed, enacted or invoked, these demonstrations of compliance with the codes of the market, gestures of homage to corporate models and displays of deference to the managerial edicts enforcing these may ultimately amount to little more than a "disciplined rehearsal of 'right attitudes'" (1985: 133–134). Indeed, although some institutional actors and participants may grow weary of that which they have come to perceive as a charade in which they are regularly required to take part, they may decide to create the appearance of playing along, in the hope that those presiding over them will be content with superficial simulations of adherence to bureaucratic requirements.

Various commentators discuss the extent to which behaviour of this kind has become an ingrained feature of present-day academia, including Peter Stewart, who describes how "a discourse of performance and compliance-based honour" has become increasingly evident at many South African universities, often shaping employees' behaviour accordingly (2007: 139; see also Ruth, 2001: 195–197). Moreover, in the UK, Ozga describes how institutional restructuring and the performance-based forms of scrutiny and evaluation that have followed in its wake may also necessitate the transformation of employees' behaviour and emotions, even if only outwardly (2011: 143, 148–150). Consequently, academic actors may study the scripts supplied to them, which may take the form of institutional guidelines and accompanying templates, among much else. Thereafter, they carry out the parts required of them, aware that their performances should follow that which is laid down in their scripts. Such enactments can take the form of ritualistic role-playing, during which employees play the parts of dutiful employees (Roper, 2004: 130; see also Hedley, 2010: 138; Hochschild, 1983: 89–91). Behaviour of this kind represents that which Arlie Russell Hochschild has termed emotional labour. Later on, we consider the consequences of this.

Connected as they are to the workings of power, the ritual-like performances brought about by corporatisation and managerialism fulfil other related functions. As a result of the way in which they are employed in higher education and in diverse professional milieus, such enactments heighten the contrasts between appearance and actuality, the literal and the symbolic, and the haves and the have-nots. In part, this takes place as a result of the way in which professional relationships and social hierarchies are reinforced and entrenched when certain rituals are enacted (Howe, 2000: 65). It has already become evident that, when various ritualistic performances take place in contemporary institutions of higher education, this reinforces and furthers the process of corporate restructuring, while consolidating the control of the managerial authorities that preside over changes of this kind, and entrenching the dominance of the external authority systems to whom they are beholden. Consequently, ritual enactments of this nature can change participants and their interactions with one another in various respects (see for instance Alexander, 2004: 537). Moreover, as later chapters will indicate, performance-related procedures, including institutional audits, performance-based assessments and other systems of performance appraisal may often perpetuate privilege and power at inter-institutional levels and reinforce socio-economic inequities.

All the while, the performance-related rites of corporate academia entail acts of literal and symbolic subjugation to external and internal authority systems that ordain them, as the performers submit to the edicts of the power structures within which they are enmeshed. As Geertz observes, the "acceptance of authority . . . that the ritual embodies . . . flows from the enactment of the ritual itself" (1973: 118). Thus, the enacting of ritualistic activities deriving from the business sector conforms to the codes of the neoliberal corporate ethos, acknowledging its supremacy over the academic domain. Indeed, the role that ritual performances can play in imposing and entrenching specific ideologies stems from the way in which the content of a ritual procedure is shaped by particular perceptions and doctrines and reinforced by the power relations underpinning them. These ideological constructs may be absorbed, sometimes subliminally, by both participants and onlookers, as their underlying meaning is expressed or implied (Tambiah, 1985: 129, 128, 156–157).

Moreover, the fact that rituals are charged with meaning has implications for those involved in them. For instance, under certain circumstances, the significance of a particular ritual may not be entirely endorsed by all the actors themselves. Yet as Alexander maintains, this may be "the meaning that they . . . consciously or unconsciously wish to have others believe". Thus, they will need to deliver convincing performances, so as to persuade their audience to accept their explanations and also their rationale (2004: 529). Such rituals, and the ideological weight they carry, may be imposed on both actors and audience from on high. Like powerful currents, they may draw those involved in them along. Whether or not the ritual is of their own choosing, or in accordance with their own convictions, they may feel compelled to become caught up in it. Consequently, ritualistic enactments, ceremonies and public displays can make such an impression and carry such weight on account of their theatrical qualities that they may seem vested with a special authority,

> [endowing] certain interpretations of reality with a legitimacy that is recognized by the social group. Ritual, by dramatic means, both declares and

demonstrates – through display and enactment – certain propositions to be unquestionably true.

(Goodsell, 1997: 942)

By this means, too, such opinions may eventually come to seem customary, commonsensical and commonplace for both actors and audience, as Goodsell contends (1997: 943). Thus, ritual performances may serve to impose certain belief systems at the same time as they express them, partly as a result of their dramatic aspects. As Geertz puts it, ritual performances may enable participants to "attain their faith as they portray it" (1973: 114). Indeed, the ritual-like procedures of corporate academia can depict and impart dominant institutional ideologies as they are enacted. Further to this, they can serve the interests of the authorities by interweaving particular ways of doing with officially endorsed ways of seeing so as to ensure that the former embodies the latter and that they lend weight to each other.

As a corollary of this, specific performance-related control technologies are employed to ensure conformity to the status quo, while the importance of adhering to officially endorsed codes of conduct is emphasised. Citing Talal Asad (1993: 62), Howe observes that the concept of appropriate ritual performance often entails developing the "abilities to be acquired according to rules that are sanctioned by those in authority" (2000: 65). For these and other related reasons, performance-related systems of surveillance and appraisal are employed to inculcate appropriate conduct in contemporary academia and other managerially-driven workplaces.

One member of Quality Assurance at a South African university corroborates this, describing how systems of performance measurement and management can serve as interlocking mechanisms of ideological control, instilling behaviour patterns that operate in the interests of the establishment:

> Performance measurement is part of performance management, so performance management is an attempt to try and manage your employees in a particular way so that they conform to your expectations and do what they're supposed to do. And, in part, it's trying to measure what they're doing and trying to make people do things that are measurable.[3]

Thus, performance is codified and regulated by means of performance-related control mechanisms, which ensure that employees conform to the company or institutional ethos, performing the duties expected of them in the way that they should. As Dave Ulrich, a public speaker, academic and business practitioner from the US, sometimes depicted as a Human Resources "guru", puts it, "[w]hat you cannot measure, you cannot manage" (cited in Fernandes, 2011).[4] In a context in which work activities are rendered down to the quantifiable, the pressure on employees to provide measurable evidence of performance is emblematic of the extent to which they and their institutions have been subordinated to the codes of the marketplace, in terms of which everything should be weighed, measured and valued accordingly (see for instance Ozga, 2011: 145; Stewart, 2007: 141).

Michael A. Peters describes how the use of performance indicators plays a significant role in bringing about subjugation of this kind. For instance, when these methods of appraisal are employed in UK universities, they often obscure influential political and ideological agendas in terms of which education is subordinated to the market (1992: 126–127). Nash corroborates this, describing how the foregrounding of performance indicators forms a key feature of the impetus to impose commercialised American models on South African academia (2006: 6). Orr's observation that these particular evaluative mechanisms are one of the core characteristics of the market university bears this out (1997: 46, 61–62).

As a result of their ideological bias, these and various other systems of performance-based evaluation further the marketisation of academia, entrenching market-oriented economic and political systems of power and control. Internally, they have become interconnected with institutional restructuring and the imposition of managerial authority.

The rule-bound rites of academia

In order to affirm and entrench internal and external systems of governance, notions of correct performance come particularly into play. Consequently, as the performance-related rites of corporatised academia are enacted, emphasis is placed on the adherence to officially endorsed rules. For example, the process of electronic submissions, often involving template completion, may be governed by stringent regulations. Certain templates, including those containing reports and funding applications, and also diverse articles, conference papers and abstracts cannot be transmitted unless the item in question has been completed in accordance with officially prescribed procedures. Numerous local universities, organisations and significant academic structures implement this, including various funding agencies such as the National Research Foundation (NRF) in South Africa. Both locally and internationally, mechanisms of this kind can serve as a means of containing and controlling individual performance. This practice may have been inherited from the commercial sector, where it is widespread. Indeed, a great many electronic transactions and processes have a certain ritual-like aspect to them, in that they involve the performance of an array of set procedures, each of which needs to be carried out in compliance with certain requirements, some of which may seem obscure. Among much else, this entails an overt submission to rules, which may sometimes appear arcane. Indeed, without submitting to the Terms and Conditions (which may often seem prolix and complex) attached to the process in question, applications, transactions and submissions may remain locked in an electronic limbo. In some respects, this may seem comparable to the void to which academics that are unable to acquiesce with certain official requirements may come to feel they have been consigned.

As an earlier chapter has indicated, the importance attached to proper procedure characterises many ritual activities, where it can serve as a means of imposing authority, while instilling conformity and compliance. Goodsell observes that this emphasis on "precise conformity" furthers the interests of the authority structures ordaining such ritualistic activities by controlling the milieu over which they preside and tolerating no deviations from the norm (1997: 944). For example, Ruth and Chetty and Merrett maintain that such forms of regulation and domination are prevalent at many South African institutions, including the Universities of the North and KwaZulu-Natal, while Parker and Jary describe how this forms a distinctive feature of UK academia (Ruth, 2001: 195; Chetty and Merrett, 2014: 189; Parker and Jary, 1995: 335–336). In higher education, as in many other domains, rule-governed enactments of this kind are indicative of a submission to the systems of power and control ordaining them and to the norms, notions and values with which they are associated. Accordingly, the correct performance of ritual-like activities in academia is emphasised to ensure deference to the corporate, managerial ethos and the neoliberal economic ideologies on which it is based.

When performers need to take special care to ensure that they conform to the prescribed procedures, these are apt to assume an overriding momentousness.[5] Thus, performers may become less concerned with the ideological content of that which they enact and more preoccupied with ensuring they carry it out correctly. This may tend to form a feature of many of the rule-bound rites of corporate academia, including many of those depicted earlier.

In the theatre of academia

While template completion and electronic submissions tend to be enacted in private, those enacting rituals in public places need to bear their audience in mind and stage their performances accordingly. For example, performers may depend and draw upon collective beliefs in various ways. For instance, they tend to engage with their audience by alluding to their common cultural frame of reference, be it institutional, community-based or organisational, thus seeking to imbue their performances with a meaningful quality. Accordingly, as Trice and Beyer observe, performers employ various culturally specific forms, including well-known items, routine behaviour patterns and familiar terminology to emphasise the extent to which their performances draw on a shared frame of reference (1984: 654).

In higher education, managerial performances draw on established iconography, discourse and conventions to create this effect. As already indicated, these objects, codes of conduct and words and phrases were introduced in the course of reform rituals, during the process of institutional restructuring. They are now employed to perpetuate particular ideological perspectives and inculcate conformity. For example, this may encompass recourse to imagery and icons deriving from the corporate world, such as the frequent invocation of oft-employed words of power and the habitual use of fetishistic images emanating from this sphere such as organograms. Customary, stylised conventions and procedures are also foregrounded, including the enactment of the particular bureaucratic processes required for specific occasions and events. These details and the other messages that are imparted in the course of managerial performances sometimes tend to be couched in the esoteric corporate jargon that has permeated many university environments. This can also foster a sense of group identity, since only those who have been steeped in this terminology may be able to interpret it, while many others may be accustomed to adopting a plausible air of comprehension.

In order to draw attention to the importance of their performance, actors may select sites that have long been imbued with a sense of collective significance. In the university context, such events may be staged in special meeting places set aside for such purposes, such as Senate Chambers, Faculty Board Rooms, and other places in or near seats of managerial authority. Moreover, during various ritual gatherings, "mundane material things" imbued with symbolic significance are often employed (Alexander, 2004: 532). For example, in higher education, certain sites in which significant rites of corporate academia take place may be adorned with the corporatised trappings of institutional identity, such as mission statements, logos and other regalia. Meanwhile, PowerPoint presentations may feature during the performances themselves so as to heighten the ceremonial seriousness of the proceedings and lend weight to the event. On occasions such as these, the symbolic importance of this visual aid may sometimes outweigh its usefulness in other respects, emblematic as it has become of professional expertise and corporate prowess. In the course of such presentations, arcane visual imagery may be displayed, such as organograms, the institutional hierarchies they depict symbolising the way in which diverse areas of institutional life are contained, commanded and controlled. Managerial presentations can include the use of that which Goodsell terms "power-enhancing furniture" (1997: 954). Arguably, this is one reason why the inner sanctums of senior university managerial staff (be they their offices, the particular areas where these are located or the chambers in which significant meetings are sometimes held) may be bedecked with furniture that is redolent of corporate power, evocative of the upper echelons of the corporate world. Partly as a result of this reliance on specific settings and iconography and the corporate fabulation relating to them, managerial performances may acquire incongruous qualities. As the US organisational theorist Karl E. Weick (1979) puts it, university managers are so frequently required to utilise "myths, symbols and labels" that they may seem to resemble evangelists, rather than accountants (cited in Trice and Beyer, 1984: 666).

Further to this, Goodsell describes how certain public performances by those in seats of state or administrative authority are preceded by widely publicised announcements, and the events themselves have an air of formality and portentousness (1997: 954). Senior managerial addresses to the entire university community or to divisions thereof may often be characterised by comparable contrivances. By these means, senior managers may draw attention to the power they wield and invest the messages they deliver with a sense of grand purpose. Then, given the predilection for elusiveness that tends to typify many of those at senior managerial level, protracted public sightings of this kind may also seem noteworthy to certain members of their academic audience. Goodsell depicts the ways in which dramatic elements can be employed in ritualistic administrative activities to capture the audience's attention and bestow a special significance on the proceedings (1997: 944). His point is also applicable to the present-day university milieu, imbued as it is with theatrical aspects. At times, some of these may seem to derive from tragedy, farce, or melodrama or even, at times, from the theatre of the absurd.

The ritual performances taking place at contemporary universities have other dimensions. A play's dramatic aspects may be heightened so as to make it seem striking and compelling, while a ritual may be staged in such a way that it commands attention and averts questions simultaneously (Moore and Myerhoff, 1977: 8). Certain managerial performances may also strive for this effect for similar reasons, by employing deliberately theatrical approaches, steeped as these may be in pomp and ceremony. When Goodsell draws comparisons between dramatic productions and the ritualistic features of public administration, he notes that if actors are able to focus their audience's attention on the performance, rather than that which it conveys, they may be less inclined to interrogate its ideological content (1997: 944).

Indeed, in the university milieu, senior managerial presentations may be carefully staged so as to capture their audience's attention, direct their gaze onto that which is unfolding before them and then, by confronting them with certain imperatives, impede their audience's capacity to adopt a more detached, critical view. For instance, managerial actors may emphasise the great significance of particular rites and ceremonials, demanding that all those assembled before them perform their stipulated roles in these procedures as a matter of urgency. They sometimes may intimate that, should members of their audience fail in this regard, this could have serious implications for their own posts while the futures of their departments or divisions might hang in the balance. Strategies of this kind have been and are often employed before and during university audits, Research Excellence Frameworks (REFs), formerly Research Assessment Exercises (RAEs), and other external and internal evaluations, and these may form a component of a process of cost-cutting. Many university employees confronting threats of this nature may become so concerned about their possible consequences and whether the performances required of them will be deemed satisfactory that they may focus upon these factors above all, losing sight of other issues at hand. Although prolonged dramatic episodes of this ilk may take a range of other forms, they all tend to have alarming, compelling qualities that ensure staff participation and compliance, lest the drama unfolding around them turn into a tragedy featuring themselves and their departments. Consequently, plays can have much in common with certain turns of events at various present-day universities. In order to sustain its dramatic impetus, a play can depict a sequence of crises, as Marjorie Boulton notes. It could, for instance, introduce certain surprising complications or predicaments, which could generate more difficulties thereafter. In this way, Boulton argues, the audiences' interest is captured and held as they become caught up in the events being enacted before them (1960: 41).

Bearing in mind all that may be required of them, senior managers need to be competent performers in order to invest the events in which they play leading roles with meaning. They may also seek to use their performances to promulgate specific agendas and impose and reinforce official power structures and systems of control in such a way that their long-term implications and ideological content will go undetected or uninterrogated. Trice and Beyer take note of this, remarking that certain ceremonial skills are required from senior managers, on account of the fact that a number of the performances on which they embark will need to be carefully staged in order to accomplish their intended purpose. These may include Faculty Board and Senate Meetings, at which significant managerial edicts are passed down from on high. Thus, Trice and Beyer contend that an aptitude for the theatrical could be advantageous to those in senior managerial positions. In fact, they are of the opinion that the ability to deliver a polished performance could be part of certain managerial job descriptions (1984: 666). Partly as a result of this state of affairs, a number of university managers may feel that it behoves them to display other dramatic abilities during their public activities, temporarily adopting the personae of corporate managers. Such behaviour patterns may become more ingrained over time, as Goodsell remarks (1997: 948). In universities, as in the corporate sector, role-playing of various kinds has become so entrenched that it takes on an almost ritualistic quality. Also, possibly, some of those in top-level managerial positions may no longer be conscious of the extent to which their behaviour is a surface display. Instead, perhaps, they may come to perceive themselves as CEOs of a kind, presiding over a company weighed down by inept subordinates.

The risks of ritual

Although the ritualistic enactments and ceremonial occasions over which senior managerial staff preside may often seem to have a predetermined quality, appearances can be deceptive. These and the other ritual activities ordained and controlled by internal and external authorities may have other, less predictable dimensions to them, some of which relate to their performative features. As Trice and Beyer note, unpredictability can be very much a feature of certain ritual performances, just as the success or failure of a theatrical performance cannot be guessed in advance (1984: 666). Under certain circumstances, then, rituals may be rule-bound yet chancy affairs, within which everything can hinge on performance and the response this evokes from the audience. As Howe observes, "[m]ost rituals are staged to achieve an end, so there is always something at stake in performances" (2000: 66–67; see also Alexander, 2004: 559).

Since the rituals of higher education involve an element of risk, much can depend on how successfully they are carried out. Moreover, as Howe notes, rituals engage with potent, unpredictable presences and energies as they are performed (2000: 67). For instance, as employees enact certain significant rites of the corporate academy, they are drawn closer to their institutional management and the external authorities to whom they are directly and indirectly accountable.

Consequently, they come into contact with those who exercise far-reaching control over their professional lives, but whose ways may appear unfathomable and whose decisions may seem capricious. By performing institutional rites before those who wield such sway over them, they may be placing themselves in a precarious position, should their performances be deemed inadequate.

Even the rites of managerialism are fraught with hazards of their own for similar reasons. On certain occasions when much may hang in the balance, skilled performances are required from those in seats of managerial authority. For instance, senior members of university management may embark on potentially risk-laden ventures when they enact the rites of managerial accountability, placing themselves and their institutions on display for external scrutiny. If their institutional performance is deemed inadequate, then their individual managerial performances may be deemed wanting too. Meanwhile, within universities, senior managers may expose their faculty or division and their managerial capabilities to the watchful, potentially critical gaze of other members of their institutional management, whether those in the upper levels of their organisational hierarchy or their managerial peers, who may seek to entrench their own positions or ascend further up the institutional ladder by displacing those around or beneath them.

Consequently, even the more powerful members of the university community may view certain important rituals with uneasiness, since not only their institution but also their own capacities to preside over it are being put to the test. This is very much a feature of ritual. For example, Howe depicts certain rituals as risk-laden performances with the potential to destabilise social order and undermine the powerful. Some Balinese rites, for instance, put rulers on public display, requiring them to prove that they can exert control over the perilous unseen forces that these events unleash (2000: 72–73). There are certain points of comparison with some ritualistic productions taking place in the recently refurbished theatre of higher education, such as the audit procedure and other external assessments, in terms of which university managers are required to display their abilities to propitiate the potentially hazardous forms of authority with whom the ritual brings them into contact, such as state officials or university auditors. Such personages are endowed with the power to overturn the existing institutional order and bring the performance to a standstill. Some of these onlookers may also act as the directors and producers of the presentations unfolding before them, while others may bestow the funding that will enable the show to continue.

Arguably, adhering to the rules may render a ritual performance less hazardous. However, Howe points out that another aspect of risk lies in this requirement, for failure to comply with the exact procedures when enacting a ritual may bring about misfortune. For instance, in various parts of South Africa it is widely believed that those who offend their ancestors by failing to perform a ritual properly may suffer in consequence, as may their families for decades thereafter. Meanwhile, failure to adhere to certain stipulations when performing some of the ritual-like activities of academia can have serious implications for the professional lives of those enacting them, or for the future of a department or division, even an entire institution. As Howe reminds us, the possibility of errors or omissions can loom large in certain rituals, and even some small ceremonies can be complicated (2000: 69). The depth of detail, the ability to identify and employ the esoteric terminology and bureaucratic minutiae required for each specific rite, and the precise adherence to the proper procedure required for many bureaucratic activities in contemporary universities renders them exercises fraught with the possibility of failure. In consequence, even the prospect of enacting mundane bureaucratic procedures can arouse apprehension.

Subversion and contradictions

Even though the performance-based rituals of corporate academia can be fraught with hazards and can compel participants to subjugate themselves to the internal and external authorities that ordain them, serving their interests while relinquishing their own, they have another dimension to them that is worth considering here. Certain features of Melanesian "cargo cults" illuminate this. Their ritualistic imitations of the ways of the colonial authorities have some points of comparison with some of the ritual-like performances in the present-day corporatised academic milieu.

Dalton maintains that sometimes ritualistic enactments that mimic the practices of those in power may – whether deliberately or unwittingly – draw attention to their irrationalities and absurdities, thereby undermining them. Making specific reference to Melanesian "cargo cult" activities that imitate features of Western society, he goes on to contend that, if such practices appear to possess idiosyncratic, farcical qualities, these derive from the nature of that which they imitate: Western capitalist culture, with all its deluded, misleading and contradictory aspects. Among much else, its economic and political vagaries and irrationalities and the strange, confusing nature of its political processes and hierarchies are symptomatic of this. Consequently, he concludes that "what passes for 'normal' reality in modern middle-class western culture is deceptive and unusual in the extreme and that Melanesians fathom this by enacting a version of it out of its 'normal' context" (2004: 193–196).

In certain respects, Dalton's observations could be adapted to fit the current university environment, within which ritual-like procedures from corporate capitalist culture are performed outside their conventional milieu. Their counterfeit aspects, contradictions and fallacies may appear less obscured by convention and familiarity when relocated to another domain. For example, some university employees may find these ritualistic enactments of the ways of the corporate sphere incongruous and feel that they are at variance with the nature and function of institutions of higher education and equally at odds with their current circumstances. There may appear to be a tension between that to which many of these ritual-like performances of academia aspire, such as excellence and world-class status (embodied, for instance, in their mission and vision statements) and the particular nature of many of the academic environments in which these enactments take place, hemmed in as these may be with constraints. To greater or lesser degrees, a variety of factors, some or all of which tend to be prevalent at many universities in South Africa and elsewhere – such as ever-decreasing staff numbers; the deteriorating, dwindling nature of infrastructural, financial and other resources; and declining staff morale – may impede individual, departmental and institutional capacities to meet stipulated targets and deliver performances that satisfy official stipulations. In a discussion of the way in which this state of affairs may manifest itself in the education system in the UK, Beckmann and Cooper draw attention to this, describing how British teachers who have become steeped in performance-related procedures may feel compelled "to fulfil competing imperatives and inhabit irreconcilable subjectivities" (2004: 3).

Contradictions and limitations of this kind may provide an inadequate basis for assumptions that performance management and measurement procedures, quality assurance observances and other ritualistic activities that have come to characterise market-driven institutions of higher education will, if enacted according to official stipulations, transform staff and university performance. Moreover, repeated invocations of corporate words of power, unaccompanied by any marked changes for the better, may ring increasingly hollow. High-sounding mission and vision statements, saturated as these tend to be with the jargon of corporate capitalist culture, may seem incongruous in an academic milieu, bearing out Dalton's observation that, when situated outside their customary context, features of Western culture may seem deceptive and peculiar. For these and other reasons then, faith in the efficacy of corporate jargon and the ritual-like performances that it frames may sometimes appear misplaced or even irrational. At times, too, it is possible that the regular use of language of this kind may leave some of those who hear it with the idea that those who employ it routinely and with serious intent may inhabit a make-believe world within which, by means of the magic of the market, all that this terminology touches turns to gold. There is also the potential that, under certain circumstances, some of the ritualistic performances of corporatised academia might acquire an edge of absurdity. Indeed, as Dalton's above-cited comment suggests, during public performances when much is placed on public display, illogicalities, inadequacies and inconsistencies that might have passed unnoticed under other circumstances and in other contexts may be rendered visible.

In conclusion then, present-day universities now function both as panopticons and public stages on which academic actors are under pressure to perform all the duties required of them while ensuring that their conduct meets the stipulated criteria. But especially as a result of their symbolic, ceremonial nature, the performance-centred rites of higher education can highlight the hollowness of that which is enacted, the bogus nature of the ethos to which such enactments are connected and the extent to which the symbolic gestures generated by the pressure to provide proof of performance serve as substitutes for actualities, while masking shortcomings and inadequacies.

Notes

1 Certain points made in Wood (2010b: 8–9) have been reworked and included on p. 110 of this chapter.
2 For example, Damian Ruth (2001) and Peter Stewart describe the authority vested in systems of performance appraisal in South African universities, including their

own institutions: the University of the North and UNISA (2007: 133–134). Shore and Wright, Olssen and Peters, Robert Cowen and Stephen Gudeman make similar observations about universities in the UK and US, as do many other academics in these and other countries (1999: 557–570; 1992: 327; 1996: 287; 1992: 1–3).
3 Interview with anonymous respondent, 2011.
4 Christina Fernandes cites David Ulrich in a report on a gathering of the Delhi Forum which focused on performance appraisals, conducted in March 2011.
5 Leo Howe makes this point when he describes how this adherence to strictly prescribed procedures manifests itself in Balinese rituals and in various other contexts (2000: 335–336; 65).

7 Kinship, collegiality and witchcraft

While the rituals of performance appraisal and the other rites of the occult academy are enacted, certain features of the shadowy side of the occult manifest themselves, metaphorically speaking. First, however, it is worth noting that the otherworldly quality of the corporate university environment is intensified by visitations from workers of magic, otherwise known as consultants. Like many established practitioners, supernatural or otherwise, they charge a high price for their services, which many of those who call on them can ill afford. (However, the underlying assumption is that market-related prices are indicative of professional excellence, esoteric or otherwise.)[1]

With the diverse, interdisciplinary nature of universities, the tasks that consultants are called on to perform are often those for which there are in-house skills, yet, like workers of magic, consultants tend to be perceived as beings set apart, authority figures possessing rarefied expertise by means of which they will perform wonders. Their status derives in part from their association – or claimed association – with the corporate world (see for instance Vale, 2009: 1). At times, ironically, the consultants employed in this capacity may be ex-academics who have become agents of the business world or, as Chris Hedges puts it, "corporate drones" (2009), some of whom may have departed precipitately from their former academic places of employment.

With the special insights to which they lay claim, consultants might profess to see into the heart of a situation, perceiving reasons for adversity and reversals of fortune, prescribing rituals for healing, and offering guidance as to the way forward, among much else. Through acts of corporate divination, consultants may, too, predict the future. Their divining tools, which often involve "the cabalistic incantations of PowerPoint presentations" (Taylor, 2003: 1), may appear to offer their audience glimpses of what lies ahead. The extent to which PowerPoint has pervaded so many institutional gatherings is indicative of the depth of the conviction that this visual aid is vested with such potency that it bestows a special authority upon all who wield it. Moreover, consultants tend to be conversant with statistics which, as Geschiere notes, have come to function as a form of divination in Western and Westernised societies. Other practitioners of special arts may lay claim to comparable abilities. For example, Geschiere draws various parallels between the modus operandi of "important experts of revelation" in Western society, such as spin doctors in the US, and certain traditional diviners, healers and workers of magic in central and southern Africa (some of whom are known as *nyangas, ngangas, inyangas* and *n'angas*). Both sets of practitioners claim to be able to manipulate events and circumstances by means of their special expertise – as do consultants (2003: 177, 1 159–182).Other professionals who have been elevated to a similar status in the business world are the prophets and holy men, "truth-makers adept at selling their wisdom," the "business gurus" periodically invoked by managers of American corporations as sources of guidance and inspiration. Such commerce and management guru figures include Tom Peters and Robert H. Waterman, the authors of *In Search of Excellence*, and Stephen Covey, among many others (Newbrook, 2005: 104). Some of these high priests of the corporate domain have become revered in corporatised academia. Roper describes how various high priests of quality management such as W. Edwards Deming (1986), Joseph M. Juran (1990) and Philip B. Crosby (1979) played an influential role during the "quality management boom" in Britain in the 1980s and 1990s (Roper, 2004: 125). However, some workers of market-oriented magic, particularly consultants, may sometimes be required to carry out tasks of another kind.

Institutional witch-finding

As a result of their status as seemingly impartial outsiders, consultants or external assessors may sometimes be called upon to perform what could be described as a process of "sniffing out", in that it may call to mind those ritualistic activities performed by those occult practitioners summoned to locate the source of the evil lying at the root of a misfortune. Consultants or other extra-institutional authorities may, for instance, be employed to produce evidence proving that specific individuals or groupings have fallen short of the mark, so that various problems that may beset a department, school or faculty, or even an entire institution can be linked to them. On many other occasions, this task is carried out by some of those who have high seats in the hierarchy of the corporate university, and are thus equipped with the authority to identify real or perceived threats, utter warnings and pronounce punishments. This is an ongoing activity, because a fundamental aspect of corporate university practice is the process of apportioning blame. Just as witch-finding often identifies the most vulnerable members of a community (for instance the elderly, the indigent or single women) as the wrongdoers, so the "sniffing out" in this context tends to zero in on the lower-level members of the university community. The academic staff, particularly those in the more vulnerable disciplines, tend to be linked to the misfortunes which the workers of corporate magic are called on to identify and address. In many universities in this country and in diverse institutions elsewhere, for example, the Humanities and some of the softest of the Social Sciences tend to be singled out for particular punishment. At times, however, other very different disciplines, including Engineering and the Sciences, have also been penalised when their academic activities have seemed too costly or not financially viable (see for instance Green, Loughridge and Wilson, 1996: 5; Deem, Hillyard and Reed, 2007: 64).

Regular witch-hunts of this nature reinforce the ever-present sense of fear. The basic function of a witch-hunt is to pinpoint the source of evil, and the authority of the supernatural practitioner in question often depends on this. Inevitably then, the innocent are picked out as the wrongdoers on a number of occasions. And, because many employees cannot be sure who will next be identified as the locus of evil, some of the most vulnerable members of the academic sector live in fear that it will be themselves or their departments.

A similar process of "sniffing out" involves detecting another harmful emanation from the spirit world: ghosts, or, to be more precise, ghost employees. Some contemporary universities may feel the need to conduct ritual-like exercises designed to detect these supernatural presences. For instance, when my institution sought to identify ghost employees many years ago, members of university staff were called on to participate in a special procedure in order to prove that they existed in flesh and blood.[2] However, the types of witch-finding depicted earlier, in which specific employees, departments and faculties are condemned (all too often for the flaws and failings of others), tend to feature more prominently in the rituals of corporate academia, intensifying managerial control and maintaining a climate of fear. Certain aspects of witchcraft accusations that cast further light on the phenomenon of institutional witch-finding are worth considering in more depth. In part, the closed, seemingly close-knit nature of academia sometimes gives rise to accusations of this kind.

The hazards of kinship

Various significant studies of witchcraft in Africa draw attention to the links between witchcraft and kinship. Within the family, the most intimate environment of all, diverse forms of ill will and anger are particularly prone to arise. By extension, academic collegiality could be viewed as a form of kinship: partly professional guild, partly a sharing of the same intellectual neighbourhood and partly stemming from a sense of belonging to an academic family of a kind. In his study of witchcraft in Limpopo, South Africa, Isak Niehaus alludes to the potential for conflict amongst those in close proximity, commenting on the tension between the ideals "of kinship, loyalty and agnatic and neighbourly harmony" and the friction that may arise within close relationships of this nature (2001a: 57).

Geschiere also describes how notions of kinship have expanded in many contemporary African societies, particularly on account of factors such as urbanisation, extending to incorporate those with whom someone is connected by other than flesh and blood ties. For example, some significant linkages may be established through involvement in civic structures, church groupings and sporting bodies. Perceptions of kinship can even encompass "urban elites": wealthy and influential people with whom it might be advantageous to be associated. In the light of these redefinitions of the concept of kinship, academic colleagues are, symbolically speaking, kin to one another. Concepts of African kinship, Geschiere also contends, are closely related to social security (1997: 212–214). In theory, the contemporary workplace is also a source of this security (although actual events may prove otherwise). For this reason, too, professional colleagues may also seem like a family of sorts.

However, when people live close beside one another, the potential for friction is heightened. This is also applicable to those who share the same workplace, where interpersonal tensions inevitably arise. Such conditions are exacerbated in the present-day corporate university, subject as it is to many tensions and pressures. Consequently, bonds of various kinds may collapse under the strain. "Witchcraft" Geschiere contends, "is the dark side of kinship. . . . It expresses the frightening realisation that aggression threatens from within the intimacy of the family – that is, from the very space where complete solidarity and trust should reign without fail" (1997: 212). In other words, someone may be accused of bewitching one of his or her own family members by his or her own kin. Éric De Rosny (1992) mentions a Duala aphorism from the Cameroonian coast: "One must learn to live with one's own sorcerer" (cited in Geschiere, 1997: 42, 212). Symbolically, this may apply to many different families, be they biological or professional.

Team-building activities reinforce such perceptions. As Trice and Beyer observe, the idea of team-building draws upon the notion that kinship bonds of a kind exist between groups of employees. Thus, team-building exercises are intended to foster notions of connectedness of this nature, in the hope that this can be turned to the advantage of a specific organisation or institution (1984: 661). The limitations of such assumptions soon become apparent. Family bonds and other close connections may be placed under strain or broken by certain turns of events, and symbolic forms of kinship are far more easily severed.

Notions of teamwork create an illusion of amicability, temporarily veiling the competition, manipulation and scheming that have long characterised the academic environment, in both its restructured and traditional forms (see for instance Ozga, 2011: 150). The atmosphere of conviviality and sociability that may arise during teamwork activities is short-lived. Just as spiritual activities may induce a brief sense of tranquillity or holiness, which soon wears thin under the pressures of daily life, so team-building rituals may foster a temporary sense of camaraderie, which soon evaporates when participants return to a stress-laden working environment peopled by authoritarian managers and insecure subordinates. Further to this, relationships between erstwhile colleagues may be destabilised in one way or another. For instance, Shore and Wright describe how internal audits draw staff into policing roles through their involvement in university structures and committees in which areas such as performance, accountability and quality are measured (1999: 566). Meanwhile, former academics who have crossed over to the managerial "dark side" (Taylor, 2003: 1) or those luckless academic staff in middle-management positions (such as heads of departments) are now required to monitor the performances of the employees over whom they preside. As a result, university employees are under ongoing scrutiny from one another, and an individual may be accused of unprocedural academic practices by her or his former colleagues, or academic kin, as a result of the latter's involvement in systems of managerial governance. Metaphorically speaking, they have become drawn into the process of institutional witch-finding.

Competition, ambition and individualism

The metaphorical parallels between perceptions of witchcraft and contemporary corporatised academia extend beyond kinship. Other aspects of the market-oriented, managerially controlled academic environment have metaphorical parallels with the dark domain of the witch. Witchcraft is sometimes believed to spring from specific urges and cravings, and present-day academic discourse and practice may often seem to be driven by comparable compulsions. In certain parts of South Africa the belief prevails that greed, covetousness and the selfish hoarding of individual material resources can be associated with the workings of dangerous supernatural forces. Adam Ashforth's Soweto respondents, for example, maintained that jealousy was the principal cause of witchcraft, as have many other individuals and communities in diverse parts of Africa (1998: 521; see also Evans-Pritchard, 1976: 55, 80; Geschiere, 1997: 212). Ashforth's respondents used the term *jealousy* to denote envy of not only the material well-being of others and a desire to undermine them but also the urge to "jealously guard" one's own wealth and possessions and bar others from sharing them (1998: 521). Similar tendencies have come to characterise contemporary workplaces governed by neoliberal economic imperatives, universities included. As Vally puts it, "[i]ndividualism, competition and consumption are the dominant values within academe as elsewhere" (2007: 23).

It is worth noting that an atmosphere of intense competitiveness may manifest itself in certain contexts in which supernatural forces are believed to be at work. For instance, in some parts of Africa it is rumoured that some political contenders employ occult forces that enable them to outstrip their competitors. Geschiere, for instance, describes how "the cut-throat competition among ambitious politicians" in parts of the Cameroon has provided fertile ground for speculation of this kind (1997: 201). Further to this, in certain parts of Africa, it is believed that various politicians have turned to occult practitioners to advance themselves.[3] These predilections have various metaphorical parallels with certain tendencies in higher education, for it is as if many universities have turned to discourse and procedures that have many metaphorical parallels with the occult in the hope that this may aid them in the forms of academic contestation within which they are enmeshed.

The competitiveness that has been fostered by university managers and agents of the state emanates from the notion that fomenting the rivalry, self-absorption and divisions brought about by contestation is constructive, contributing to the expansion of the knowledge economy and enabling universities to become more economically self-reliant and to compete more effectively in global markets. Indeed, as Burrows reminds us, in market-driven capitalism, the market is envisaged particularly as a place of competition, rather than exchange (2012:

357). Further to this, as Olssen and Peters observe, heightened competition is synonymous with enhanced quality in terms of neoliberal ideologies (2005: 326).

Vally alludes to the "discourse of competitiveness" that has come to constitute one of the dominant languages of present-day academia worldwide. It has also made its presence felt at a deeper level, reshaping the culture of the academic workplace. For instance, Grossman contends that South African institutions of higher education "are infused with a deeply rooted competitive individualism, promoted at almost every point" (2006: 100). This state of competitiveness extends through this country's university hierarchy and through many other higher education environments elsewhere. For instance, in 1999 the University of Witwatersrand, one of South Africa's more prestigious institutions, emphasised in its strategic plan that the university would need to compete with other institutions for staff, students and potentially precarious sources of funding (cited in Pendlebury and van der Walt, 2006: 82).

Academic competition may take different forms in diverse countries, and degrees of profit and prestige accruing from this may be subject to variation. Yet some comparable pressures tend to prevail globally. In the UK, for instance, a Research and Development Report noted in 1996 that "to a much greater extent than ever previously, universities must now compete with each other for resources" (Greene, Loughridge and Wilson, 1996: 4). Similarly, when making reference to the market-oriented nature of NPM and related new managerial practices, Deem, Hillyard and Reed depict UK universities as domains within which competition is foregrounded (2007: 14). Moreover, Bok maintains that academic competitiveness has long been a particular feature of higher education in the US (2003: 14). Citing another US academic, Sheila Slaughter (1990), Orr corroborates these statements, describing how globalised economic contestation is reflected in the present-day higher education milieu, as universities vie with one another for lucrative contracts in the industrial and commercial sectors and at state level. For instance, they also compete with one another to arrive at scientific and technological discoveries with innovative, profit-generating potential, among much else (1997: 54).

Besides institutions being compelled to compete with one another for material support, both from the state and from external funding bodies, contestation extends to other areas of academe. As globalisation erodes national boundaries, institutions of higher education in many countries worldwide have become caught up in competition for status (for instance in terms of their positions in international university rankings), students, financial support and prominent academics to add lustre to their institutional profile. The term *world-class university*, with its implication that the institution that lays claim to such an accolade should become globally competitive, is suggestive of this. This academic rivalry can also infect inter-institutional relationships within one country. For instance, an online newspaper article described how Kenya's seventeen private universities are striving to outdo one another in their attempts to lure students (Waruru, 2013: 1–2). Further examples of this tendency will be considered in this chapter in the following pages.

As many local and international commentators observe, this contestation for restricted economic and material resources not only takes place between institutions but also extends right into the heart of universities themselves, permeating campuses, faculties, schools and departments and generating interpersonal tensions. Shore and Wright contend that this has become a chronic condition in UK academia, for instance, while Stewart describes how the South African higher education environment has also become contaminated by tendencies of this kind (Shore and Wright, 1999: 568; Stewart, 2007: 137).

For instance, various South African institutions have become sites of contestation due to the university mergers. At present, many universities in this country consist of several separate campuses endowed with varying degrees of status and privilege. Thus, employees from two very different campuses of one university, such as the Alice and East London campuses of the University of Fort Hare – the former an HDI located in a small town at a distance from urban centres, and the latter, an urban HAI – may also view one another as competitors for limited institutional resources. Moreover, both locally and internationally, other new hierarchies have emerged within restructured universities at managerial and academic levels, heightening inter-institutional and intra-institutional divisions. This condition is intensified by the extent to which universities themselves are characterised by an unequal distribution of financial and material resources, and an ever-widening gulf between university managers and academics and among those departments, faculties and institutions that are viewed as significant and those that are deemed lacking in certain respects (see for instance Stewart, 2007: 140).

Other distinctions in status have also come to the fore, including those based on the ratings accorded to different institutions, departments, journals and individuals, which generate hierarchies and divisions at institutional, departmental and individual levels, exacerbating the climate of competitiveness. For example, Shore and Wright highlight the way in such contestation is intensified by the significance now attached to the audit system, and the performance indicators upon which it draws and the institutional hierarchies it entrenches:

> The new audit norms focus on adherence to selective performance indicators to produce a quantifiable score that is then used as the basis for pitting department against department and institution against institution. Thus a pecking order is created between those departments ranked as 3, 4, and 5*('international excellence').
>
> (1999: 569)

Shore and Wright go on to observe that these and similar ranking systems prevalent in the corporatised higher education milieu foment interpersonal divisions by providing academics with new ways of envisaging their fellow academics, for instance as "'a 3b', or a '5' researcher" (1999: 569). In South Africa, the ratings bestowed on researchers by the NRF have effects of this kind. For instance, NRF-rated researchers in South Africa enjoy varying degrees of prestige, while unrated researchers may be made to feel that they lack academic substance. (NRF ratings are partly determined by factors such as publications, patents, other measurable research outputs and the impact thereof.)

League tables and other university ranking systems play a key role in establishing other related hierarchies at international and national levels, consolidating differences between institutions, and reinforcing a sense of inter-institutional competitiveness all the while. For example, many universities have become caught up in inter-institutional struggles revolving around rankings. In South Africa, for instance, it was reported that the University of the Witwatersrand was seeking to displace the University of Cape Town as Africa's foremost tertiary institution in 2011 (Govender, 2011: 13). University rankings are based on a variety of features, such as research assessments, entry standards, student–staff ratios, graduate career prospects, institutional resources and facilities and perceived prestige of universities. Consequently, as various local and international commentators observe, institutional rankings can serve as "proxies for privilege", favouring the elite universities at the cost of the less affluent and privileged institutions, including those in the developing world. (Amsler, 2013: 4. 6; see also Chapman, 2013). Such rankings have become more influential during the last decade and can exercise far-reaching effects. In many countries, the UK included, they have an impact on an institution's status and funding and tend to guide students, particularly foreign applicants, in their choice of universities and courses, for instance (see for instance Chevalier and Jia, 2013; Shore and Wright, 1999: 570).

Just as university rankings embody the state of competitiveness that has taken hold in higher education, so does the discourse often employed to depict them. Featuring headlines like "Why the University of Surrey Is on the Rise", "SA Varsities Slip Down in Global Rankings" and "UCT Drops 13 Places on World University Rankings", the media coverage of the rise and fall of diverse universities' fortunes sometimes evokes sports event commentaries or stock market reports. Moreover, an Australian online newspaper recently described how the University of Melbourne "tumbled six places from 28 to 34 in just a year" (Hare, 2013). In the UK, university rankings are often referred to as "League Tables": lists displaying the current standing of sports teams.

All too often, the condition of ongoing contestation tends to have been accepted as an integral feature of the present-day university environment, while its damaging aspects are all too often elided. As Collini puts it, the facile assumption that universities are caught up in a struggle to surpass one another now constitutes one of the dominant notions in academia, infecting many universities in the UK and elsewhere:

> In Britain, the discussion mostly reduces to whether Oxford and Cambridge and Imperial College are "competing" with Harvard and Stanford and MIT; in certain other countries, attention is focused on getting one or more universities in the world's "top 50" or "top 100".
>
> (2012: 17–18)

Both locally and internationally, this emphasis on competition tends to take place at the cost of much else. For instance, as Collini remarks, this is indicative of a self-absorbed desire for individual advancement, irrespective of the personal and wider social costs involved, of "a kind of mercantilism of the intellect, a fear that the stock of national treasure will be diminished, rather than augmented by the success of enterprises elsewhere" (2012: 17). Moreover, the current obsession with competition obscures other significant concerns. Orr notes that only two years after South Africa's political transition, at a period when remedying the inequities of the past was of paramount importance, various policy documents, including the Government Green paper and the 1996 report of the South African National Commission on Higher Education (NCHE), placed greater emphasis on the need to become internationally competitive than on the need for redress and equity (1997: 62).

In countries such as South Africa, in which affluence and widespread poverty coexist, the divisions and disparities that this inter-institutional competitiveness engenders are exacerbated by the stark divisions between the contenders. On the one hand, there are the relatively well-endowed South African institutions, many of which are former HAIs, precarious bastions of academic privilege and influence, targeting the intellectual and economic elite. On the other hand, the institutions lacking resources and adequate academic infrastructures, formerly many of the HDIs, draw their students especially from the underprepared and the rural poor.

Alluding to the Comaroffs' research into contemporary manifestations of the occult (1993, 1999), Moore and Sanders contend that present-day forms of witchcraft and other occult practices are symptoms of the precariousness, unease, inequalities and unfulfilled expectations in contemporary societies (2001: 3). Indeed, some of the metaphorical parallels between the present-day, market-driven academic environment and the sinister side of the supernatural have some of their roots in the inequities, imbalances and anxieties that pervade the daily lives of universities. All too often, these conditions are intensified by the obsession with competitiveness.

The rankings and ratings accorded to individual researchers, including those bestowed by the NRF in South Africa, and various measurable, officially approved research outputs such as publications and patents, reap monetary rewards, as do numbers of graduates, particularly at postgraduate level. Universities receive state funding on the basis of these, and faculties, departments and employees in question tend to benefit financially in turn (Ministerial Statement 2012/3 and 2013/4). These financial incentives intensify the climate of competitiveness in academia, bringing various damaging tendencies associated with witchcraft, such as greed, covetousness and selfishness to the fore.

Monetary incentives, selfishness and greed

Macdonald and Kam describe how academics at a range of universities (including some in France and Australia) are paid large amounts of money for publishing articles in high-ranking journals and varying amounts for other publications, depending on the journal's status.[4] Indeed, many other international and South African universities tend to award cash incentives for publications in accredited journals. This, as South African academic John Aitchison observes, has spawned a wave of "university 419" scams: dubious peer-reviewed journals, often with fake "impact factors", that publish articles, irrespective of their quality, provided their authors pay them to do so (often in US dollars). Nonetheless, since such publications have employed one stratagem or another to acquire accreditation, these authors benefit materially, receiving financial rewards from their institutions, while accumulating more research outputs and enhancing their promotion prospects. Meanwhile, although their employees' work – often of such a shoddy nature that it would not be publishable elsewhere – is on public display, universities do not object, since they receive subsidies for publications in accredited journals, and a number of these 419 journals appear on the lists of officially approved journals. (The *Mediterranean Journal of Social Sciences*, favoured by a number of South African academics, is one such publication.) Moreover, incentive funding often tends to be bestowed on academics for the graduation of postgraduate students under their supervision. (Unsurprisingly, in a context of this kind, a number of postgraduate students whose work is flawed and inadequate have degrees bestowed on them nonetheless.) Aitchison observes that the cash incentives that are now bestowed on universities and thereafter on academics for publications and postgraduate degrees have intensified greed and corruption within academia (2015: 31).

Payments relating to systems of performance appraisal may also feature at diverse institutions in the UK, South Africa and elsewhere (see for instance Parker and Jary, 1995: 320). For instance, my institution offered a bonus to employees who completed their IPAs. Meanwhile, NRF-rated researchers have access to special funding sources. These monetary incentives heighten academic rivalry at various levels. Researchers vie with one another as they strive to publish their work, for journal space is limited and journal status is partly determined by rejection rates. Furthermore, those who outstrip many others in their academic field derive prestige and enhanced publication opportunities from this, and thus more monetary rewards. Accordingly, the pressure to publish research findings in specific areas or generate patents before other academic competitors do so often tends to be fuelled by material self-interest (see for instance Ozga, 2011: 147). Partly as a consequence of this focus on monetary matters, competition now extends to human capital of a kind, as more affluent universities strive to outbid one another in their efforts to lure prominent researchers. Potential cash cows producing profit-generating publications and enhancing institutional prestige, they may perhaps elevate their institution's ranking.

The sense of stress and desperation permeating many market-driven universities fuels the compulsion to accrue that which may safeguard them in troubled times. A compulsion of this kind may often manifest itself in a preoccupation with scores, ratings and ranking levels and points bestowed on individuals, departments and institutions by internal and external assessors. Moreover, many academics may become so caught up in that which Stephen Gudeman describes as "the new fetishism of numbers" (1998: 1) that they may base their own sense of self-worth, perceive the value of their colleagues and the success of their institutions in terms of numerical (and sometimes alphabetical) units of measurement.[5] The "obsession with league tables" in the UK is symptomatic of this (Collini, 2012: 17). More broadly, that which Parker and Jary depict as a "fetishism of rankings" is prevalent in many market-oriented university environments worldwide (1995: 331).

Accumulation and deprivation

The economic exigencies with which many market-driven universities are beset tend to give rise to an emphasis on fiscal restraint. Yet paradoxically, this is often combined with a squandering of financial resources as the ethos of privatisation and individual accumulation is promoted. Other professional domains that have been pervaded by forms of consumerism and commodification may be characterised by comparable tendencies. One conspicuous feature of the appetite for accumulation has already been highlighted: the extent to which restructured, corporatised universities are characterised by inflated salaries for those in the upper echelons of management and conspicuous expenditure at senior managerial level. Indeed, as Ginsberg notes, many senior managerial staff at US universities appear to have a predilection for ostentatious status symbols, including costly vehicles and lavishly furnished offices (2011: 71–87). Ginsberg's point is also applicable to many other societies that have fallen under the sway of consumer capitalism and commodity fetishism, the UK and South Africa included. For instance, in recent years the dean of one UK business school launched a "corporate ID programme" complete with a whole array of items bearing the new corporate brand. The dean also had his office redecorated, at considerable cost, as if he were the CEO of an affluent corporation (Parker, 2014: 284–285). In circumstances of this kind, it may sometimes seem as if some of those exercising authority feel compelled to accrue various economic and material resources, partly by diminishing the extent to which others have access to them. Sometimes it may also seem as if they seek to instil similar urges in those over whom they preside.

However, excessive expenditure by those in powerful positions was also a feature of many university environments in the past. A former vice-chancellor at my institution, for example, held lavish parties at which a large quantity of expensive alcohol was served, favoured expensive clothes and purchased a Mercedes Benz, partly to symbolise his affluence and status. Such predilections were by no means restricted to my institution or indeed, to South Africa. Nowadays, however, the valorisation of material accumulation and commodity fetishism that has come to characterise many corporatised university environments and the societies within which they are located has reached far greater proportions, providing a fertile breeding ground for tendencies of this kind. Moreover, many present-day vice-chancellors' salaries and perks would allow ample scope for such extravagances.

Yet in many countries, South Africa included, the academic condition may seem to be one of deprivation. Salaries, internal budgets and staff numbers are restricted, while infrastructures supporting academic activity have diminished, often because the funding required to sustain these is no longer available or has been channelled elsewhere. Ironically, although budgets have been devolved to schools, departments and centres, all too often very little in the way of adequate financial support has trickled down to these levels. According to the findings of Deem, Hillyard and Reed's survey, for instance, there is "little scope for anything but essentials" in many areas of UK academia (2007: 54). However, in diverse universities in many other parts of the world, including numerous South African institutions, particularly HDIs, it sometimes seems as if there is insufficient financial wherewithal even for such bare necessities. Such tendencies call to mind two interconnected, opposing impetuses that are said to be key features of sorcery: accumulation and deprivation. Contemporary witchcraft practitioners are said to be driven by a selfish craving to accumulate whatever it is that will provide material well-being, generally obtained at the cost of others (see for instance Geschiere, 1997: 5, 16; Niehaus, 2001a: 9).

The malevolence of sorcery

While the malevolence of witchcraft may differ in depth and intensity from the damaging tendencies that the market-driven university environment has brought to the fore, various metaphorical parallels are worth considering. UK academic Danny Dorling (2011) maintains that present-day social and economic injustice is validated and perpetuated by means of several interconnected, widespread notions. Elitism is equated with efficiency; exclusion and prejudice are normalised and greed is valorised while despair is depicted as inevitable (cited in Amsler, 2013: 6). In certain respects, these forms of selfishness, avarice and arrogance manifest themselves in the market-oriented university milieu, with its emphasis on competitiveness and the-winner-takes-all capitalist ethos. Here, as elsewhere, privatisation and individual accumulation are promoted.

Moreover, the present-day academic climate of rivalry and insecurity can foster ill-will, encouraging malicious impulses. The stakes are high in market-driven universities; this often gives rise to an anxiety to excel – even, if need be, at the cost of colleagues, other departments, divisions or institutions – combined with a fear of the possible consequences of failure. Inclinations of this nature have become an endemic feature of numerous university environments in South Africa and elsewhere, generated by the nature of the corporatised university milieu, in which incentives and punitive measures are often implemented simultaneously. For instance, Shore and Wright allude to the way this manifests itself in UK academia, remarking that "[i]n a regime of competitive allocation of declining funds, failure must be punished if 'excellence' is to be rewarded" (1999: 569). Further to this, the precarious, embattled nature of the market-oriented university environment can increase the desire to accumulate that which may bestow temporary material security and stability, while heightening a resentful awareness of others' relative security and prosperity. Such tendencies foster insecurity, envious rivalry and covetousness. For instance, some university employees and managers may be gladdened when certain institutions, departments or colleagues suffer setbacks or calamities if there is a possibility that the disadvantages of others may work to their advantage.[6] Collini, among others, depicts the greed, suspicion and selfishness that this climate of stress-laden competitiveness has fostered. Many universities may now come to perceive other institutions as their opponents in an ongoing struggle for monetary incentives, prestige, institutional security and ever-diminishing resources, and this kind of "educational Darwinism" breeds mistrust and tension (Collini, 2012: 163). While such malicious tendencies have long been features of academia, the present-day market-driven university environment, with its endemic climate of fear and its focus on competitiveness, lends itself particularly to harmful inclinations of this kind.

It is worth noting that witchcraft is not always perceived as an act of conscious malice in Africa. For instance, some of E. E. Evans-Pritchard's Azande respondents in South Sudan maintained that some witches were capable of acting without a full awareness of their destructive intentions (1976: 56–60). And arguably, perhaps, some of those in positions of authority at corporatised universities may not always be fully aware of the damage they may be doing to the professional and personal lives of others by means of their utterances and actions. Nonetheless, some may wish misfortune on others, seeking to benefit from this, and may attempt to harm them. Indeed, much damage can be inflicted in the course of many of the routine procedures and processes in the corporate university milieu. For example, audits and other external and internal forms of evaluation and monitoring may offer ample opportunities to highlight the shortcomings and failings of others, whether actual or imagined. (At such times, for instance, certain departments may perhaps be deemed to be overstaffed or non-viable, while specific employees' performances may be found wanting, even if there are insufficient grounds for allegations of this nature.) Ruth notes that performance appraisals are often feared, for employees are frequently assessed by diverse people, some of whom are strangers. Although appraisals may sometimes draw on "nothing but rumours, ignorant opinions, hearsay evidence, misinformation, prejudice and outright character assassination, or friends shielding one another in order to build up their empires and inflate their egos", such assessments may carry weight and may destroy careers (2001: 199–200).

Moreover, those who preside over institutional hierarchies may emphasise the power that they wield and the hazards that may await those departments and employees that are deemed unsatisfactory or unproductive. Incidentally, various occult practitioners in South Africa and elsewhere are said to make use of some similar strategies to draw attention to their powers. For example, the South African inyanga Khotso Sethuntsa employed tactics of this kind, while Evans-Pritchard observes that those who make unpleasant allusions to others, or threaten them with misfortune should they displease them, are often suspected of witchcraft among the Azande (1976: 51). Meanwhile, both menacing manifestations of the occult and various university managers may display a certain degree of vindictiveness. This appears to be an essential attribute of malign occult beings, and the authoritarianism that often tends to form a feature of the corporatised university environment may involve bullying tactics, which can slide all too easily into spitefulness and malice (see for instance Southall and Cobbing, 2001: 13; Thornton, 2004: 161–164).

The corporate university environment encourages the growth of damaging tendencies in other related respects. Images of consumption can characterise malevolent occult agencies, and African witches are often renowned for their obsession with eating. A belief also prevails in certain parts of Africa that malign supernatural forces reside within the belly (see for instance Geschiere, 1997: 7; Evans-Pritchard, 1976: 49). Thus, witchcraft is often perceived as a form of spiritual and psychic devouring (Geschiere, 1997: 203). For instance, Pamela G. Schmoll discusses accounts of soul-eaters among the Hausa in Niger. Driven by greed, soul-eaters drain their victims of their life-essence, dehumanising them (1993: 193–220). Another example is provided by Bastian, who observes that the *amoosu* (the witch) is perceived by Igbo-speaking people in Nigeria as a "psychic cannibal . . . [who] treats other human beings as though they were meat" (1993: 133). Meanwhile, the mamlambo devours blood: literally the blood sacrifices it requires and, metaphorically speaking, the hearts' blood of those who are bound to it. The nature and consequences of a pact with this being will be discussed in more depth in a subsequent chapter. There are certain points of comparison between this occult urge to consume and the spirit of consumerism that has come to characterise many market-driven higher education environments.

Universities in capitalist countries were bound up with consumerism in the past, in that they served the interests of the bourgeoisie, thus forming part of the machinery of capitalism. However in the present-day globalised world, pervaded by neoliberal economic approaches valorising consumerism, marketing strategies permeate many societies more powerfully than ever before, the competition between nations and organisations and institutions and the individuals within them has taken on new proportions, and consumerism has engulfed far more areas of life, transforming all it encompasses. In the global knowledge economy, students are the consumers, higher education is a consumer good and academics the human capital feeding consumer forces. Trajectories of this kind are sometimes taken to extremes when terminology from the manufacturing sector is employed, involving images of production and consumption which may extend to incorporate human beings. For instance, graduates may be converted from consumers to items for metaphorical consumption, depicted as "end products", intended to reap benefits for "the final consumers", generally in the commercial sector (Ite, 2004: 251).

As a result of these factors, it could be contended that restructured, market-driven universities that have taken on the procedures and practices of the corporate capitalist workplace have entered a hazardous realm, within which potentially damaging forces, both mercantile and metaphorically magical, hold sway at both seen and unseen levels. As the symbolic parallels with sorcery in this chapter suggest, the process of corporatisation and marketisation can contaminate many university environments, reducing them to places of sorrow and fear, in which forms of envy, suspicion, self-centredness and greed run rampant, fuelled by the forms of market-driven corporate capitalism that diverse universities have embraced.

High priests and agents of redemption

Meanwhile, those at the pinnacle of the occult hierarchy preside over this milieu, with its fractured network of academic kin. Although power structures of this nature have always been a feature of university life, the high priests and holy men of today's managerialised university (the majority of whom still tend to be male) have acquired an awful – in various senses of the word – authority, in terms of the extensive forms of power and control vested in them. Moreover, their status as beings set apart from the rest of the university community is reinforced by the general awareness among staff members that management earns far more than they do, in terms of direct salary payments and perks. Geschiere discusses the extent to which new forms of affluence and power can disrupt domestic and extended family networks in Cameroonian society (1997: 10). His point has bearing on the current academic context, in which new types of authority and economic privilege have become concentrated at managerial level, exercising a divisive effect. Moreover, Geschiere's and Fisiy and Geschiere's analyses of the way in which new elites have been associated with the occult in the Cameroon and various other African states has some points of comparison with the nature and effect of current power dynamics in higher education (Geschiere, 1997: 6–10; Fisiy and Geschiere, 2001: 241).[7] Symbolically speaking, the occult features of contemporary university discourse and practice emanate from and reinforce the prestige and status of the managerial elite, thereby consolidating the dominion of the economic and political authorities whose interests they serve.

Within an occult system of this nature, there are other, subsidiary players at work. Just as agents of redemption fulfil a key function in certain mystical and spiritual doctrines, so they also play an important role in the occult academy. In this context, they may take the form of Quality Assurance personnel, emissaries from the corporate realm, those employed at Teaching and Learning Centres, consultants, representatives of university committees, and managerial staff performing related functions.

These officially sanctioned agents of redemption offer various forms of guidance and salvation to those who seek to mend their ways by becoming efficient, productive components of the "new-generation" corporatised academy. On one level, their agency is necessary for acolytes who wish to rise higher in their institutional hierarchies. For instance, staff members seeking promotion at various universities, including some of those in South Africa and the UK, may be required to complete Teaching and Learning Centre teaching modules. Moreover, agents of redemption may offer staff members counselling during times of ritual trial. For instance, university staff may be directed to Quality Assurance personnel,

Teaching and Learning Centres or to presentations by various consultants for assistance in preparing for the ritualistic ordeals of audits. Periodically such agents also provide instruction in the correct performance of other ritual-like procedures, such as the completion of templates. They also preside over institutional rites of passage, such as the annual induction courses which newly appointed academics may be required to undergo. Moreover, they can play prominent roles in various institutional rites of renewal, especially those said to promote organisational development. On such occasions, they may share their wisdom with individuals and groupings that aspire to transformation.

However, these agents of the occult academy and the unseen external forces to which it is in thrall are not always to be trusted. Just like certain mystical teachers to whom some seekers after the truth turn in times of need, some of their wisdom may be inadequate or of dubious provenance. At times, some such personnel may even seem little more than "parasitical operators", drawing significance and sustenance from the academic community upon which their continued existence is reliant (Taylor, 2003: 5). Comparably, some spiritual teachers may depend on their devotees for material support and a status that they would otherwise lack.

There are further parallels between the agents of corporate managerialism and those with expertise in the otherworldly. Certain academic occult practitioners who offer instruction in the norms and practices of corporate managerialism may resemble members of cults or religious fundamentalists who take on the initiation of newcomers so as to ensure that they conform to the codes of the collective. Shore and Wright discuss the role played by individuals who fulfil functions of this nature in higher education and in society at large. (For instance, certain psychiatrists, educationalists and medical specialists can perform tasks of this kind.) Within their institutional or broader social contexts, these experts are believed to have access to specialised knowledge which they share with those who seek "to engage in the process of self-improvement in order to modify their conduct according to the desired norms" (1999: 560). Thus, they may form part of structures of social control and confinement, ensuring conformity and compliance. Alluding to Foucault's *Discipline and Punish* (1977), Shore and Wright draw attention to the way in which these practitioners can constitute part of the control mechanisms in institutions that impose order and inflict discipline at individual and collective levels (1999: 560). In other words, to cite Foucault again, these agents of redemption are a component of the carceral mechanisms that exercise "a power of normalization" over members of a social context who are regarded as disrupting or deviating from the norms, or regulations, governing their milieus (1977: 308). While appearing to offer salvation, such agents of redemption in the corporate university may act as conduits for managerial authority, and the unseen, omnipresent forms of economic and political power and influence that hold sway over the institution as a whole.

Notes

1 Many of the issues discussed on pp. 126–140 in this chapter are also examined in Wood (2010b: 9–12) and Wood (2014b), Kinship, Collegiality and Witchcraft:

South African Oral Accounts of the Supernatural and the Occult Aspects of Contemporary Academia. *Tydskrif* 5 1 (1): 153–159. However, various points from these sources have been developed further in the light of more recent research findings. Pages 129, 137 and 141 mention information from Wood, Felicity with Michael Lewis. 2007. *The Extraordinary Khotso: Millionaire Medicine Man of Lusikisiki.* Johannesburg: Jacana: pp. 161–165.

2 In order to prove that they still inhabited the physical world (sometimes ghost employees may no longer do so) and their institution, staff members were required to present themselves at a stipulated site during certain times, bearing documentary evidence proving that they were bona fide university employees.

3 For example, Jean-François Bayart (1996) maintains that various political leaders in Africa, including Sékou Touré, Mathieu Kerekou and Jean Bédel Boukassa, sought to become more politically influential by drawing on aspects of sorcery (cited in Geschiere, 2003: 159, 321). In South Africa during the apartheid era, some prominent Afrikaner Nationalist politicians, including premiers J.G. Strijdom and H.F. Verwoerd, visited the widely renowned inyanga Khotso Sethuntsa. Friends and family members claim that they sought his medicines for good fortune and political power.

4 For instance, Stuart Macdonald and Jacqueline Kam describe how some French universities paid around €12000 for an article published in a high-status journal in 2007, while Melbourne Business School paid A$15 000 for publications in the Top 40 journal list drawn up by the *Financial Times* (2007: 644).

5 Although Gudemann considers this new valorisation of numbers particularly in relation to the University of Minnesota, his points are widely applicable.

6 Ruth describes the ways in which this tendency manifests itself in the University of the North, South Africa, for instance.

7 According to Geschiere, for example, rumours abound in a number of African societies that various powerful politicians and certain members of the *nouveaux riches* owe their wealth and power to their dealings with certain shady supernatural forces (1997: 6–10).

8 Secrecy, publicity, confusion and power

In higher education, as in so many other areas of life, power is reliant on that which is unseen and obscure. Taussig observes that "politics is played out in the shadows" (2003: 145; see also 273, 295–300), while Geschiere describes how "concealment and secrecy" form an integral part of the workings of power (2003: 182). As Shore and Wright remind us, many political thinkers (including Machiavelli, Marx and Gramsci) have described how power is most effective when it is hidden from those it controls (1999: 559).[1]

In order to delve into the occult mysteries of managerialism, let us consider how some forms of magic are bound up with secrecy and mystery, exerting part of their power by this means. Nowadays, senior managerial staff at corporatised universities may exercise part of their authority covertly, while sometimes taking it to exceptional levels. Thus, institutional managerial systems may seem characterised by concealment. Chetty and Merrett depict one instance of this, describing how policymaking at the University of KwaZulu-Natal in 2006 and thereafter was often engineered by means of "rubber-stamping forums hidden from both public and private view" (2014: 134). Further to this, the use of arcane, convoluted jargon and the hierarchical complexities within which managerial activities are often enmeshed heighten the mystique within which numerous systems of managerial governance may seem to be steeped.

Mystery and publicity

The aura of mystery often surrounding managerial rationale and procedure is deepened by the way in which, both literally and figuratively, many senior managerial staff in diverse institutions in this country and elsewhere appear to have a predilection for setting themselves beyond the reach of the employees over whom they preside, by means of verbal and physical strategies of elusiveness and evasiveness. Then, even when they are physically present, university managers may remain absent in a significant sense. For instance, one academic interviewed in the documentary *Luister*, which investigates racism at the University of Stellenbosch, maintained that the vice-chancellor did not seem to be speaking as an individual. Instead, she intimated, the voice of marketing was heard, rather than his own. Her point could be applied to various members of senior management at diverse corporatised universities, both locally and internationally. In a sense, they may often seem to serve as mouthpieces of the market, into which their individual voices are subsumed.

From a managerial perspective, there is much to be gained from appearing aloof and remote. By distancing themselves from other employees often on account of the urgent matters to which they are required to attend by virtue of their positions, various senior managerial staff members symbolically elevate themselves above those around them. In certain respects, then, senior university managers begin to resemble ever-present, yet inaccessible emanations from another world, with the power to determine the destinies of the lesser beings that are subject to their control. For these and other reasons, managerial staff may often appear to have acquired the ability to seem ever-present even when they are absent, by virtue of the extent to which they may loom large in the minds of their subordinates even when they are far removed from them. Yet again, this bears out Geschiere's observations about the interconnectedness of power and the imaginary (2003: 179–182). His point also holds true for many workers of magic. For example, the South African inyanga Khotso Sethuntsa deliberately cultivated a sense of mystery and secrecy around himself, generating many rumours about the extent of his powers. "He was an elusive man", someone who knew him well remarked. "He'd never tell anything straight" (Wood and Lewis/ Yako, 2004).

The son of someone who once knew Khotso once said,

> My father used to say that Khotso was quite clever, because he refused [to divulge his secrets] . . . . He didn't usually reveal his powers publicly . . . what he usually did was to show off his wealth. . . . [So] he was clever in the sense that his powers were kept quite secret. By showing people his powers, he could end up quite powerless. The mystery [was tied up with the power].
> (Wood/Mabongo, 2002)

A *n'anga* from Harare, who was rumoured to sell wealth-giving beings (termed chikwambos), also preferred to create a sense of mystery about his work and about the wealth-giving spirits he and others were said to supply. For example, he once observed, "I cannot go into detail about the process that one has to undergo to finally become the owner of a chikwambo". He also said: "I myself cannot comment on that . . . and neither can I tell you which form of chikwambo I would recommend people to obtain" (Muswaka/Sekuru, 2010). Someone in the Eastern Cape town of Alice, South Africa, who claimed to supply wealth-giving creatures, was similarly evasive about his modus operandi (Muswaka/anonymous respondent, 2010). By weaving an aura of secrecy, these and other workers of magic seek to create the impression that they have access to extraordinary powers that ordinary mortals would not be able to comprehend or control. They also highlight the rare and special nature of their knowledge by this means. As has been indicated in the opening chapter, other specialised practitioners, including academics, may emphasise the arcane nature of their work for similar reasons.

There are, however, other dimensions to this issue for, as Geschiere points out, a combination of secrecy and publicity can form part of the workings of power (2003: 181). Similarly, Pels contends that various forms of influence and control in present-day societies appear to derive a significant part of their power from an interplay between mystery and publicity (2003: 6, 3). The paradoxical blend of concealment and public exposure that characterises many present-day corporatised universities is one facet of this. For instance, Benjamin Ginsberg describes how many of those in the most prominent positions at universities in the US may often be veiled in degrees of obscurity, with names and faces that even students and alumni may fail to recognise (2011: 5). This state of affairs is often a feature of institutional life at many other corporatised, managerially governed universities elsewhere.

While an aura of mystery tends to surround senior university managerial staff in many respects, they are simultaneously promoted as high-profile figures by the institutional publicity apparatus, including the divisions of Marketing and Communication. In many universities in South Africa, the UK and elsewhere, the faces of the top university managers are frequently displayed in institutional promotional material, on the university website and in other institutional documentation. For example, photographs of executive deans once adorned the covers of faculty prospectuses in my institution. At the same time, managerial voices are often heard. This frequently takes electronic form, when managerial announcements, exhortations and edicts are regularly broadcast over university computer networks, while at some institutions vice-chancellors may share their thoughts with the university community on a regular basis. William Makgoba, a former vice-chancellor at the University of KwaZulu-Natal, was wont to do this, for instance (Chetty and Merrett, 2014: 160–173). All the while, the institutional media may regularly feature articles about the activities, aspirations and achievements of members of senior management. Sometimes this may be combined with blatant self-promotion at senior managerial level. For instance, Chetty and Merrett remark that displays of self-aggrandisement of almost embarrassing proportions became a conspicuous part of the institutional culture at their university during their tenure (2014: 143). This is by no means an isolated case. Instead, similar managerial tendencies may be a distinctive feature of diverse university environments in South Africa, the US, the UK and elsewhere (see for instance Ginsberg, 2011: 76–77; Parker, 2014: 286–287).

Yet again, various university managers and certain occult practitioners may have some aspects in common in this regard. For instance, although the inyanga Khotso Sethuntsa surrounded himself with a sense of mystery, as depicted earlier, he also carried out various forms of highly effective self-advertisement and self-aggrandisement. Other occult practitioners, such as the n'anga from Harare and the ukuthwala practitioner in Alice, South Africa, have made use of similar strategies. For instance, the Alice ukuthwala practitioner ensured that the advertisements promoting the wealth-giving magic that he supplied were publicly displayed throughout the town, although he remained an elusive, secretive figure. Thus, these and many other workers of magic rely on interweaving secrecy and self-promotion, in order to draw attention to their supernatural expertise while surrounding themselves with an air of mysterious power, wielding an influence over many of those around them by this means.

While publicity of this kind plays a significant role, other forms of mystery and mystification may be employed to heighten the mystique surrounding senior managerial staff. Above all, the occult quality of corporatised universities feeds on an ever-prevalent sense of mystery. University salaries are a closely guarded secret, for example. Southall and Cobbing, for instance, observe that there was a lack of transparency around salary issues – particularly those of senior management – at Rhodes University in 2001 (2001: 19, 40). Meanwhile, the University of Fort Hare's salary list was duplicated and distributed in 2006, revealing striking salary discrepancies. However, a local newspaper, the *Daily Dispatch*, reported that the university management declined to disclose how salaries were determined.[2] Yet even when salary details are revealed, the largesse bestowed on senior managerial staff may remain shrouded in obscurity. It has already been noted that many senior managers at diverse institutions in South Africa and elsewhere tend to receive significant parts of their salaries in the form of perks.

Then other areas of mystery may prevail around certain disciplinary codes that may be used to enforce managerial authority. For instance, Rhodes University managers were reluctant to discuss such issues with the academic staff union, the National Tertiary Education Staff Union, in 2001 (Southall and Cobbing, 2001: 19). Furthermore, an employee who falls foul of senior management may be subjected to disciplinary action for breaching what may seem to be an obscure or even problematic institutional regulation. Duncan cites several examples of South African academics who have been dismissed from their institutions for reasons of this kind, including University of KwaZulu-Natal academic Fazel Khan (2007: 10–14).

Two other academics from this institution, Nithaya Chetty and John van den Berg, were subjected to disciplinary proceedings for sharing information about Senate meetings with members of the university community outside Senate and for revealing this information to the media. Van den Berg and Chetty's case highlights the extent to which secrecy surrounding university documents and meetings may become so extreme that even the most commonplace institutional documentation may become confidential, while publicising the most unremarkable discussions may generate disciplinary proceedings. As Chetty and Merrett indicate, restrictive measures of this kind are by no means unique to the University of KwaZulu-Natal (2014: 122, 147–151, 173). Instead, they form part of a growing trend, both locally and internationally.

These conditions are exacerbated by a lack of information. This may especially concern important decisions and developments that affect employees and students. For instance, Duncan describes how the South African Ministry of Education released a National Plan for Higher Education in South Africa in 2001, advocating increasing student enrolments in Commerce, the Sciences, Engineering and Technology, and business-related and career-oriented programmes. Various departments in the Humanities were somewhat disturbed by this, although the minister assured them that they would not be unduly affected by this development. Notwithstanding this, however, a number of Humanities departments were subsequently closed down (Duncan, 2007: 6). This is indicative of the extent to which information may be obscured or withheld from those whom it most directly concerns, both by senior managerial staff and sometimes by those external authorities who preside over them. (Sometimes the lack of clarity at senior managerial level may stem in part from this.) Unsurprisingly then, various South African university employees may discover more about current conditions at their institutions from the media than from members of management and the university publicity apparatus. For instance, various employees at my university tend to glean much information about the state of affairs at their workplace from the pages of *The Daily Dispatch*. As commentators such as Ginsberg remind us, comparable conditions are prevalent at many other institutions of higher education in the US and elsewhere (2011: 4).

Unfathomable upheavals, inexplicable edicts and incomprehensible procedures

On another, related level, the reasons for the introduction of new procedures and sudden, dramatic policy changes with far-reaching implications may seem unfathomable. Such conditions abound in many universities, including those in South Africa, the UK and the US (see for instance Southall and Cobbing, 2001: 14–21; Gudeman, 1992: 2). For instance, Chetty and Merrett noted in 2014 that their institution had undergone a process of seemingly endless and senseless change since the 1990s. They also maintained that disruptions of this nature could impede dissent, thus serving the interests of the university authorities (205–206). Meanwhile, Parker describes the sudden, destructive nature of the changes that took place at the European business school where he was formerly employed when a new dean took charge. Although the new dean was appointed because the business school was said to be failing in certain respects, there seemed to be insufficient grounds for accusations of this kind (2014: 284).

Indeed, the reasons why particular changes and edicts are suddenly and unexpectedly enforced may sometimes seem to border on the inexplicable. New sets of commandments (often relating to the performance of various complex bureaucratic rituals, the practical functions of which appear to be fully comprehensible only to those who have been initiated into the secrets of managerialism) regularly descend from on high. These upheavals and areas of obscurity have become widespread academic phenomena. Moreover, such mutations and permutations can suddenly strike without warning. On these and comparable occasions, the style of managerial governance may seem simultaneously hands-off, heavy-handed and offhand.

If university procedures seem inscrutable and confusing, then university employees may begin to lose a sense of direction and purpose, and their work itself may begin to seem devoid of significance. For instance, a report produced in 2006 by a University of KwaZulu-Natal academic Fazel Khan, dismissed for bringing his institution into disrepute, highlights the sense of meaninglessness prevalent among academics at his institution during that time. According to his report, this feeling arises when "the function, purpose and meaning of your work do not make sense" (cited in Duncan, 2007: 11). This state of affairs is a widespread malaise, infecting many academic environments in South Africa and elsewhere. For example, Hedley remarks that managerial structures in the UK often seem in a process of flux and change, creating the impression of instability and uncertainty. He also describes the effect of the recurrent restructuring programmes, the rationale and purpose of which may seem obscure and bewildering to many university employees (2010: 137, 140). In his novel *Deaf Sentence*, dealing in part with academic life at a contemporary UK university, David Lodge alludes to the confusion and disarray wrought by the frequent forms of institutional reconfiguration to which the university authorities seemed devoted (2008: 27). As Lodge's comment suggests and as Parker also remarks, the reasons for the frequent changes and disruptions that characterise much contemporary university life in the UK and elsewhere may be so incomprehensible that they seem to stem from forces beyond human ken, or from a comparable source: the inscrutable sphere of institutional management (Parker, 2014: 284). This reinforces the impression that the university management is a secret order of the elect and chosen, driven by unfathomable principles of its own.

However, the confusing, mutable nature of managerial policy and procedures plays another, more straightforwardly practical function, which tends to remain part of the hidden workings of managerialism and the systems of power and authority to which it may be accountable, as an undisclosed policy (Shore and Wright, 1999: 569). Nonetheless, Shore and Wright indicate that the HEFCE once alluded to this stratagem directly, acknowledging that it would be preferable to retain specific performance indicators for a two-year period only, since "after that time people get wise to them". Thus, Shore and Wright conclude, the intention "is to keep systems volatile, slippery and opaque". They mention that, like many other features of corporatised academia, this draws on American corporate notions. For instance, they note that Peters and Waterman's *In Search of Excellence* encapsulates this principle (Shore and Wright, 1999: 569). Arguably perhaps, some of the obscurities surrounding senior managerial policy and procedure also may stem from the deliberately designed complexities and mystifying aspects of the milieu within which it operates.

Confusion of this nature can fulfil certain functions, which have been employed for comparable purposes in certain mystical practices. For instance, those who purport to possess otherworldly powers, performing magical acts of dubious provenance, as well as those who carry out fraudulent conjuring tricks rely on baffling and bewildering those who behold them, so as to deceive them into believing that they are in the presence of superior individuals endowed with exceptional abilities that transcend those of ordinary mortals (Pels, 2003: 7). Once again, this may call to mind Geschiere's observations about the relationship between publicity, secrecy and power. An ancient example of this is the cryptic nature of the Delphic oracle's predictions, which cast light on the uses to which mystification and confusion can be put. In part, the obscure, fragmented nature of the Oracle's prophecies could have served as a safeguard. By making it difficult for the exact meaning of an enigmatic statement to be definitely established, it could render it impossible for the Oracle to be subsequently proven wrong. Above all, though, the opaque Sphinx-like nature of the Oracle's utterances reminded those who heard them that they were witnessing the workings of an otherworldly form of power, which they lacked the intellectual and spiritual capacities to comprehend.

The maze of managerialism

In the present-day corporate university environment, such forms of managerially-induced mystification are compounded by the complicated requirements with which university staff are regularly required to comply, many of which appear to fulfil no rational purpose. Nevil Johnson, for instance, alludes to "the paraphernalia of futile bureaucratization required for assessors who come from high like emissaries from Kafka's castle" (1994: 379; cited in Shore and Wright, 1999: 567). The world of Franz Kafka's castle is presided over by multilayered hierarchies, as is the corporatised, managerially governed university milieu. Various forms of economic and political influence and control are also at work at national, international and multinational levels, far beyond the reaches of university managerialism, shaping the nature and direction of higher education and using institutional managerial staff as their agents in various respects. The obscurity surrounding those who wield the most significant managerial authority adds to the layers of complexity and mystery in which institutional managerialism is steeped.

Shore and Wright discuss the market-driven restructuring of UK universities in the 1990s, observing that the degree of state intrusion was obscured by numerous intermediaries. These included external assessors, consultants, managerial staff and other employees who conformed with and promulgated the edicts issued by the institutional authorities (1999: 563). A similar state of affairs is still prevalent in the UK and elsewhere. Then internally, the extent of senior managerial control over the daily lives of university employees often tends to be concealed by a network of complicit subordinates who serve as conduits for senior managerial authority. Consequently, the nature and workings of senior managerial structures may come to seem bewildering or even impenetrable.

Hedley discusses the extent to which the state of confusion now prevalent at many contemporary universities is closely connected to their internal hierarchical complexities. Universities now consist of multi-tiered structures of administrative authority, and each level may deal with different types of issues. However, when they discuss the same issue, they may perceive and respond to it in diverse ways, depending on the exigencies of their specific context. Thus,

> mutual incomprehension grows. . . . (As an example, try asking a random sample of university employees what the recent "restructuring" exercise was designed to achieve.) Certainly the production of a university strategic plan,

most of the content of which is incomprehensible to most of those supposedly guided by it, is likely to promote cynicism, rather than the sense of communal purposes which is presumably its aim.

(2010: 136)

The opaque nature of managerial authority is intensified by this lack of clarity. Bruce Baker's description of the complex organisational systems in the "modernised" public services in the UK has some bearing on this. He observes that the fractured features of their institutional structures conceal the managerial chains of accountability. Ultimately then, the extent to which those who preside over a process can be held accountable for what takes place beneath them becomes unclear (2004: 47). Therefore, paradoxically, the new managerial and administrative chains of command in restructured universities, purportedly imposed to bring about greater accountability, have diminished this in various respects. All in all, the hegemonic nature of senior managerial dominion, its hierarchical complexities and its shadowy, imprecise workings have rendered it both aloof and elusive and thus less accountable. Ironically enough, however, the mysteries of managerialism are often enacted at the same time as the corporate fables of transparency and accountability are invoked.

The stylised, ceremonial nature of senior managerial procedure heightens this sense of mysterious remoteness, as does the aura of special significance surrounding it, which can distance it from the ken of all those employees who do not form part of the upper echelons of senior management. Goodsell describes how the rituals of public administration can be "full of contrived and calculated presentation . . . [and] endowed with the evocative mystique of state sovereignty" (1997: 948). Senior managerial staff in other areas of the public domain, higher education included, also ensure that the procedures over which they preside are characterised by these qualities. On account of these and other previously-delineated features, managerial practices can obfuscate, intimidate and complicate simultaneously.

Kafka's work recurrently comes to mind in the current academic context. There is, for example, the university decision-making process, which can become a Kafkaesque bureaucratic labyrinth in which coherence, efficiency and rational outcomes are lost. One committee meeting may give birth to another committee meeting at another level, which generates yet another in its turn, leading on and on to further meetings. No decision can be taken until the final committee meets. All this is imbued with ritual solemnity, since the correct procedures, as stipulated by university policies, are dutifully adhered to. As time passes, and the final pronouncement continues to be awaited, the last, decisive committee meeting becomes an event that takes on almost mystical, even mythic proportions. This is partly because it presides over the entire process, offering a way in which an outcome can be disentangled from the administrative maze in which it is trapped, but even more on account of the way in which this decisive event can be so long awaited that it seems to exist in the realms of hope and prophecy, rather than in actuality.

Many belief systems, including numerous established religions, spiritual movements and cults, are sustained not so much by the present as by the future: the expectation of things to come and the anticipation that predictions will come to pass. Indeed, if a devotee can be persuaded to feel that she or he has a stake in the future at some or other level, their present-day adherence may be maintained. Possibly then, university managements and the external authorities to whom they are accountable may be guided by a similar principle. By directing staff members' attention towards the future through an ongoing process of delays and deferments, these employees' focus could be shifted away from their current situations and present-day sources of dissatisfaction. Moreover, they might become inclined to believe that their obedience and submissiveness might eventually facilitate favourable outcomes.

Manipulation and deception

For their part, like Alice in Wonderland, many academics may feel that they inhabit an unstable, unpredictable world within which the ground rules constantly change. Along with a number of other factors, this serves to undermine the myth that corporatisation and managerialism will bring about greater efficiency and productivity. To university employees blundering around in a shadowy world of managerialism, such qualities may seem hard enough to envisage, let alone attain, just like the mythic constructs of excellence and quality.

It is especially worth bearing in mind an issue that seems to turn current university procedure topsy-turvy: the extent to which various dominant discourses and perceptions appear to be based on myths, fantasy and arbitrary notions. One distinctive occult feature of the corporate university is an unshakeable belief in the power and effectiveness of something that may seem, to all appearances, to exist in the world of the imagination. Even if, empirically, magic does not seem to work, the belief that it does – or might – is the cornerstone of the workings, or the perceived workings, of magic. For example, Levi-Strauss observes that "the efficacy of magic implies a belief in magic" (1963: 168). Comparably, a managerialised, corporatised university, with its top-heavy, unwieldy bureaucracy, its lack of administrative accountability and its chains of command as intricate and rigidly ranked as orders of demons or angels in medieval cosmology (sometimes depicted in university organograms, with each level of authority confined in a box outside of which it is not permitted to think and act) may not necessarily carry out its work more swiftly and efficiently than that institution did in former days, but the belief that it does so is all important. Thus, the conviction that supernatural or corporate, managerial magic is effective makes it effective, at least in the eyes of those whose world views accommodate one or other of these forms of potency.

Yet magicalities of this kind and other forms of enchantment and the mystical practices now prevalent in corporatised academia may seem only temporarily efficacious, while the inadequacy of many others is evident from the outset. In consequence, the question arises: what transpires when this becomes apparent? Managerial authorities either ignore this or resort to time-honoured tactics widely favoured by various occult practitioners in a diversity of contexts. They may claim that a procedure did not work on account of the workings of external forces beyond their control, or they may argue that the fault lies not in the procedure itself or in those who preside over the process but in those who carry it out. Consequently, they may claim that other employees, often the academics, are to blame for this state of affairs. This strategy has various advantages. When subordinate employees are undermined, this renders them more insecure, and thus potentially more malleable. However, certain university managers may sometimes be held accountable, and this has comparable benefits for some of those above them in the managerial hierarchy. Not only does this remind various managerial staff of the precarious nature of their positions, but it may also incite them to carry out their duties with more rigour. Similarly, it serves to warn other employees that they cannot escape scrutiny and possible censure.

At times, however, members of senior institutional management may employ additional approaches. They may maintain that if all the necessary bureaucratic rituals are re-enacted, the desired results will follow, as if by magic. Sometimes they may even recommend that some new, even more efficacious (and possibly more complex) ritual procedures be carried out. It is possible that sometimes they may adopt this line of action in the hope that the mental effort and onerous labour that the required process will entail will so drain staff members of psychological, emotional and physical energy that they will become inadequately equipped to focus upon the problems at hand in any significant way. This method is thus liable to erode their capacities for effective dissent.

Similar strategies have been employed by various workers of magic when their occult arts did not deliver the desired effects. For instance, Evans-Pritchard describes how certain rain-makers in Africa maintained that their rituals had not been properly performed, or that they needed to be carried out again, or over again in order for the magic to take effect (no date, cited in Etzioni, 2010).[3] Tactics of this nature have also been employed in certain Melanesian "cargo cults". When rituals were conducted to bring about the arrival of the much-desired "cargo", but that which was sought-after did not materialise, it sometimes tended to be claimed that "false" rituals had been carried out (Kohl, 2004: 88). Khotso Sethuntsa employed comparable techniques when clients who had paid him "rain money" to work his magic on their behalf complained that rain had not fallen and his wealth-giving magic had failed them. However, he informed his clients that the fault lay with them, not with him, because they had failed to follow his instructions. Furthermore, when the money came pouring in but the rain did not come pouring down, Khotso let it be known that this state of affairs had arisen because not everyone in the area had paid for rain. Accordingly, many people in the district began handing in "rain money" all over again and encouraging those around them who had not yet done so to do so as well.

When the magic of the market fails, and the promises of enhanced efficiency and productivity proffered by corporate managerialism prove hollow, similar stratagems are sometimes employed by certain members of senior management and agents of the corporate sector. This took place, for instance, when systems of performance management and measurement filtered down to universities in South Africa after having taken hold elsewhere in the world. When employees began receiving instruction in the arts of performance management at various local universities, including my own, they were sometimes told that it was their duty to exhort their fellow employees to "buy in" to this system. In other words, if performance management proved unsuccessful, then various staff members (such as heads of departments) might be held to blame for this, on the grounds that they failed to persuade their colleagues to endorse it. This resembles Khotso's weather-working wizardry in certain respects in that his clients were informed that they needed to persuade all those around them to "buy in" to his magic, by purchasing hail insurance or rain money, in order for these forms of enchantment to take effect.

Manipulation and deception of this kind may fulfil additional functions. Sometimes, for instance, these tactics may be used to obscure the damage wrought by institutional restructuring. As the following chapters show, certain damaged and damaging denizens of the supernatural can cast light on the positions of contemporary academics and on current conditions in corporatised university environments.

Notes

1 Information adapted from the following sources has been revised, expanded upon and included on pp. 142–147 of this chapter:
Wood, 2015b. Secrecy, Publicity and Power: Strategies of Occult Practitioners and University Managers. *Southern African Journal for Folklore Studies* 25: 46–54.
Various points mentioned on p. 143 and pp. 148–152 of this chapter were also noted in Wood (2010a: 234–236) and Wood with Lewis (2007: 75–76, 208).
2 See Baatjies, Spreen and Vally (2013: 156). See also George (2006) and Deal with the Problem (2006).
3 Similar stratagems have been adopted elsewhere in other contexts. Amitai Etzioni, an academic in the United States, compares the explanations provided by the rainmakers cited by Evans-Pritchard to the excuses given by US generals for the failure of the war in Afghanistan (2010).

9 The zombies of corporate academia

This chapter turns to one of the distinctive features of occult economies as defined by the Comaroffs: the appropriation and commodification of human beings and their productivity.[1] The Comaroffs describe how occult economies lay claim to not only "the bodies and things of others, but also the forces of production and reproduction themselves" (1999: 297). As Leslie A. Sharp reminds us, this is a long-standing historical and intercultural phenomenon (slavery is one feature of this). Subsequently, this has been adopted by the manufacturing and corporate sectors (2000: 287, 295). Further to this, the commodification of human bodies, and the appropriation of human productive and reproductive capabilities, is a distinctive feature of witchcraft in Africa (see for instance Sanders, 2001; Geschiere, 1997; Fisiy and Geschiere, 2001; Niehaus, 2001a; Auslander, Rosalind Shaw, 2001; and the Comaroffs, 1993, 1999).[2] This tendency has been perceived as being closely connected to forms of colonial and postcolonial control, and it has become interwoven with magical ways of generating illicit wealth.[3]

Human Resources

In the corporate world, this reduction of human beings to wealth-generating commodities finds its parallel in the concept of Human Resources. (Employees are also envisaged in this light when the phrase "human capital" is used.) This terminology, which has now found its way into higher education, is suggestive of a core feature of occult economies, and also of the market-driven ethos. Employees can be viewed as resources to be utilised until they are exhausted, downgraded, downsized (or rightsized) and discarded. The focus on human capital that may often form a feature of the corporate workplace has a certain irony to it, for it tends to be accompanied by an emphasis on the beneficial consequences of disposing of substantial parts of that human capital by means of downsizing (see for instance Olssen and Peters, 2005: 332). One feature of this is the non-renewal of contracts. Indeed, many staff members may feel they inhabit an environment in which they are reduced to expendable resources.

Steven Poole critiques the term *Human Resources* (first documented in 1961), describing how it can be used to disempower and dehumanise. He maintains that this phrase has the effect of depriving groups of human beings of independent thought and volition, reducing them to objects to be exploited:

> People considered as "Human Resources" are mere instruments of a higher will. Consider the Nazi vocabulary of "human material" (*Menschenmaterial*) and liquidation (*liquidieren*, recasting murder as the realisation of profit).
> (2006: 67)

The word *corporate* itself, denoting the body, is suggestive of various forms of control and command wielded over employees in the corporate and the manufacturing contexts as well as currently in the academy, where it has permeated aspects of discourse and practice. This is suggestive of the extent to which many employees may seem little more than minor body parts, controlled by the higher organs. At the University of KwaZulu-Natal, for instance, the division of Public Relations is known as Corporate Relations.

If employees are envisaged as expendable objects serving the needs of others, their bodies and minds appropriated for material gain, they have a metaphorical counterpart in the sphere of the supernatural. Indeed, the earlier-depicted images of physical and psychological exploitation and control are embodied in the figure of the zombie. In certain perceptions of the supernatural in South Africa and elsewhere, a group of zombies is envisaged as a mindlessly obedient, unquestioning labour force, functioning mechanically and tirelessly, requiring minimum sustenance (thin porridge, in South Africa) and housed in cramped quarters, such as cupboards. In parts of Africa, Fisiy and Geschiere note, the witchcraft of wealth is related to the "witchcraft of labour" (2001: 241). For example, certain rich individuals who exhibit the trappings of Western-style prosperity are believed to have zombie labour forces at their disposal.[4] Zombies have a symbolic resonance in the corporate realm, where the wealthy and powerful rely on the labours of underlings to retain their positions and accrue more affluence. Such patterns repeat themselves in corporatised academia.

For instance, there is the contrast between the spacious, shiny domains of senior university managers and the inferior, poorly maintained work spaces inhabited by their subordinates – metaphorically, sometimes, cupboards in comparison. There are also the disproportionate salaries: the rich four-course dinner of managerial packages in stark contrast to the thin gruel doled out to those at the lower levels of the company or institutional food chain. Although these discrepancies derive from corporate practice, they have now become distinctive features of the academic sector, underpinned by two parallel delusions.[5] There is, first, the fallacy that inflated salaries will lure managers who will prove to be models of corporate excellence; second, the illusion that since employees are drawn to academia out of love for the profession rather than a desire for economic remuneration, they will be content with a pittance. In consequence, this has given rise to a state of affairs that led a former South African minister of education, Naledi Pandor, to admit that academic salaries were "disgraceful" (cited in Coldwell, 2008: 3). Habib, Morrow and Bentley also comment on the "embarrassingly low remuneration of academics" in South Africa, while Stewart makes a similar point (2008: 151; 2007: 138). However, conditions of this kind are by no means restricted to South Africa. More broadly, there are certain parallels between the zombie and the corporate body of the university, labouring to further the interests of the market forces controlling it.

Zombies are not in a position to object to their situation, since they exist only to carry out the commands of their owners. Meanwhile, the managerial ethos encourages consensus and obedience. In its most extreme form, it exacts unquestioning submissiveness from employees who become spellbound with panic at the spectre of retrenchment, or disciplinary action that could ultimately provide grounds for dismissal.

Instruments of labour

The conditions under which present-day employees labour is by no means a recent phenomenon. For example, Andrew Ure's depiction of the British factory system in 1835, shaped by his philosophy of utilitarianism, depicts the way the demands of the workplace can reduce individuals to a zombie-like state. Ure's rhapsodic descriptions of the concept of the automated factory contain echoes of the ethos of managerialism, and they are also suggestive of the figure of the zombie. Ure envisages a factory workforce as "a vast automaton, composed of various mechanical and intellectual organs, acting in uninterrupted concert for the production of a common object, all of them being subordinate to a self-regulated moving force" (Marx, 1976: 544).

As Marx observes, Ure's description converts factory workers into zombie-like, mechanical components of the production process and as such, they are "subordinated to the central moving force". The workers become mere "instruments of labour", performing their duties mechanically, reduced to a robot-like state and controlled by centralised forms of authority. Later on, Marx describes how perceptions of this nature extend beyond the factory into other workplaces where workers become stripped of independent volition and subordinated to the means of production (1976: 358, 544–545, 1004). Thus, workers fall under the control of those who command the means of production, just as zombies are controlled by their owners.

Such conditions have persisted, acquiring new dimensions. A century later, Michael Taussig considers the dehumanising role played by the market culture, where the worker becomes "a reified object of labor and . . . command over persons is effected through the anonymity of market mechanisms" (1997: 135). In contemporary corporatised higher education, for instance, employees are reduced to Human Resources, subjugated to the demands of the market. All the while, they labour on the university factory floor, rigorously controlled by and subordinated to a unified, centralised managerial chain of command.

This state of affairs affects the lives of teachers as well. For example, UK academic Nafsika Alexiadou describes how the changing role of education has altered the way in which teaching staff are perceived, reducing them from professionals to factory labourers to components of the industrial machinery itself. Utilising terminology that evokes Ure's description, she observes that teachers are viewed as "production workers, 'raw material', or part of the 'machinery' of the institution" (1999: 427). For his part, Norwegian academic Nils Christie describes academic staff as "puppets" controlled by the agents of academic capitalism (1997; cited in Beckmann and Cooper, 2004: 8). As a corollary of this process of commodification and corporatisation, academics may, to adapt Elizabeth Young-Bruehl's expression, find themselves in the grip of forces that seek to "methodically eliminate speaking and acting human beings" (2006; cited in Giroux, 2007: 10). These descriptions have certain parallels with the image of a zombie: a being characterised by its passivity and powerlessness, manipulated and controlled by an unscrupulous owner.

Ritzer expands on this, commenting on the dehumanising effect of rationalisation, describing how many university employees may feel reduced to automatons in the factory-like environment of their workplaces (2015: 147). The labour exacted from them tends to be foregrounded, while their individual emotions, needs and aspirations may be downplayed or dismissed. In such contexts, Marx maintains, the worker is forced to sell "his own labour-power as a commodity" (1976: 1003). Commodification of this nature finds its ultimate expression in zombies, who are envisaged purely as embodiments of profit-generating labour power. Then, academics themselves exist as commodities on the contemporary corporate academic market, as units of labour to be purchased (or disposed of) in terms of their income-generating capacities. Thus, university staff may seem reminiscent of zombies not as a result of the direct workings of sorcery, but by means of an indirect magic of a kind: the pervasive potency of market forces. In work environments over which they wield sway "most everything, especially human labor, has become a commodity for purchase on the market" (Taussig, 1997: 131).

Some of the above-cited comments are suggestive of the way in which the relentless work ethos prevalent in the globalised corporate sphere has the effect of reducing many present-day private- and public-sector employees to a state that is a reminiscent of the plight of the labour-driven zombie. Guy Standing discusses this further:

> In modern industrialised societies, it is almost as if the labouring ethic has imprisoned or drugged people. The job becomes a commitment, while home is a distraction to be avoided as much as possible, a place where "chores" (work) must be done as quickly as possible. Work at home has become perceived as constraining labour in the job, rather than part of leisure.
>
> (1999: 190)

For many individuals employed in contemporary higher education, this situation is compounded by the fact that they may also feel under pressure to labour unremittingly as a result of the unstable nature of their work environment. Situated on the many fault lines of the contemporary capitalist system, rendered vulnerable by its nature as a public service and subject to threat as a result of its nature as higher education, their places of employment are prone to sudden, unforeseen upheavals and collapses, which have the potential to assume seismic proportions for the lives of those caught up in them. The possibility of sudden, unexpected economic downturns looms large in this milieu, as does the risk of retrenchment. This engenders a sense of insecurity in the minds of many employees, some of whom may resort to gearing their lives primarily towards their work, in a desperate attempt to keep this threat at bay. Moreover, paradoxically, they may allow themselves to be controlled by their employers' demands in an equally frantic attempt to assert a measure of control over their working lives. By labouring incessantly, they attempt to ground themselves as solidly as possible in their places of employment in order to bestow an illusory sense of stability on them. In this way, they endeavour to reassure themselves that the conditions under which they labour have not spiralled beyond their control. But by reacting to the precarious nature of their work environments in this way, employees relinquish their individual needs and desires in various respects, becoming comparable to zombies, the lives of whom are reduced to the work imperative, as they labour unceasingly on behalf of their unseen owners. Furthermore, academics often tend to become so bound up in learning the new requirements of corporate academia and adhering to its strictures (Giroux, 2007: 128) that they may feel deprived of the intellectual and imaginative space to adequately explore alternative possibilities and freer, more fulfilling ways of being.

Ironically, however, the more many academic employees' lives may become geared towards their work, the more they may feel alienated by their workplaces. For example, their institutional culture may seem at variance with their own value systems, while the duties they are required to perform may become less and less meaningful. For instance, the myriad bureaucratic burdens imposed upon them may far outweigh those tasks for which they have an interest and aptitude. Moreover, the professional activities that may once have seemed most significant to them may now seem to have been drained of much that once gave them with value and meaning. Instead, they may seem to have been reduced to conduits through which the waves of bureaucracy can flow, and down which the ever-lengthening arm of official control can reach. All in all, then, certain members of the academic community may feel that they inhabit a soul-destroying environment, resembling the soulless, dispirited world of the zombie.

Certainly, many academics may come to view themselves as zombie-like beings: depersonalised "units of resource whose performance and productivity must constantly be audited", thus becoming "docile auditable bod[ies]" as Shore and Wright observe (1999: 559, 563). Thus, they perceive themselves as Human Resources labouring under the control of the audit culture. In terms of this system of evaluation, the body of academic enterprise is broken up into discrete components to which varying degrees of worth are accorded and, as Gudeman puts it, "converted into units of currency" (1992: 1–2). This is comparable to Sharp's description of the way in which the human body has sometimes been fragmented into productive units in the corporate and manufacturing sectors.

Charles Dickens depicts one instance of this in *Hard Times*, in which the factory workers are reduced to "hands" (Sharp, 2000: 293). The metaphorical parallels with the muti trade in South Africa, in which human beings are reduced to separate, marketable commodities in the form of their body parts, are evident here.

Spiritual resources and emotional labour

Commodification extends beyond bodies, encompassing the human spirit itself. In present-day corporate environments, employees' spiritual resources can sometimes be perceived as sources of energy to be harnessed for commercial purposes. In these secular contexts, definitions of spirituality can sometimes include areas such as self-realisation, personal fulfilment, direction and purpose in life, as UK academics Peter Case and Jonathon Gosling remark. They go on to observe that spiritual resources have their particular uses in the corporate capitalist workplace. For example, qualities that can be spiritually inculcated, such as patience, kindness and service to others, may be bent to serve economic ends in various workplaces in which such qualities are much in demand, including the service, hospitality and teaching professions (2010: 258, 262, 275). Then, in an article titled "Spiritual Power: The Internal, Renewable Social Power Source" published in a journal with the somewhat disquieting title of *Journal of Management, Spirituality and Religion*, Sonia Goltz suggests some further reasons why it can be potentially profitable to harness spiritual energies. Spiritual resources, she maintains, do not diminish as they are drawn upon. Instead, they replenish themselves from within, while generating themselves in similar fashion (2010: 341). Thus, as a self-generating, "renewable" source of energy, spirituality has its particular advantages in an environment in which commercial imperatives are predominant. In such contexts, employee spirituality can be viewed in functional terms, as a cost-free item enhancing performance and profit.

Case and Gosling contend that various studies of workplace spirituality, including Goltz's paper, seek to convert spirituality into a commercial item. They describe how the harnessing of employee spirituality for material ends stems from a broader compulsion to control and commodify the physical, emotional, psychic and spiritual lives of employees (2010: 257–259). This tendency, enforced by numerous control mechanisms, is now prevalent in many corporate capitalist workplaces, especially those in which employees experience limited autonomy (see for instance Webster and Mosoetsa, 2001: 16; Morris and Feldman, 1996: 1001).

Employees' emotions can be put to commercial use when they are required to carry out emotional labour by suppressing their feelings and exhibiting the particular emotions and behaviour that their institution or company may deem desirable. In a study entitled *The Managed Heart: the Commercialisation of Human Feeling*, Hochschild discusses the way in which emotional labour involves "managing feeling" and outward appearances, concealing one's true feelings from others and even at times from oneself (1983: ix –x, 3–7, 34–48, 89–90, 146). The appropriation of the human mind, body and spirit is particularly pertinent here, bearing in mind the physically, mentally and psychically enslaved nature of the being that forms the focal point of this chapter.

The zombie-like state into which many university employees may descend is also connected to the dreary, wearisome nature of many of the tasks they are required to perform. These may frequently take the form of repetitive bureaucratic labours that may seem to swamp many individuals' professional lives. Duties of this kind may wear down many of those who perform them, on account of their arduous, tedious nature and also since they may seem interminable. Internationally, a range of executives and business psychologists have made reference to a condition depicted as brown-out which, it has been contended, has become a distinctive feature of many contemporary workplaces and is particularly caused by a heavy, monotonous workload. Thus, the term depicting this malaise is suggestive of the dullness of the labours that induce it. Employees suffering from brown-out slump into a state of listless depression, and become "disengaged, demotivated and lose interest in their jobs".[6] Arguably then, while sunk in this state of gloom and apathy, a zombification of a kind takes hold.

The parallels between various contemporary employees and zombies encompass the practice of outsourcing. Indeed, one individual who purported to put zombies to work for him depicted this as a type of outsourcing to the South African anthropologist Robert Thornton (2007). Various large corporations, universities included, have come to rely on outsourcing, since it is low maintenance and cost-effective (provided the human cost this practice entails is not factored into the equation). Not only does outsourcing not require the burden of long-term economic responsibility and enabling managers to discard staff at will, but companies that pay their contracted workers a pittance can also, in turn, charge less for their services, thus gaining the edge on their competitors when submitting tenders to institutions and corporations.[7]

Baatjies describes how the growing inclination to outsource work, combined with the casualisation of much academic labour, has contributed to an ever-increasing tendency to reduce employees to disposable Human Resources in the "international human capital economy". Eventually, he contends, faculties are likely to be reduced to "dungeon-like spaces where all are treated as faceless workers who have to justify their cost to the institution" (2005: 30). This depiction of the commodification of labour in the corporate university environment suggests that the state of intellectual, psychic and emotional incarceration that has been manifesting itself in this milieu for some time is liable to intensify, while all those held captive become increasingly dehumanised. Arguably then, it is intimated that the position of the academic will draw ever closer to that of the zombie.

Notes

1 Various points in Wood (2010a: pp. 237–238) have been included on pp. 153–155 and pp. 157–158 of this chapter and combined with information drawn from more recent research.

2 Geschiere, for example, investigates the way in which this tendency manifests itself in the Cameroon, observing that not only material goods but also people become viewed as commodities in certain forms of sorcery (1997: 258). In her study of accounts of supernatural were-creatures and cannibalism in Sierra Leone, Rosalind Shaw also examines the connections between new forms of the occult and commodification (2001: 50–70).
3 For instance, Shaw maintains that rumours of cannibalism, human sacrifice and the manufacturing of wealth-generating medicines from human body parts in contemporary Sierra Leone can be related to older tales of cannibals in West Africa and the lucrative trade in human beings in that region. She contends that such accounts are suggestive of contemporary forms of power and control, including the reduction of young people to disposable resources, expended by leaders in the pursuit of power and wealth in the course of the civil conflict in Sierra Leone (2001: 51, 67). Moreover, Luise White explores the relationship between vampire stories from Central and East Africa and forms of "colonial bloodsucking" (2000: 6). Geschiere examines another manifestation of this in the Cameroon, when discussing contemporary rumours of ekong, a form of wealth-giving magic. It is said that ekong practitioners seize control of human beings, using their bodies and their labour to generate wealth. Geschiere argues that accounts of ekong draw on old memories of forced colonial labour recruitment practices and the slave trade (1992: 171, 177).
4 Geschiere, for instance, comments on the belief in the Cameroon that zombies are controlled by present-day witches, such as certain nouveaux riches who derived their wealth from their labour. His respondents maintained that zombies were a new form of witchcraft, and often related them to the arrival of Westerners and Western-style symbols of material affluence (1997: 139).
5 For example, Stiglitz draws attention to the disproportionate salaries received by CEOs and corporate employees in the US and the UK in the 1990s and 2001:

> During the nineties . . . [c]ompensation of American executives was completely out of line relative to the salaries of middle management, relative to the salaries of workers, relative to anything imaginable. . . . Even in 2001, a disaster year for profits and stock prices, executive CEO pay increased twice as fast as the pay of the average worker (2004: 124).

In the UK, executive salaries were generally 25 times those of average employees; while the salaries of CEOs in the US amounted to 500 times more than the salaries of ordinary workers by 2000 (2004: 124).
6 So "Browned-Out" by Work That You Look Forward to a Heart Attack". 2015. *Sunday Times.* 20 September: 19.
7 The exploitative features of outsourcing in South African higher education have been widely discussed (see for instance Bertelsen, 1998: 147; Pithouse, 2006: 86, 88). These have sparked off protests at many South African universities since 2015. For instance, the #Outsourcing Must Fall protests formed a component of the #Fees Must Fall movement in 2015 and 2016. Comparable forms of resistance have erupted in the UK, the US and elsewhere, indicative of the extent to which outsourcing has become a widespread source of discontent.

10 Sacrifices and suffering

While zombies are to be pitied, another South African occult presence even more closely associated with economic prosperity than zombies, invites fear.[1] This being, known as the mamlambo, brings wealth to those who enter into a pact with it, but at a terrible price. The Xhosa term for ownership of a mamlambo is ukuthwala.[2] The mamlambo is a shape-changer but is often envisaged as a seductive mermaid, a beautiful woman or a snake or a handsome man. It frequently adopts these alluring forms because it is associated with that for which many yearn (Morrow and Vokwana, 2004: 92). It is sometimes said that this being manifests itself as a white woman or man, and it favours fashionable Western clothing and expensive accessories, suggestive of its association with the forces of Western capitalism (Wilson, 1936: 287). The Comaroffs depict Hausa soul-eaters in rural Niger, said to devour the soul essence of those around them, as "the personification of capricious commodities, the sirens of selfish desire" (1993: xxv). This is also applicable to the mamlambo, the forms of material affluence with which it is associated and the dangerous temptations it embodies.

The mamlambo has been associated with socio-economic and political imbalances and inequalities, as have various other African wealth-giving spirits, such as the Zimbabwean chikwambo, the Malawian *njoka* and (under certain circumstances) the West African Mami Wata. Dilley notes that, in certain parts of Africa, marked inequalities in the distribution of wealth and power, as well as exploitative political and economic practices are sometimes believed to be brought about by malevolent supernatural presences (1992: 6). The corporatised academic sector tends to be characterised by these qualities, so some might regard it as an environment in which a being like the mamlambo might not seem entirely out of place.

As Dilley's previously cited point intimates, it is believed that the corrupt influence of malign occult spirits such as the mamlambo can infect the lives of not only those individuals who enter into pacts with them but also those around them and society at large. In the specific case of the mamlambo, this results in part from the morally abhorrent behaviour that is needed to sustain a pact with this being. For example, in exchange for wealth, the mamlambo demands blood sacrifices, including the sacrifices of those closest to its owner.

Alliances with wealth-giving supernatural beings elsewhere in Africa require offerings of a similar kind. For instance, it is sometimes said that when Mami Wata bestows affluence on her consorts she may require the life of a family member in return (Frank, 2008: 331). The wealth-giving chikwambo in Zimbabwe is rumoured to thrive on the blood of individuals in its owner's family or community; as is the Malawian njoka. However, the mamlambo is a more distinctive, fully fleshed-out figure than the chikwambo or the njoka, and its nature and desires tend to be more vividly depicted in various oral accounts describing it, heightening its malign, menacing qualities. The mamlambo has also been particularly closely associated with blood sacrifices, and it is certainly a more malevolent being than Mami Wata, a paradoxical spirit who afflicts, heals and rewards her followers. It will also become evident that the mamlambo's particular attributes cast light on certain features of the occult academy.

The belief that the mamlambo feeds on the blood of those whom its owner holds dear is symbolically appropriate, for the lust for individual accumulation may exact a price from those closest to the accumulator. It is also said that a pact with a mamlambo ultimately brings about misery and disaster. Those who undergo ukuthwala become enviably wealthy, but it is rumoured that their lives end unenviably in suffering and despair, as do the lives of many of those closest to them. So how can this be compared to the way in which universities have wedded themselves to the corporate world? There are certain striking metaphorical parallels between the two.

Insatiable desires, incessant sacrifices

Viewed from some perspectives, the corporatisation of higher education may seem reliant on faith in wealth-giving magic of another kind, influenced as it is by a conviction that financial well-being will descend, as if from high, by this means. In certain respects, corporatised universities could be compared to the owner of a mamlambo, who enters into a pact with this being believing that it will work its magic for his or her benefit, only to fall under its control. Alluding to both occult economies and forms of consumer capitalism, Nyamnjoh observes that the promises of economic freedom and empowerment that both supernatural agencies and agents of capitalism proffer are illusory. Indeed, he observes that "[a]gency as independence only creates dependence" (2001: 46). This form of entrapment is especially applicable to universities which, seeking to attain economic security through seemingly independent means, embraced market forces to accomplish this yet have found themselves in thrall to these very same forces. As a result of the wealth that it offers and in its sexually irresistible qualities, the mamlambo arouses desires that cannot be readily satisfied and ensnares its human victims by this means. While it may bestow money or brief sensual pleasure, it leaves the one who falls under its spell ever hungering for more.

Lindstrom contends that an insatiable yearning (for wealth, power, fame, love or security, among much else) is a persistent form of desire in the west (2004: 18, 31–33). A longing of this kind is insatiable, for aspirations of such a nature cannot readily be fulfilled. Marshall Sahlins (1972: 39) describes how modern Western culture has fostered this state of greedy, dissatisfied wanting. In part, this inclination has been generated by the expansion of Western consumer capitalism and it helps sustain it. Consequently, desires of this kind have been celebrated, rather than interrogated (cited in Lindstrom, 2004: 34).

The figure of the mamlambo, market forces given beguiling form, symbolises the perils and temptations of an economic system that is sustained by the suffering of many in order to benefit a few. Individual prosperity comes at a broad social cost. In this respect, oral accounts of the mamlambo highlight the damaging aspects of the self-absorbed pursuit of individual affluence that the Western capitalist economic system promotes. Various writers have discussed the way in which certain beings, discourses and practices associated with the occult embody critiques of capitalism, which tends to foster a selfish striving for wealth at all costs. Niehaus's description of witchcraft familiars in the South African Lowveld touches on this, for example, while Parish examines the way in which witchcraft discourses among the Akan of Ghana convey comparable criticisms of individual material accumulation (Parish, 2001: 118). Frank also describes how oral accounts of Mami Wata convey a critique of this kind. Accordingly, certain disastrous consequences of the ownership of a mamlambo are suggestive of the damage that the alliance between universities and the marketplace has inflicted on institutions of higher learning and thus (to employ one of the key terms of corporatised academia) on knowledge production.

First, there are the sacrifices the mamlambo demands. The Comaroffs argue that sinister occult presences such as the deadly, seductive mamlambo "provide disconcertingly full-bodied images of a world in which humans seem in constant dangers of turning into commodities, of losing their life blood to the market and the destructive desires it evokes" (1993: xxix). One aspect of this is evident in universities, where staff members become Human Resources to be sacrificed to the imperatives of the market. In the current academic climate, one inhales the miasma arising from the sequence of sacrifices that form an integral part of the worship of the corporate divinities. Indeed, the necessity of staff retrenchments, non-renewal of contracts, freezing of other posts and budget cuts is repeatedly stressed, as a reminder that regular sacrifice is a cornerstone of market-oriented university practice.

Another related sacrifice is the notion of academic collegiality, which wilts and shrivels in a working environment that operates in terms of a system of managers and subordinates. When former colleagues are relegated to these positions, the bond between academic kindred spirits falls away.[3] Moreover, in the face of ongoing academic retrenchments, there has become less and less space for the luxury of collegiality, as the institutional climate encourages betrayal. When co-workers become aware that the ritual sacrifice of some of their number might temporarily propitiate the high priests and oracles of the market forces, they cease to be colleagues. Consequently, ties of friendship, loyalty and collegiality may have to be sacrificed in the interests of the presumed economic advancement of an institution or the survival of a department. As we have already seen, although universities have inherited many morally dubious practices from the past (including the backstabbing that has long been a feature of academia), they have expanded on and intensified these while also importing whole new array of ethically problematic features.

As this indicates, the sacrifices required in corporatised universities encompass ethical concerns. This is ironic in the light of the emphasis that now tends to be placed on the idea of ethics (embodied for instance in university Ethics Committees and Ethical Clearance Certificates now mandatory at many institutions). However, structures and procedures that invoke the idea of ethics often tend to serve as a means of entrenching the authority of those in positions of power and influence, be they institutional, state-related or corporate. For example, those applying for an Ethical Clearance Certificate may be required to indicate that they comply with the norms and values endorsed by the internal and external authorities that preside over a process of this kind. Meanwhile, university ethics committees may encourage research that furthers their specific sets of interests, or those of the particular power players, both internal and external, to whom they are beholden (see for instance Goldacre, 2012: 34–44, 81). Indeed, the way in which the concept of ethics can be used to further the interests of those in positions of power, be they institutional, state-related or corporate, may call aspects of certain religions and political ideologies to mind. In such contexts, notions of morally acceptable behaviour may come to denote submission to the strictures of a specific religious or political doctrine. More often than not, such perceptions of worthy conduct are contextually shaped by the dominant figures in one or other religious or political hierarchy, as well as by various social norms, so that ethical behaviour tends to denote obedience and conformity.[4] In the university context, when they are sanctioned by managerial rather than moral authority, such perceptions of virtue can be employed to fulfil a function of this nature.

In a work titled *The Corrosion of Character* (1998) Richard Sennett examines the way in which former work-related values such as "endurance and loyalty", firmness of character and personal integrity have been eroded by the requirements of contemporary workplaces, shaped as these often are by the pressures of market capitalism. Thus, short-term profit-oriented partnerships tend to be favoured, and employees may feel under pressure to adjust or relinquish personal convictions, values and codes of conduct in accordance with present exigencies.

Accordingly, the "market morality of profit" now tends to exercise sway over much academic activity (Mamdami, 2007: 76). In 2003, Bok posed the following question: "If more and more 'products' of the university were sold at a profit, might the lure of the marketplace alter the behaviour of university officials in subtle ways that would change the character of Harvard for the worse?" (2003: x). Even in Bok's day the moral contamination of which he spoke had infected diverse areas of academia. But now, more than a decade later, the tendencies to which Bok alludes have become a more deep-seated, widespread malaise at individual, institutional and external levels.[5]

Research is tainted by this, for example. Ben Goldacre describes how large corporations may bestow funding in exchange for research findings that promote their products, for instance. Alternatively, they may produce "research" papers themselves, or "revise" an existing body of work, then require selected academics to submit the papers in question for publication under their names. Moreover, an academic may receive an "honorarium" from a particular company for delivering promotional speeches to help market a specific company's wares. Academics may also be paid to act as consultants in order to perform a similar function (2012: 294–299, 334–335). Although such circumstances were a feature of academia before market-oriented restructuring, they have now taken on a more overt form and flourish in an academic climate that lends itself to research fuelled by mercenary incentives.

Conversely, research that draws attention to problematic features of a corporation's products may have to be suppressed by the university authorities or by their corporate sponsors (see for instance Goldacre, 2012: 38–40, 92, 340–341). For instance, Bok, Klein and Giroux describe how a University of Toronto researcher, Dr Nancy Olivieri, produced research indicating that a drug produced by Apotex, Canada's largest pharmaceutical company, was not only ineffective but possibly also toxic. Apotex tried to suppress her findings, while the university suspended her from her position as programme director, issuing her with a warning that she and her staff were not to publicise the case. As Bok notes, Apotex and the University of Toronto had been discussing the possibility of a multimillion-dollar "donation" to the university and its teaching hospitals for some years (2003: 75; see also Klein, 2000: 99–100). Giroux, moreover, cites the case of Ignacio H. Chapela, a professor of Ecology at the University of California, Berkeley, who was denied tenure possibly on account of his criticism of a multimillion-dollar research grant agreement between the university and the biotechnology company Novartis. Prior to this, Chapela had also co-published a paper with graduate student David Quist critiquing genetically modified crops, which was criticised by another "scientist", a fake persona generated by a public relations company linked to the biotechnology giant Monsanto. Then *Nature*, the journal that published Chapela and Quist's study, subsequently published a disclaimer calling some of their conclusions into question. Chapela maintained that *Nature* had been placed under pressure by scientists co-opted by the biotechnology industry (Giroux, 2007: 113–116). Although these are North American examples, they are symptomatic of a far more extensive corporate-intellectual disease that infects many academic environments worldwide.

The extent to which numerous universities, both in South Africa and internationally, have been infiltrated by corporations has been noted near the outset. Not only have universities proved lucrative sites for diverse companies to set up shop and market their wares, but they may also sign sponsorship contracts with corporations, undertaking to endorse their products on campus in exchange for remuneration. Companies accorded preferential marketing opportunities have included a number of those that have been linked to human rights violations, environmental destruction and animal experimentation, including Nike, Shell, McDonald's, Pepsi and Coca-Cola (Klein, 2000: 307–408). Many universities, it seems, have no qualms about entering into partnerships with morally problematic implications provided they reap material rewards for this.

Giroux and David H. Price draw attention to other aspects of this issue, investigating forms of collaboration between universities, systems of state control and surveillance and the military. Price depicts the extent to which research in anthropology and other related areas of the social sciences has been co-opted into the service of the US military, the FBI, the CIA and other intelligence agencies. Insight into and an understanding of other cultures and languages have long been perceived of strategic significance by these groupings. For instance, Price mentions the Minerva Consortium, a programme linked to the Defence Department, which funded research projects in areas relating to military matters. Minerva's initial areas of interest included "Studies of the Strategic Impact of Religious and Cultural Changes in the Islamic World" and "Studies of Terrorist Organisations and Ideologies". He observes that since the nature and purpose of this research would be determined by the Defence Department and shaped by its ideological assumptions, the project outcomes would be distorted accordingly. Moreover, he describes how Human Terrain Teams have utilised anthropologists and other social scientists to provide anthropological, socio-cultural and linguistic information to facilitate the military occupation of Iraq. Price also notes that higher education funding programmes such as the National Security Education Program, the Pat Roberts Intelligence Scholars Program and the Intelligence Community Scholars Program are intended to ensure that universities produce scholars whose ideological approaches are in keeping with those of the Defence Department (Price: 2011: 60–61, 134). Giroux discusses further examples of this trend. For instance, citing William G. Martin (2005), he mentions that the University of Southern California established a "Homeland Security Centre of Excellence" after receiving a $12 million grant. Academics from a range of US universities, including Berkeley and New York University, became involved in the work of the centre (2007: 22). Such forms of collaboration between military-industrial bodies, state security structures and academia are by no means restricted to the US.

A Faustian pact

Just as the owner of a mamlambo is consumed by an overriding hunger for wealth, so market-oriented universities are driven by a desire for economic profit. They pay a high price for this, as there are other kinds of sacrifices involved. Georg Simmel (1978) draws attention to the extent to which economic exchange can be characterised by sacrifices, for an individual who desires an object may be required to relinquish something that is dear to her or him (cited in Appadurai, 1986: 3–4). As more and more universities develop features in common with commercial emporia, Simmel's point acquires a growing resonance. Just as a mamlambo demands that its owner sacrifice those dearest to him or her, many universities are required to sacrifice that which was, in essence, closest to their hearts: the workplace ethos that makes for effective teaching and research. Both the ukuthwala pact with a mamlambo and universities' uneasy alliances with the corporate world are sustainable only if they strike at their souls. South African academic Adèle Thomas examines a related phenomenon, arguing that many universities' ability to affirm and maintain an ethical culture has been eroded because universities now copy corporate practice, which tends to focus on results, rather than values (2009: 4–5). Moreover, those who place that which is close to their hearts, their own academic ideals, before managerial decrees and the pursuit of corporate goals place themselves at risk.

In part, the yearning for success and material security, be it individual, departmental or institutional, is potentially dangerous because it can become a predominant force driving academic practice. Sometimes desires of this nature may come to seem all-consuming, engulfing the lives of those individuals who become entrapped by them and also the environments they inhabit. It is said that those who take on the ownership of a mamlambo are reduced to a comparable state.

Once again, the story of Faustus springs to mind. Marlowe's Faustus, we recall, also enters into a pact with commercial as well as spiritual aspects, selling his soul to further his own intellectual ends. However, like an owner of a mamlambo, he does not benefit from the transaction. During the rest of his career, he does not prosper as he sought to do. He desires to enhance the store of earthly knowledge by embarking on this pact, yet significantly, one of the areas in which his failure is particularly evident is that of knowledge production.

Academic malcontents

Next, it is said that sorrow and misfortune tend to be visited upon the households of those who embark on a pact with a mamlambo.[6] Just as a pact with a mamlambo brings misery in the end, so a career at a corporatised university may ultimately offer neither security nor contentment. Indeed, such institutions often also seem to be characterised by a climate of anxiety, despondency and despair.

An inordinate number of university staff members suffer from depression or chronic stress-related ailments, some of them life-threatening. Indeed, tension, exhaustion, distress and low staff morale seem to have become widespread, endemic features of academic life. In South Africa, for example, Pendlebury and van der Walt observe that misery and angst are rife at their institution, the University of the Witwatersrand (2006: 88). As other local commentators indicate, this forms part of a broader phenomenon. For instance, Bertelsen and Orr, Southall and Cobbing, and Webster and Mosoetsa examine the impact of globalisation and corporatisation on the academic workplace and the emotional and psychological toll this exacts. Ruth (2001) and Habib, Morrow and Bentley also depict the tensions and insecurities in diverse South African academic environments (2008: 203, 205). Then, citing other local academics' findings, Stewart discusses the extent to which "a sense of malaise, stress and cynicism" has taken hold at numerous universities in this country, mentioning that an increased use of tranquilisers has become prevalent (2007: 137, 135, 138).

An emotional climate of this kind pervades numerous institutions of higher education in Africa and beyond. For instance, Mamdani's account of conditions at Makerere University, Uganda is indicative of this. In general, Paul Tiyambe Zeleza and Adebayo Olukoshi maintain that "morale has never been lower" at many African universities (2004b: 602). There are many other international examples. For instance, Hedley indicates that numerous Irish academics have become dejected and confused, while Giroux depicts the fear, anxiety and resentment prevalent in US academia (2010, Giroux, 2007: 122). Malcolm Saunders observes that feelings of this nature are widespread in many Australian university environments, citing research findings of other Australian academics, including Thornton, in this regard (2006). Meanwhile, Burrows describes how many UK academics are suffering from stress, exhaustion and unhappiness, and mingled feelings of remorse, inadequacy and aggression and emotional and psychological pain (2012: 355). Other academic commentators in that country corroborate this, including Collini, who alludes to "the distracted, numbers-swamped, audit-crazed, grant-chasing" nature of many academics' lives (2012: 19; see also Amsler, 2013: 7; Shore and Wright, 1999: 570).

Further to this, Webster and Mosoetsa cite a *Times Higher Educational Supplement* report conducted in the UK in 2000, which indicates that "more than half of those who work in British universities are on the brink of depression or anxiety, while a quarter have suffered a stress-related illness in the past twelve months". The report concluded that conditions of this kind stemmed from the changes that had taken place in higher education in the UK. In general, however, as Webster and Mosoetsa remark, the findings and conclusions of the preceding report have wider relevance (2001: 2). The Higher Education Supplements of international and local newspapers, including the *Times* in the UK and the South African *Mail & Guardian*, indicate that many academics at numerous universities elsewhere in the world, including those in this country, are similarly afflicted. In general, as Bertelsen concludes, "confidence, loyalty and commitment" are ebbing away (1998, 144). A few of the factors that have given rise to this state of affairs will be touched upon here.

A great deal of tension and worry is generated by job insecurity. Guy Standing, from the University of London, depicts academics as part of the precariat class. According to Standing, this grouping, a product of neoliberal economic agendas, is characterised by a shared sense of anxiety and vulnerability concerning career prospects, income stability and job security. Many of the precariat are employed on a temporary basis or have been relegated to ancillary positions, often of a short-term nature. In general, as the term denoting them suggests, members of the precariat tend to occupy precarious positions. Marginalised in numerous respects, they may lack access to labour-related and social securities, including protection against arbitrary dismissal, trade union protection and reliable health care and pensions. As part of the precariat, university employees are "on the edge", often precariously distanced from secure employment and sources of income, while experiencing the steady erosion of their rights, whether socio-political or health- and welfare-related. Along with many members of the precariat, academics may experience deep-seated feelings of insecurity and disquiet, alienation and anomie: a sense of "passivity born of despair . . . a listlessness associated with sustained defeat" (Standing 2011: 69–71, 6, 10–20; Jenvey, 2013).

The sense of uncertainty and anxiety that has become a chronic condition in the academic workplace is caused in part by the terror of retrenchment, which hangs over many staff members, many of whom occupy temporary or contract posts. Also, many employees are beset by an ever-present dread that as a result of the climate of ongoing surveillance, grounds might be found for their dismissal. "I constantly fear for the future," an academic colleague at my institution told me, "because I do not know whether my contract will be renewed, and whether or not I will be able to support my family next year".

The future is a source of fear for other reasons. University audits inflict severe stress on a recurrent basis and, even when an audit is not in progress, the prospect of the next dreaded visit from the auditors looms large in many employees' minds. However, from a managerial point of view, audits have the advantage of reducing academic staff to a state of anxiety and weariness, thereby rendering them more malleable. In this respect, regular audits constitute a distinctive feature of the general managerial principle which Mike Parker and Jane Slaughter term "management by stress" (1988; cited in Roper, 2004: 134). Other forms of external and internal monitoring and evaluation compound this. The extent to which they may seem ever-present and ongoing wears staff down further. As Dibben and Higgins note, importing systems of performance measurement from the private sector into the public services has resulted in more stress-laden and exploitative working conditions (2004: 31). Thus, many employees may passively accept the dictates and judgements of managerialism out of sheer emotional, psychic and physical exhaustion.

Present concerns weigh heavily on many staff members' minds in other respects. Making reference to a survey carried out at selected African universities in 1994, Uwem E. Ite notes that inadequate remuneration is one of the foremost sources of discontent among academic staff in this continent (2004: 251). For instance, Webster and Mosoetsa cite the results of a survey conducted at a Nigerian university, which drew attention to the psychologically damaging effects of low pay (2001: 3). Stewart makes a similar point about South African universities (2007: 138), while Habib and Morrow point out that academic morale is further eroded by the message conveyed through the discrepancy between academic and managerial salaries, which implies that managerial activity is more highly valued than teaching and research (2006; cited in Habib, Morrow and Bentley, 2008: 151). In their discussion of UK universities, Deem, Hillyard and Reed highlight a widespread problem when they describe how academic salaries and status have declined concurrently, simultaneously undermining staff members at financial and psychological levels (2007: 40). Further to this, Southall and Cobbing draw attention to both the physically and psychologically exhausting consequences of low pay, as "academics are required to supplement their salaries by selling themselves on the marketplace" (2001: 11).

Erosion and immiseration

As we have seen in earlier chapters, the diminution of money and resources is interconnected with the erosion of time. As a head of department in the UK remarked, "the salaries have fallen behind . . . the workload has gone up exponentially" (Deem, Hillyard and Reed, 2007: 55). This has given rise to a combination of debilitating factors that have become such deeply ingrained parts of corporatised academic environments worldwide that they have featured repeatedly in preceding chapters. These elements include the combination of a dramatic increase in student numbers at many institutions, a heavier bureaucratic load, funding cuts, greater demands to meet performance requirements and deliver quantifiable outputs, longer hours, combined with a reduction in staff numbers, lack of administrative support, inadequate infrastructure and insufficient academic and institutional resources.

Other factors compound the pressures under which university employees labour. Coldwell describes how academics are trapped between two unrelenting forces: massification and managerialism, with its interminable bureaucratic demands. This leads to what he describes as immiseration: "the erosion of academics' discretionary time to think, conceptualise and postulate new ideas" (2008: 3). Indeed, as the term suggests, immiseration has the potential to reduce many academics to a state of misery and frustration, in it that deprives them of that which drew them into an academic career in the first place. In his novel *Deaf Sentence*, Lodge alludes to this, vividly depicting the state of despondency and futility that descends on academics at a UK university who feel the effects of immiseration.

Many academics find this situation both physically and psychically exhausting. Webster and Mosoetsa describe one individual's reaction to this, citing a report that appeared in a South African newspaper, the *Eastern Province Herald*, in 2001. The article describes how a professor who had been carrying a heavy teaching and administrative load walked out of his department, without even turning off his computer, and disappeared (2001: 2). However, even when employees are present, they may be absent in a significant sense. First, many employees may still go to work when they are ill, in the face of limited paid sick leave, the possibility of non-renewal of contracts or disciplinary action for not carrying out their duties. This phenomenon – depicted as a "new office plague" – is known as presenteeism (Wild, 2015: 19). Indeed, as an academic colleague remarked,

> The psychological and physical health of academics, especially when failing, is part of what we feel compelled to disguise out of fear. . . . The very fact that one is working in an environment where everyone is overloaded makes it difficult to "confess" to unwellness, which also, culturally, is seen as weakness (moral as well as psychological) and judged accordingly.[7]

Yet even when they are physically healthy, increasing numbers of university employees may feel afflicted by a more deep-seated type of malaise. Anxious, stress-laden, demotivated and even resentful, they may be burdened at emotional and psychological levels, becoming increasingly alienated from their workplaces and their professional lives.

Control and consumption

Academics often tend to succumb to depression, feeling that they now function in a context in which academic professionalism is valued primarily in terms of the extent to which it can serve the interests of corporate managerialism. For instance, citing Australian academic Rodney Nilsen (2004), Saunders describes how "teaching and research have been not merely degraded and devalued but totally subordinated" to the university administration (2006: 10). Many academics from diverse countries have corroborated this (see for instance Hedley, 2010: 139; Habib, Morrow and Bentley, 2008: 140–141). Webster and Mosoetsa examine the damaging effects of this phenomenon, stating that occupational psychologists are generally of the opinion that the principal cause of work stress stems from the loss of control over one's work situation (2001: 4). Indeed, as Deem, Hillyard and Reed maintain, numerous academics at restructured universities in the UK and elsewhere may feel that the core areas of their professional lives have slipped beyond their control (2007: 2). There is, especially, the way in which what Greene, Loughridge and Wilson depict as "the academic heart-lands, teaching and research" (1996: 1) have, in effect, been colonised by outsiders. External and internal assessors impose new, sometimes apparently alien criteria to determine what should be taught and researched and whether it is being taught or researched adequately.

There are certain metaphorical parallels between the position of academics in corporatised universities, who are required to support and submit to managerial authority, thereby sustaining the sovereignty of the economic and political power structures to which their institutional managerial systems are bound, and the victims of sinister supernatural forces and those in alliance with them, such as the mamlambo and the witch, and the owners of zombies. Like those who fall prey to malign occult agencies, numerous academics may feel they are being drained of their physical, emotional and psychological energies. Not only do they become physically exhausted, but emotional labour is often also exacted, while employee spirituality may be harnessed for commercial gain. It is worth recalling that the mamlambo, the witch and other malign occult beings are believed to be obsessed by the urge to consume: an act that can take place at physical, psychic and spiritual levels. The extent to which consumerism has permeated present-day higher education has been described in preceding chapters.

It is also worth noting that neocolonialism has sometimes been metaphorically depicted as a form of consumption. For instance, the Comaroffs describe how, as "a new form of imperialism, the affluent West siphons off the essence . . . of impoverished Others". They go on to contend that

> [p]ostcolonial Africa is replete with accounts of the way in which the rich and powerful . . . appropriate the life force of their lesser compatriots in order to strengthen themselves or satisfy consuming passions.
>
> (1999: 282)

These images of the destruction wrought by the consequences of Western neocolonial economic and political control have metaphorical parallels with the results of a pact with the mamlambo, which is said to deprive its victims of their moral capabilities, their emotional, psychic and physical well-being and, ultimately, their lives.

Sanders makes a related point when discussing the effects of the "free" market on Tanzanian society, describing how this has given rise to a widespread sense of vulnerability. Citing Elizabeth Colson (2000) he contends that many people now feel defenceless against "a system which they see as draining them of their resources to the benefit of remote others" (2001: 178). Meanwhile, the Comaroffs allude to a widespread "fear of the creeping commodification of life itself . . . of a relentless process that erodes the inalienable humanity of persons and renders them susceptible as never before to the long reach of the market" (1999: 291). These observations cast some light on the state of many university employees. To varying extents, they may feel physically exhausted and disempowered, and sometimes also so drained of their psychological and emotional energies that they lack the physical and psychic resources to withstand the "creeping commodification" engulfing present-day academic environments. Moreover, they may feel defenceless against the whims of seemingly unassailable, sometimes remote systems of power and authority that exercise far-reaching control over their workplaces and their personal lives.

Disillusion and despair

The symbolic parallels between employees at market-oriented universities and the victims of the mamlambo extend further than this. The Comaroffs depict menacing occult presences such as the mamlambo as "modernity's prototypical malcontents", symbolically associated with the disillusion and despair generated by forms of Westernised modernity, including "perceptions of money and markets" (1993, xxix). In various respects, those that become spellbound by the enchantments surrounding the market and captivated by dreams of all that can be wrought by money, believing that these can fulfil desires and work magic on their behalf, can ultimately be reduced to an emotional state of this nature. In their disenchantment and despondency, they become metaphorically comparable to those who fall prey to the allure of the mamlambo. Certain aspects of the malaise of anxiety and depression that afflicts present-day university environments can be viewed in relation to this condition.

Those who trust the false promises proffered by the mamlambo are doomed to disappointment, and wealth acquired by means of an ukuthwala pact proves temporary and unreliable. Meanwhile, those who believe that market forces and corporate capitalism will bring about their salvation may find that they have invested their hopes in dreams that bring disillusion in their wake.

Nyamnjoh's analysis of development and witchcraft in the Cameroon illuminates this. Citing the Comaroffs, he observes,

> In contemporary Africa, development is presented as the way to salvation, promising concrete and visible results; but the more it is pursued, the greater

an illusion it becomes. . . . [D]isappointment grows by leaps and bounds. Development or modernity seems to excel in churning out 'malcontents' through unilinearity and zombification.

(2001: 32)

This passage hints at the danger of persisting in the belief that Western development and recourse to market-driven capitalist models will almost magically bring about deliverance from economic predicaments and socio-economic instabilities and inadequacies. Those that fall prey to illusions such as these risk not only dismay but diminution. They may become disempowered when they discover that they vested their hopes in that which was essentially a mirage, or they may forfeit their independent volition, becoming subjugated to systems of influence and authority that do not operate in their favour.

There are thus certain parallels between Nyamnjoh's description of the seductive, deceptive aspects of development and the tantalising promises of affluence proffered by the mamlambo, which ultimately prove hollow. In various respects, the marketisation of present-day universities (periodically depicted as a developmental strategy of a sort) is fuelled by comparable illusions. Sometimes it entails a similar pursuit of that which Lindstrom terms "the bounty of modernity" (2004: 24). This is also driven by convictions that the development (or "modernisation") of a kind in higher education, influenced by Western economic models of commodification, competitiveness and corporate managerialism, will deliver all that it promises.

Thus, the accoutrements of corporatisation and managerialism in which contemporary universities have bedecked themselves acquire another layer of meaning. They may serve as expressions of desire for that which is not readily accessible or which may be well-nigh unattainable, such as excellence, world-class status and quality. In consequence, disillusion has pervaded the contemporary academic milieu, while many of those who inhabit it may feel entrapped in an alien environment that runs counter to their interests and values. Like the visions of material affluence proffered by the mamlambo, the image of streamlined "modernity" to which numerous corporatised universities aspire is a chimera. Instead, it has generated many academic "malcontents".

Nyamnjoh's observation casts light on market-oriented institutions of higher education in other respects. The "unilinearity" to which he alludes is suggestive of qualities on which the smooth functioning of corporatised universities depends, as is his reference to "zombification". The extent to which numerous present-day institutions of higher education have become characterised by a culture of conformity and constraint, operating by means of those agents and mechanisms that exercise a "power of normalization" (Foucault, 1977: 308) to enforce compliance with corporate norms has been depicted in previous chapters.

Nonetheless, despite the extent to which they can undermine and subjugate those who subscribe to them, images of Western material advancement and the economic practices allied to them continue to exert their enchantment. Meanwhile, the being that embodies their magic, the mamlambo itself, exerts a similar spell, despite the fact that pacts with this spirit are said to bring more suffering than satisfaction in their wake, and wealth acquired by means of an ukuthwala pact proves temporary and unreliable. Similarly, although corporatisation and marketisation have intensified over the decades, the longed-for economic security and stability that such processes seemed to promise still remain dreams. Thus, both the ukuthwala procedure and the market-oriented restructuring of academia are fuelled by desires that remain unfulfilled. These analogous forms of enticement fail to deliver that which they promise, and both are ventures laden with failure.

The price to be paid

Not only can a career at a corporate university decline into disillusion and despair, but ultimately it can even culminate in calamity, just as a pact with a mamlambo eventually leads from disappointment to disaster. When individuals receive money in abundance from the mamlambo, the wealth they receive gives rise to a greater loss than gain, its dangers outweighing its benefits. The mamlambo strikes at the heart of the family, depriving its consorts of their spouses, their fertility, their human sexual relationships, their children, and their domestic happiness and harmony, sowing suspicion and discord in the family circle. Ultimately, it may even bring about its owner's destruction. Metaphorically, this is indicative of the human cost involved in the pursuit of wealth. In various respects, too, this has certain symbolic parallels with the price of corporatisation in present-day higher education.

In the end, contract positions may not be renewed, threats of retrenchment may no longer be held at bay, departments may be closed down and even those in management may find their positions uncomfortable and precarious. Yet again, Marlowe's Faustus could be borne in mind. Although his pact with the devil appears to promise much, his "tragical history" ends in darkness and horror. Eventually, he is compelled to relinquish his grandiose aspirations and the spiritual price that he is required to pay looms large. There is another dimension to this. Just as readily as the devil and his lieutenants welcomed Faustus into their midst, so, too, did they turn on him, inflicting terror and torment when they felt inclined to do so. Then in the end, having toyed with him for a while, they discarded him, abandoning him to his fate. Comparably, the mamlambo lavishes temporary affluence, but it can suddenly and capriciously turn against its owner, transforming wealth and good fortune into poverty and suffering. Meanwhile, senior university managers serve the interests of those to whom they are beholden, but the benefits of a pact of this nature are not always lasting or binding. Power can be withdrawn as readily as it was extended, along with the privileges that accompanied it. This can take place for several reasons, one of which may be financial expediency. Alternatively, for example, some senior managers may find themselves at the receiving end of a restructuring process or they may become a focus of inter-managerial tensions.[8] There is another factor, which also has a certain bearing on the mamlambo and the agents of Satan in *Faustus*.

Managerial and diabolical forms of authority and other sinister spiritual agencies tend to have a predilection for punishing those close at hand. In part this serves to prove that they will tolerate no deviations from their specific codes of conduct, even from those within their midst, as well as to send out a broader signal that they are forces to be reckoned with and should not be treated lightly. However, this may also spring from a certain degree of vindictiveness. As we have already noted, this is an essential feature of malign manifestations of the occult, and it can also be a by-product of certain corporate managerial strategies of bullying and intimidation.

Other earlier points are worth recalling here. These relate to the process of apportioning blame that constitutes a key feature of corporate university practice. Given the Kafkaesque nature of the present-day university environment and the fact that much goes astray in the managerial labyrinth, much that is blameworthy may accumulate. Consequently, certain problems may eventually become such obstructions that they can no longer be ignored. There are, however, the hierarchical complexities of institutional structures, which can make it more difficult for the error to be traced back through the ramifications of the university hierarchy to its source. Thus, members of academic departments tend to be identified as the principle offenders. Disempowered by their lowly status, they tend to be less able to mount any effective objection. Nonetheless, the blow may occasionally fall on certain individuals in university management. There is an outside possibility that every once in a while the most conspicuous figure in a particular institutional hierarchy, the senior manager (sometimes perhaps a dean or a director of a division) may be held responsible, sometimes due to the fact that he or she represents the terminus of all the subordinate lines of management in the department or division in which something went awry. Alternatively, he or she may seem a convenient scapegoat.

Thus, some of those in senior managerial positions may perhaps learn that their positions are Faustian ones in these respects. In a manner of speaking, they have turned "to the dark side" of managerialism (Taylor, 2003: 1), only to discover that management does not look after its own; just as the owner of the mamlambo may learn that this being can bring about a reversal of fortune as dramatic and disproportionate as the startling elevation to prosperity that it originally engineered. A contradiction of this nature constitutes one of the many paradoxes within which corporate universities are steeped. One of the most significant of these is worth considering further, partly because it gives rise to various riddles that lie at the heart of present-day higher education.

Notes

1 Ideas and information in parts of pp. 161–164, 167–172, 174–176 of this chapter have been adapted from these sections of the following sources:
    Wood, F. 2013: Faustian Pacts and False Promises: the *Mamlambo* and the Market University. *Southern African Journal for Folklore Studies* 23 (1): 158–167.
    Wood (2014a: 77–78).
    Wood (2014b: 159–160).

176 *Sacrifices and suffering*

   Wood with Lewis (2007: 65–66, 253, 263–310).
   Many of these points have been revised in the light of more recent research, and most of the previously cited studies examine other occult aspects of corporatised universities and different features of the South African supernatural.
2 The mamlambo originated among the Xhosa-speaking peoples in South Africa. This being is believed to reside in water, and its full name in Xhosa is *uMaMlambo*, the mother of the river. A great many accounts of female mamlambos have arisen, partly because men were traditionally the breadwinners and they also tended to be the narrators of these stories. However, accounts of male mamlambos are now increasing, indicative of various socio-economic changes. For instance, the role that a considerable number of South African women play as the principal family breadwinners has grown in importance; and many women are unmarried heads of households.
3 One academic interviewed by Webster and Mosoetsa made this remark: "I did not see them as management before. I saw them as colleagues. Now I feel I am on the other side of the divide". Another academic observed, "The 'us' and 'them' syndrome . . . has resurfaced again" (2001: 12).
4 For example, during the apartheid era in South Africa, the term *Christian civilised values* came to mean adherence to the edicts of the white minority government.
5 Mamdani describes the extent to which such tendencies contaminated Makerere University, for example: "The income-generating units . . . were so systematically getting soiled with a market ethic that many of their staff were no longer willing to do anything that was not directly paid for" (2007: 76). Such inclinations are prevalent in many other universities elsewhere.
6 There are numerous oral accounts that testify to this (see for instance Niehaus, 2001a: 57–62; Wilson, 1936: 287). Some of the best-known deal with the eventual fate of one of the most prominent sellers of ukuthwala in southern Africa, Khotso Sethuntsa (commonly known as Khotso), who was said to be a millionaire. His sons died young, one of them declining into depression and alcoholism long before his death. A number of his wives suffered from chronic diseases. Khotso himself was beset by suffering and pain near the end of his life, and after his death his family was riven by bitter legal battles for his estate.
7 E-mail from colleague in the Humanities (name and institutional affiliation withheld).
8 Chetty and Merrett describe how these inter-managerial tensions manifested themselves at their institution, for instance (2014: 144).

11 Smoke and mirrors and wind money

All in all, the fact that many distinctive aspects of the supernatural have permeated contemporary corporatised universities gives rise to certain questions. In their very emphasis on utilitarianism and steel-edged, functional corporate pragmatism, in their very desire to cut through the mysteries of academia with its ideals, its dreams, its visions and strange quests, universities have become deeply esoteric and obscure, ruled by complex hierarchies of authority of extraordinary, almost medieval intricacy, thriving on secrets and mysteries as well as strange ritual practices. These can sometimes be best understood in terms of the occult. There is some dark humour in the irony of this. However, there is also a serious issue at stake: Why have universities, in their quests to become more efficient, functional and goal-directed, become more shadowy, complex and abstruse?[1]

Ironies and equivocation

There are several possible reasons for this. For one thing, the confusing, opaque nature of contemporary university practice is reinforced by the discourse of managerialism, which relies heavily on the jargon of the corporate world. This is a language of smoke and mirrors, distanced from actuality and thriving on equivocation and evasion. Newbrook describes it as "a language that is not designed for clear communication. It is a language of avoidance, . . . half-truths and outright lies" (2005: 10). Euphemistic expressions, for instance, have long been used to soften some of the harsher features of the modern-day workplace. The term *rationalisation*, for instance, tends to be invoked as justification for "retrenchment" (a euphemistic expression in itself). Then, as Shore and Wright note, "budget cuts" have been converted into "efficiency savings" (1999: 564). In addition, as Hedley observes, "incentives" denotes bribery to enforce compliance, in that it entails paying employees to do as they are told (2010: 138).

As this suggests, the discrepancies with which managerial jargon is fraught add further layers of confusion to present-day universities, turning them into Humpty-Dumpty worlds in which words' meanings are twisted to suit the users' interests. As a result, some of the most oft-invoked terms in the corporatised academy acquire several different, sometimes conflicting meanings. For instance, *incentive* can have paradoxical qualities, encompassing punishment as well as rewards. While obedience is "incentivised", negative incentives are employed as disciplinary measures to bring about conformity by means of coercion. Moreover, to many employees in restructured university environments controlled by those in positions of privilege and power, the word *accountable* has come to mean "You are accountable to us, but we are not accountable to you". Shore and Wright refer to one instance of this, describing how universities in the UK are expected to be accountable to the HEFCE, yet this body does not regard itself as accountable to them. For instance, the HEFCE gave the London School of Dentistry a low grade in the 1996 RAE; and when the School of Dentistry asked for reasons for this grading, the HEFCE refused to disclose them (1999: 566).

The concept of accountability also encompasses that which Shore and Wright describe as "the panopticon model of accountability", in terms of which university staff members are expected to be constantly visible and inspectable amid ongoing internal and external forms of evaluation. Thus, *transparency*, a related term in certain respects, does not so much denote democratic openness as exposure to continuous scrutiny of this kind (1999: 566). Moreover, like *accountability*, this term tends to hold different meanings for those at various levels of the institutional hierarchy in that it may seem to apply particularly to those in subordinate positions and less so to those who preside over them. Hedley, for instance, observes that many employees at Irish universities were inclined to believe that "transparency tended to run in one direction only, from the bottom of the organisation to the top, but not the other way around" (2010: 138). His point holds true for many corporatised, managerially governed institutions of higher education elsewhere.

Transparency has taken on additional layers of the paradoxical, as previous chapters have indicated. By means of regular enactments of transparency (including the audit procedure, the rites of performance appraisals and bureaucratic rituals bestowing the appearance of efficiency and productivity while seemingly laying all open to scrutiny) combined with ritual-like incantations of terms such as *transparency* and *accountability*, that which is depicted or enacted in the name of transparency serves to obscure more than it discloses. Thus, the extent to which the concept of transparency has been foregrounded in corporatised universities casts further light on the mysterious, ritualistic aspects of such institutions, in that this promotes forms of concealment by weaving an illusion of openness. Once again, this bears out Pels's and Geschiere's aforementioned points about the ways in which certain kinds of enchantments, some of which are at work in contemporary societies, are reliant on a skilful interplay between secrecy and revelation. For instance, the franker and more open a magician may appear to be, seemingly disclosing all about his or her arts and equipment, the more he or she may be concealing. Thus, his or her apparent transparency may serve as a means of dissembling (Pels, 2003: 7; Taussig, 2003: 273, 295–300).

There are other levels of irony and illusion at work. As Shore and Wright have mentioned, terms such as *accountability*, *transparency* and *efficiency* have frequently been depicted as empowering and emancipatory, despite the way in which they have been used to reinforce forms of control and constraint (1999: 559). Ironically, too, as universities have become weighed down by new complex layers of bureaucracy, this has been depicted as a way of replacing the bureaucratic hierarchies of old-style universities with streamlined, more efficient systems.[2] In these and other respects, that which was termed "the efficiency model" during the implementation of NPM in the UK public sector has made its presence felt in higher education (Deem, Hillyard and Reed, 2007: 36). Further to this, as numerous academics in the UK, South Africa and elsewhere have indicated, the discourse describing the efficiency and productivity brought about by corporate restructuring is often at variance with the actual effect of this process. This is evident, for example, in Bertelsen's description of how "more and more of our time is taken up by lengthy meetings whose recurrent agenda is how to do more for less" (1998: 140). Pendlebury and van der Walt also describe how the restructuring process at the University of the Witwatersrand was purported to transform their institution into a smoother, more streamlined workplace. Yet as a result of its intricate managerial hierarchies and its extensive bureaucratic demands, it clogged, confused and convoluted the work process, generating disruptions and instabilities, just as it has done elsewhere (2006: 90–91). Deem makes comparable points about the "modernisation" of UK academia (2001: 10). Moreover, the implementation of additional bureaucratic requirements in order to ensure accountability and efficiency can undermine the very qualities that such procedures are intended to enhance. Although, as Collini notes, "[w]e certainly *report* on ourselves much more fully", this may prove counterproductive in certain respects, distracting employees from other university-related duties and eroding their time (2012: 134–135).

As the above arguments suggest, the concept of rationalisation has paradoxical implications. Ritzer, for instance, describes how workplaces governed by core features of rationalisation, including efficiency, may undermine these very same qualities. He speaks of the "irrationality of rationality", in other words, the contradictory consequences of attempts to adhere to purportedly rational approaches in consumer capitalist practices, contending that that which may seem practical and reasonable may prove illogical and potentially damaging (1999: 78, 93):

> [W]e are in danger of being seduced by the innumerable advantages already offered, and promised in the future, by rationalization. The glitter of these accomplishments and promises has served to distract most people from the grave dangers posed by progressive rationalization. In other words, we are ultimately concerned here with the irrational consequences that often flow from rational systems.
>
> (Ritzer, 1983)

The market-oriented restructuring of academia has been shaped by dangerous enchantments of this kind. Indeed, the occult aspects of corporatised universities, with their ambiguities, contradictions and obscurities and strange and sinister qualities, have been brought about by the irrational features of rationalisation of which Ritzer speaks.

Furthermore, the incongruities and illusions with which some of the most oft-invoked power words in contemporary higher education and the policies and procedures associated with them are suffused are suggestive of the elusive, illusory aspects of the ideologies shaping the restructuring of higher education, drawing as they do on free-market capitalist principles, with their arcane, ambiguous and deceptive aspects and their reliance on mystery and magic.

This state of affairs is compounded by the vague and confusing nature of corporate managerialism, with its predilection for delays and deferments, which have not only rendered the future uncertain and imprecise but also obscured and destabilised the present. All the while the mystic secrets of managerialism sow confusion and disorientation, and corporate mythologies continue to be disseminated, their illogicalities and fallacies infecting academic discourse and institutional environments with organisational and intellectual disorder and disarray.

Some of these areas of mystification are evident in one of the principal power words of corporate academia: *innovation*. *Modernisation*, a related term, is also fraught with incongruities and ironies. When applied to the contemporary restructuring of institutions of higher education, "innovation" can indicate potentially (or purportedly) profitable research developments, or the introduction of that which is claimed to be more effective and productive, such as new procedures and organisational structures, for example. But when it becomes viewed as an aspect of that which has been depicted as knowledge capitalism, the term *innovation* can acquire some contradictory implications. For instance, Orr mentions that *innovation* can sometimes come to denote not so much the production of new knowledge, but rather the commodification of existing knowledge (1997: 54). *Innovation* has also acquired an aura of enchantment because, like various other terms, including *excellence* and *world-class*, this word appears to be endowed with a transformative magic. It can imply that universities have cast off old ways, remaking themselves as "new-generation" institutions.[3] The concept of modernisation, when associated with NPM and related initiatives that set out to "reform" or "modernise" the public sector, has similar associations. In the specific context of higher education, this term implies that through a process of improvement and upgrading, public institutions – universities included – have been remade anew, becoming part of the "modern" world. In various respects, however, the opposite has taken place.

Ironically, despite the way in which they profess to have superseded outdated academic leadership structures and practices, restructured universities have various antiquated aspects, some of which they draw from the corporate sector and its hierarchies of managerial control, as well as the cumbersome complexities of public service bureaucracy. Paradoxically, for example, elements of academia have become medievalised during the course of that which has sometimes been depicted as an innovation process.[4] For instance, the complex, hierarchical structures of authority at managerially governed universities not only call to mind the hierarchically ranked orders of beings in both the visible and invisible worlds of medieval cosmology, but also the feudal system in the Middle Ages. Newbrook's assertion that corporate power structures are "based on [levels] of deference that would shame a medieval court" is also applicable to present-day higher education (2005: 9). Furthermore, some of the ideas underpinning certain core concepts and procedures in "new-generation" universities, such as "total quality" and vision and mission statements have been described as somewhat outdated, based on organisational development strategies in the 1970s (Parker and Jary, 1995: 324).

Next, innovation and antiquity are combined, in that both modern sorcery and certain longstanding enchantments have become integral aspects of present-day university discourse and procedure. Not only has this added a novel, sinister dimension to contemporary occult economies, but it has also bequeathed new forms on some ancient aspects of magic and ritual. In these respects, then, the corporate restructuring of contemporary universities, while drawing on certain systems and procedures reminiscent of those of bygone days, has introduced unprecedented features into the shadowy sphere of the occult.

Deception, disparities and dissonance

Modernity and aspects of the occult are interconnected in other respects. The ambiguous, paradoxical features of the ethos and discourse of "modernised" institutions of higher education have certain areas of commonality with the ideologies and the terminology utilised to justify Western colonial and neocolonial hegemony. They are also suggestive of the extent to which corporatised universities have become sites of ideological, discursive and psychological dissonance. This has heightened their strange and shadowy qualities.

The Comaroffs argue that some Eurocentric concepts of modernity imposed on colonised peoples made the colonisers seem strange, inscrutable, almost occult presences, since colonisation had its own irrational, even mythic aspects, including various alibis, such as "civilization", "social progress", "development" and so on (1993: xxx). Peter Gay makes a similar point, alluding to the "alibis for aggression" fostered in Western bourgeois culture to justify the exploitation of the non-Western world (1993; cited in Dalton, 2004: 201).

Dissimulation of this nature continues to be employed to advance Western neocolonial agendas. For example, the allure of the market is intensified when commercialisation and commodification are harnessed to the superficially appealing notion of development.[5] This latter concept is an unequally untrustworthy construct, invoked as it has been to serve the interests of the forces of globalised capitalism. The World Bank, for instance, employs this alibi to further its own agenda. In the university context, invocations of high-sounding ideals such as quality, excellence, accountability, team-building, ethics and so on are imbued with enchantment, functioning, in a sense, as "alibis" for corporatisation, commodification and authoritarianism. In various respects, these notions are informed by aspects of the market-oriented, corporate mythos that numerous restructured universities have adopted as their master narrative. Like many myths, this has various impenetrable, ambiguous features.

The Comaroffs describe another myth of Western provenance with similar qualities, contending that Eurocentric notions of modernity evolved occult aspects particularly as a result of the strange, paradoxical qualities they acquired when apprehended by other peoples:

> For modernity ... carries its own historical irony ... the more rationalistic and disenchanted the terms in which it is presented to "others", the more magical, impenetrable, inscrutable, incontrollable, darkly dangerous seem its signs, commodities and practices.
>
> (1993: xxx)

A comparable situation has arisen in higher education. The more the proponents of market-oriented restructuring claim this process is based on rational, practical principles, the more such processes may seem to become steeped in shadowy forms of mystery, mythmaking and magic. Furthermore, the pragmatic businesslike discourse now employed in academia can be so fraught with the discordance between the corporate context from which it arises and the academic concerns that it purports to address that it becomes equivocal, slippery and even unfathomable, as do the corporate, bureaucratic practices that this discourse frames. As a result, both discourse and practice slide away into areas of mystery and potential menace.

Nonetheless, the confusing, impenetrable aspects of current university policy and practice may fulfil certain practical functions. At times, these may serve as a way of masking the true features of corporatisation and managerialism, depicting them in grandiose, generalised terms as the result of a transformation process fuelled by visionary strategic plans, rather than by exposing them for what they are: a surrender to globalised neoliberal economic pressures. Readings, for instance, remarks that, in the final analysis, the corporatisation of universities amounts to "the generalised imposition of the rule of the cash-nexus" (1996: 3). This has been played down, as has the extent to which the transformation process at many South African universities draws especially on the Thatcherite reconstruction of institutions of higher learning in the UK and the corporate ethos of the US. As one dimension of this, the extent to which features of consumer capitalism have shaped the commodification of intellectual activity has also been elided.

In order to effect this, some of the rhetoric of restructured academia has acquired an aura of enchantment in that, like a magical garment that transforms the outward aspect of its wearer, it serves to cloak the market-driven, neoliberal ethos of contemporary universities in the appealing garb of democracy. For instance, many institutional mission statements (such as some of those cited in the opening chapter) with their claimed commitment to egalitarian principles and the greater good of the societies around them, may fulfil a function of this nature. As Bertelsen contends, there is a discrepancy between the apparently democratic language describing that which has been depicted as a transformation process and the trend towards corporatisation and commodification that this discourse justifies (1998: 135–137). These tensions between democratisation and marketisation tend to give rise to equivocation and inconsistencies, as the need for the former can easily become submerged by the imperatives of the latter. For instance, it is worth noting that the academic president of Monash University, South Africa, recently stated that, while "inclusive and quality education for all" was one of the United Nations' 17 Sustainable Development goals, other issues, especially serving the needs of the knowledge economy, would need to be prioritised (Louw, 2017: 27).

Consequently, market-oriented institutions in the UK, the US and elsewhere have acquired paradoxical qualities. In South Africa, for example, university managers may invoke democratic concepts such as redress and equity, yet their institutional ethos, based as it is on neoliberal economic convictions, does not operate in the interests of those most in need of such ideals (for instance, the economically and educationally deprived communities from which various local universities, particularly the HDIs, draw many of their students). Indeed, egalitarian notions are sometimes propounded at the same time as student exclusions increase and tuition fees grow ever more costly.[6] All the while, performance-based assessments that tend to benefit the educational elite at prestigious institutions take place.

As earlier chapters have indicated, when quantifiable features such as graduation rates, research outputs, qualifications of faculty members and financial viability are assessed, this tends to reinforce racial and class-based disparities. A significant amount of the state funding allocated to universities is based on evaluation of this kind, yet this method of assessment favours the traditionally privileged institutions equipped with the wherewithal to provide satisfactory proof of performance in these areas. A South African newspaper article entitled "Lacklustre Means, Miniscule Output" draws attention to this, for example (Maluleke, 2011: 29). Making specific reference to the South African situation, Nash concludes that instead of remedying the imbalances imposed by apartheid, this reliance on quantitative methods of appraisal often furthers that which has sometimes been described as Merton's Matthew Effect. As in the Gospel according to Matthew, Chapter 13, verse 12, more is bestowed upon those who have in abundance, while those who are lacking may risk being stripped of the little they have (Merton, 1988: 608–609; see also Nash, 2006: 6; Macdonald and Kam, 2007: 650). In this country, underperforming universities are inevitably those upon which the burden of the past rests most heavily, the historically disadvantaged institutions for those from lower-income urban districts or remote rural areas, attended particularly by African students.

But it is evident that unequal distributions of power, status and wealth are a ubiquitous feature of diverse systems of higher education worldwide, although these distinctions may manifest themselves to varying degrees and take on differing forms. In 1993, for example, the Association of University Teachers in the UK described the way in which various audit systems, RAEs and Teaching Quality Assessments penalised those institutions that were not in a position to excel in evaluations of this kind, sometimes on account of financial problems and infrastructural limitations. Shore and Wright remark that this tendency is in keeping with neoliberalism, in which those "deemed to be underperforming must be punished, rather than aided" (1999: 565). Consequently, as Portuguese academic Antonio Nóvoa observed in 2014, various European universities "lend themselves to policies that reproduce fractures and divisions in Europe" by benefiting the more affluent countries and institutions at the cost of the economically embattled ones (5–6). Thus, whether in South Africa, the UK, Europe or elsewhere, performance-based assessments of educational institutions tend to operate in favour of relatively privileged institutions, while undermining the disadvantaged, thus trapping them in the categories they seek to transcend (see for instance Orr, 1997: 61–62; Cooper, 1997: 39).

Discrepancies of this kind intensify the impenetrable aspects of the restructured, corporatised university milieu. The discourse, ethos and practices of this environment are often veiled in varying degrees of deception and self-deception, whether deliberate or unintentional, which conceal their nature and effect, the type of ideologies that gave rise to them and the vested interests underpinning them. For example, various aspects of the "transformation" of South African universities tend to be kept concealed within the thickets of managerialism, because rather than looking towards the future, they hearken back to a reactionary past. As University of KwaZulu-Natal academic Murthree Maistry puts it, a "silent colonisation" has taken place (2013; cited in Jenvey, 2013). Restructuring higher education in accordance with neoliberal economic approaches and in the interests of globalised capitalism acts as a form of neocolonial control in the African context and elsewhere.

The structural adjustment programmes imposed on many African countries by the IMF and the World Bank in the 1980s and 1990s, as a consequence of such countries' reliance on loans from these bodies, have had similar effects, as have their more recent manifestations, such as the Poverty Reduction Strategy Papers. These systems have bound many African nations more closely to systems of neocolonial, neoliberal economic and political control, locking them into ongoing patterns of cost-cutting and commodification, which have extended to encompass higher education (see for instance Chang, 2010: 118). For example, Zeleza and Olukoshi describe how the World Bank and other comparable bodies have promulgated neoliberal economic agendas, in terms of which many African universities have been condemned for being ill-equipped to meet the demands of the market. As a result, they have suffered economically (2004a: 2–4).[7]

East African legal theorist and activist Issa Shivji comments,

> Then came the . . . neoliberal offensive. . . . Imperialism and capitalism masquerading as globalisation and free market set the rules of the game. . . . We did not need thinkers, asserted our erstwhile benefactors. . . . Universities are not cost-effective, decreed the World Bank. Education, knowledge must be sold and bought on the market. . . . The colonised mind resurfaced.
>
> (2005: 34)

For instance, there are certain parallels between the type of narrow, vocationally-oriented instruction favoured at many market-oriented universities and the apartheid-style system of Bantu Education, designed to train South African learners to perform limited workplace-related forms of labour, becoming instruments of those in positions of economic control.[8] Desmond Ryan's critique of the current higher education system in the UK is pertinent to this. He maintains that the reductionist, utilitarian approach that often tends to be promulgated, which emphasises functionality and solid, practical results and outputs, and the fulfilling of certain closely stipulated criteria, is outdated and has limited commercial applicability (1998: 1–8, 16–17). A range of commentators corroborate Ryan's assertion, including Mamdani in his analysis of the impact of neoliberal "reforms" at Makerere University, Uganda between 1989 and 2005.[9]

But the strange, convoluted aspects of corporatised academic discourse and practice do not simply arise from an urge to obscure inconvenient issues such as these. They cover a void, disguising the essential hollowness of the corporate, managerial ethos. Situated on its shifting sands, the jargon and praxis of corporatisation and managerialism is rendered precarious, destabilising that which they encompass. This gives rise to various instabilities and paradoxes while intensifying the state of confusion and mystification that has become endemic to corporate academia.

On one level, this reflects the extent to which universities have become bedazzled and confused by the "meta-narrative of globalization" (Vale, 2004: 10), a master narrative that had begun proving hollow decades ago. More broadly, the forms of enchantment and fabulation upon which managerial, market-driven academia is based also derive their precarious, ambiguous aspects from the extent to which they draw on that which is ambiguous, elusive and unstable: such as the market, aspects of free-market capitalism and the essential item at its heart: money itself.

Transitory money

Marx draws attention to the paradoxical aspects of money, highlighting not only its centrality in the capitalist system of economic exchange but also the fact that this cornerstone is provisional and mutable, as a result of the function it fulfils.

"All commodities are only transitory money", Marx observes, "money is the permanent commodity". Expanding on this point, he observes that the significance vested in money lies in its capacity to vanish as soon as it appears, by playing its role in the exchange process. Consequently, it can only be used if it is given away. Therefore, "money appears only fleetingly, or its substance consists only in this constant appearance as disappearance" (1973: 149, 231, 209). Money thus occupies both the realms of the seen and unseen, fulfilling its most important function as it disappears from view.

In certain respects, various perceptions of money in diverse parts of Africa may stem from similar ideas. In particular, there is a widespread sense that financial security and stability is, to an extent, a chimera. Schmoll cites one example of this, noting that the Hausa in Niger allude to "wind money": magical money that vanishes after it is used to purchase an item, leaving the individual who received the payment with nothing (1993: 198). In southern Africa, there is a similar belief that money that magically materialises after an encounter with the mamlambo can vanish as swiftly as it appeared, as can this being itself. Moreover, it is said that wealth obtained through ukuthwala disappears after the one who acquired it dies, depriving those close to them of lasting economic protection.[10]

Both Marx's points and the earlier-mentioned examples from the African supernatural are expressive of a deep-seated conviction that money is fleeting and ephemeral, and cannot be relied upon to provide long-term security or stability. The high heels on which the mamlambo is sometimes said to teeter and the flimsy garments this being is said to favour are suggestive of the precarious nature of financial security and the inadequate protection that money can provide. More broadly, the mysterious, unpredictable features of globalised capitalism, some of which have been mentioned previously, offer certain grounds for beliefs of this nature.

Yet money, as transient and unreliable as it is, is the keystone of corporatised universities, founded as they are on a belief in the market, with hard cash as the seemingly solid, stable point to which their discourse and praxis are fixed. But the unreliability and instability of this foundation is a significant factor that destabilises corporatised academia, rendering both its discourse and practice elusive and enigmatic.

Thus, the perplexing, obscure nature of corporate university practice is expressive of the extent to which some of those in internal and external managerial positions have had their heads turned by the magic of the market yet been bewildered by the way that the market and money itself can betray them – or simply become so dizzied by the incongruity of reconfiguring academia as a corporate enterprise – that they have lost clarity of vision and critical focus.

Notes

1. Points adapted from the following sources are included in pp. 180–181 and 186–187 of this chapter: Wood (2014a: 71–72), Wood with Lewis (2007: 286–310) and Wood (2010a: 238–239). The majority of the preceding points originally appeared in other contexts, furthering different arguments.
2. Parker and Jary (1995; 319, 325–326) and Deem (1998: 51) point out that this has often been the case in restructured universities in the UK, for instance.

3 For example, when the Vaal University of Technology in South Africa hosted a conference on new-generation institutions of higher learning in 2010, Professor Alwyn Louw (the then deputy academic and research vice-chancellor) claimed that, in their combination of academic and vocational training, theory and practical application, such institutions met the needs of industry, "[providing] solutions to competency requirements in the knowledge society" (2010: 2). In the same year, the vice-chancellor of the University of Johannesburg lauded this academic model in a promotional newspaper insert, depicting his institution as a new-generation university, intent on "building a winning brand" (Rensburg, 2010: 3).

4 My thanks to Professor Nhlanhla Maake from the University of Limpopo, South Africa, for drawing attention to this point in 2009.

5 One example of the perceived connection between development and marketisation in higher education is evident in David Kaplan's arguments in favour of "research that helps overcome developmental problems . . . *and in a capitalist society this inevitably means business enterprises*" (1997: 75).

6 In South Africa and internationally, the issue of fees has become a contested one, separating many universities even further from the communities they claim to serve. In this country, for instance, proposed fee increases in 2015 and 2016 sparked off nationwide #Fees Must Fall protests, while many similar forms of organised resistance have taken place internationally. For instance, the documentary *Kettling of the Voices* (2015), depicts the student protests caused by the prospect of university fee hikes in the UK in 2010. Tuition fees have also been an ongoing source of discontent in the US. Two documentaries, *Ivory Tower* (2014) and *Starving the Beast* (2016), illustrate this, for instance.

7 Mamdani depicts an instance of this, describing how development aid donors, particularly the World Bank, put pressure on poorer African countries, including Uganda, to focus on primary education. Higher education funding drained away in consequence (2007: vii).

8 Various students at the University of Fort Hare made this point when I presented part of this study as a seminar paper in 2009. They expressed the concern that the market-oriented restructuring of South African universities meant that they were being "sold short". As African students, the parallels with the old apartheid-era Bantu Education system sprang readily to mind.

9 For example, Mamdani draws attention to some of the ironies arising out of the valorisation of skills-based courses in Uganda. At Makerere University, for instance, the Faculty of Education was one of the losers in the "reform" process, despite the fact that it taught practical vocational skills. Paradoxically, too, the attempted marketisation of courses in the Faculty of Science generated economic problems for the Faculty. The formulaic, multidisciplinary approaches in the new market-related courses created in 2000–2001 confused and alienated a number of students (despite extensive attempts to promote these courses at student level). By 2002 it became clear that student intake in the Faculty had been steadily dropping. Similar problems were experienced in another faculty, which offered training in practical, utilitarian skills, the Faculty of Technology. In 2003, Mamdani concluded, "Many of the science-based Faculties had been convinced that, rather than being an answer to the Faculty's problems, the market-oriented strategy was the source of them" (2007: 71, 98–101).

10 The events that took place after the death of Khotso Sethuntsa, who was rumoured to have entered into an ukuthwala pact with a mamlambo, were widely perceived as evidence of this. Although Khotso, as he was commonly known, was said to be a millionaire, his fortune vanished mysteriously after his demise, and his family were left in a near-destitute state. Many cited this as evidence that wealth accumulated by means of ukuthwala does not outlast the accumulator.

12 Conclusion: breaking the spell

In conclusion, corporatised universities have not simply entered the market but have become drawn into the occult component of the marketplace. The poisonous metaphoric presence of wealth-giving spirits and corporate divinities infects university policy and practice, rendering the discourse and rituals of managerialism unpredictable, ominous and enigmatic. Meanwhile, teams of academic zombies perform endless bureaucratic rituals.[1]

As the preceding descriptions suggest, "modernity generate[s] its own enchantments" (Pels, 2003: 32). Sometimes, paradoxically, conceptions of Western modernity may bring forms of magic into being by denying them. Pels contends that while "modern [Western] discourse reconstructs magic in terms that distinguish it from the modern, this at the same time creates the correspondences and nostalgias by which magic can come to haunt modernity" (2003: 4–5). In certain respects, this calls to mind present-day higher education, in which parallels with the occult have arisen from attempts to cast off various long-standing features of academia, with their rarefied, esoteric qualities, and to refashion many universities as forward-looking, businesslike institutions, following global trends towards corporatisation, commodification and managerialism. Yet, as a result of this, universities have acquired arcane aspects and evolved new magicalities of their own.

Indeed, numerous corporatised institutions of higher education provide examples of the ways in which new forms of magic can be generated or longstanding beliefs and practices can either be reinvented or adapted to suit contemporary conditions. Kaplan, for example, observes, "The sites may change, but surely we also (as Clifford Geertz [1973: 5] once put it) live in webs of meaning that we spin ourselves and vest magical potencies in our newest familiars too" (2003: 199). Recent ethnographic studies, including those by Pels, Taussig, Meyer, Geschiere and the Comaroffs examine this tendency, and this study investigates its hitherto unexplored dimensions.

As universities have been ensnared by the perilous enchantments of the marketplace, entranced by the aura of power and wealth surrounding the corporate sphere, and entangled in the mazes of managerialism, they have begun to pay the price for this. Accordingly, a question now arises: Are there any liberatory possibilities available in a situation of this kind? Or, to adopt more otherworldly terminology, can the malign spell be broken?

Dissent

In response to this question, let us consider this exploration of the occult aspects of corporatised universities. Its critique of market-oriented restructuring and managerialism is not intended as an end in itself. Instead, it is interconnected with broader issues: the need for resistance to free-market capitalist systems of influence and control and the neoliberal economic approaches that impose and perpetuate them, infiltrating even the academic workplace. A striving towards freer, more equitable economic and socio-political dispensations should form a core component of a struggle of this kind.

Changes of this nature are of vital importance, for Merton's Matthew Effect – where the affluent and influential are rewarded while those in disadvantaged, economically precarious positions are penalised – is at work in present-day higher education and in other domains. Indeed, it is evident that prestigious, privileged universities have more to gain from the current dispensation than institutions in more financially straitened circumstances that draw the majority of their students from economically deprived communities. In South Africa, for example, the contrasts between HAIs such as the University of Cape Town, the University of Johannesburg and the University of the Witwatersrand, on one hand, and HDIs like the University of Zululand, the University of Venda and the University of Fort Hare, on the other, are indicative of this. Such patterns play themselves out more broadly in today's globalised world, in which the more powerful, prosperous nations enrich themselves at the cost of the more vulnerable, economically embattled ones, South Africa included. As Giroux observes,

> [i]f solutions to the problems facing higher education are to be effective, then they cannot be abstracted from the growing inequality between the rich and poor that is taking place at a global level. This type of rabid capitalism must be confronted both at home and abroad on multiple levels, including the ideological, cultural, economic and political.
>
> (2007: 208)

It is worth noting that various political struggles, including anti-apartheid activism in South Africa, have taken place on many levels, extending from mass mobilisation to armed resistance, non-violent direct action, symbolic protests and intellectual and cultural dissent. As political events in this country have shown, a multifaceted movement challenging the established order can be harder to crush on account of its hydra-like qualities. Moreover, such an initiative can draw in a range of individuals and communities and be more wide-ranging, extending through diverse spheres of society.

When viewed from metaphorical perspectives, the figures of the zombie, the witch driven by greedy, covetous impulses, and those so consumed by a desire for wealth that they fall prey to malign wealth-giving spirits cast light on some of the consequences of the "rabid capitalism" mentioned by Giroux. Arguably then, as they illuminate the damaging effects of market-oriented academia, these diverse beings highlight the importance of opposing the established order and the neoliberal economic approaches that have brought it into being, and striving for economic and socio-political alternatives.

Standing describes the important role that democratic professional associations, in alliance with worker and student organisations, could fulfil in resisting the systems of power and control in restructured higher education and other domains (2011: 159). Giroux also maintains that there is much that academic employees could learn much from student movements about broadening and intensifying organisational resistance (2007: 205–206). These observations are very pertinent to South African universities at present, and indeed to many other institutions in diverse countries, including those that have often been discussed in this book. Certainly, such organisational activism is much needed, and it could play a key part in confronting and challenging marketisation and managerialism. In South Africa, for instance, the nationwide #Fees Must Fall student protests in 2015 obstructed the proposed fee hikes for the following year, temporarily at least.

On the other hand, the limitations of various South African student protests, such as the #Fees Must Fall and the #Outsourcing Must Fall campaigns of 2015–2016 and other related initiatives, such as the Open Stellenbosch movement, are also worth considering. While they served as powerful forces for student mobilisation, the impact they exerted appears to have been short-lived. For instance, further proposals for fee increases gave rise to more protests, and even more are liable take place. In part, perhaps, these campaigns may have lacked a vision for the future. This could have encompassed strategies for future directions; and clearer conceptions of the socio-political and economic alternatives to the neoliberal economic approaches and the systems of state authority that have brought about the privatisation of the public domain and imposed and consolidated corporatisation and market-oriented managerialism.[2] Moreover, the students involved in these movements might have been able to take their struggles further by forging alliances with university workers and professional staff. Political mobilisation of this nature might have posed a more sustained and forceful challenge to the status quo.

Notwithstanding the role that could be played by organisational alliances of this kind, the building of effective employee associations is not always easily accomplished in the contemporary climate of corporate authoritarianism. In South Africa, for example, many university organisations and the individuals within them have been cowed into silence, co-opted or corrupted. Giroux describes how similar situations occur in various institutions of higher education in the US and many other corporatised university environments (2007: 5, 19–20, 185). Indeed, as preceding chapters have shown, the climate of fear that tends to be prevalent at restructured universities may often stifle defiance. This is frequently sustained by punitive measures and threats, both overt and covert, many of which have been depicted above, and reinforced by the myriad control mechanisms that infiltrate employees' working lives.

Therefore additional forms of dissent are needed to help foster a sense of resistance that could lend itself to the growth of alternatives. Consequently, marketisation, corporatisation and managerialism need to be challenged on various levels. As one dimension of this, some of the concepts most dear to many internal and external managerial authorities, often employed as control mechanisms, could be re-appropriated and interrogated. For example, the notions of excellence and productivity, along with mission statements, have been revisited and reinterpreted, in South Africa and elsewhere.

Since the concept of excellence may seem to encapsulate some of the key ideas driving neoliberal university restructuring, this idea has come under particular attack from various opponents of the corporatisation of higher education. For example, staff and student bodies in France, Belgium and elsewhere have sought to express their opposition to the corporate restructuring of their universities by challenging the concept of excellence. For instance, in an article titled "Down with Excellence!" Julie Le Mazier, a postgraduate student at the University of Paris, describes how this tactic formed a key component of student resistance to marketisation and corporatisation at French universities (2012). Moreover, corporatised, commodified notions of excellence have been challenged and reformulated in the *Chartre de Désexcellence* (2014), drawn up by staff and students in Belgium and France.[3] The charter constructs an alternative concept of *désexcellence*, which is concerned with the true quality of academic work: the nature and significance of what it achieves and the satisfaction gained by those who produce it.

Furthermore, the Slow Science Manifesto (2010), promulgated by the Slow Science Academy in Berlin, maintains that the foregrounding of the quantifiable has impaired academic research, particularly in certain disciplines. The Manifesto contends that the focus on short-term productivity and the valorisation of quantity at the cost of quality has undermined and reduced thorough research and significant developments in scientific knowledge.[4] Instead, the Manifesto declares that "[s]cience needs time to think. . . . Scientists must *take* their time".

Next, the Manifesto for Universities That Live Up to Their Missions (2012), drawn up at the University of Liège and endorsed by many university employees worldwide, takes issue with another cornerstone of corporatisation: university mission statements, individual institutional declarations with an aura of sameness. The Manifesto critiques the extent to which restructured corporatised universities fulfil the core business of higher education: teaching, research and community service. These areas could perhaps be regarded as their missions, but the Manifesto suggests that the ethos and practices at many corporatised institutions tend to undermine these.

Arguably these previously-delineated initiatives might seem like a kind of escapism: an attempt to construct a private realm of academic ideals untouched by corporatisation and managerialism. Yet they are significant in that they promulgate alternative perceptions at a time when many staff and students may feel they inhabit an environment in which consensus has become compulsory and their voices are stifled. Moreover, they compose part of a multifaceted culture of dissent that could lend itself to the growth of organised resistance. This study represents a facet of this multidimensional opposition to the corporatisation and commodification of academia and the economic and political forces underpinning it, as will become evident below.

Yet alternative approaches may seem hedged in by limitations. We have seen that corporate control is sustained by submissiveness – and, in particular, by inculcating conformity and compliance. So how can staff members counter this? Standing argues that a sense of independent agency needs to be restored to academics, equipping them with a sense of power and control over their working lives (2011: 159–160). Thus, they need to resist zombification and the neoliberal economic tendencies that have fostered it, evolving a heightened insight into the authority systems and control mechanisms in their workplaces, their societies and their lives and the ways in which they exercise their power and bend others to their will. Certainly, by this means, employees at restructured institutions would be better equipped to withstand the "creeping commodification" of their workplaces (Comaroffs, 1999: 291) – which all too often distorts their own inner lives – and strive for alternatives. These may encompass not only institutional transformation but also the socio-economic changes of which Standing and Giroux speak. But given the constraints under which numerous university employees labour, how can the strengthening of individual resolve and the growth of collective opposition be brought about?

Defamiliarisation

There are additional strategies that academics could employ to encourage the growth of that which Readings depicts as "a community of dissensus" (1996: 180–194). For instance, the tactic of defamiliarisation can play an important role in this regard. According to Viktor Shklovsky, this technique serves to remove dulled, automatised perceptions of the familiar by making it seem new and strange. This may result in a re-appraisal of well-known, commonplace features of our experience (1965: 11–12).[5] Defamiliarisation has an important role to play in the corporatised academic milieu. For instance, Amsler analyses concepts like performance, efficiency and value for money, drawing attention to their underlying ideological agendas and contending that "this deeper doxa . . . must be made visible, denaturalized and confronted" (2013: 11). We can put our own academic disciplines to work here, drawing on them for guidance and sources of insight as we expose and interrogate the systems of power and control in our societies and workplaces. For example, Shore and Wright consider the way in which anthropological approaches and insights can be harnessed to confront and critique the doctrines, discourse, perceptions and practices of corporatised, audit-driven institutions of higher education (1999: 571).

This exploration of the occult aspects of market-oriented, managerially governed universities employs techniques of this kind. By juxtaposing elements of the southern African supernatural and other aspects of mystery and magic with the ethos, structures and praxis of corporate academia and the economic systems of power and control underpinning them, parts of the status quo are defamiliarised. In the process, the strange, contradictory and damaging features of market-oriented, managerially governed universities have been highlighted, along with their ominous absurdities and areas of unseen menace. Interconnected with this, the ways in which such institutions have become pervaded by fabulation, false magic and mystification has been brought to the fore.

Diverse studies of mystical, magical beliefs and practices in Africa employ similar approaches in order to invite us to re-examine and interrogate the nature and the workings of the forms of Western capitalist power to which they are related and which they illuminate. The Comaroffs' article on occult economies is one such example, as is Geschiere's research into beliefs in wealth-giving magic in the Cameroon (1992, 1997, 2003). Meanwhile, White describes how certain accounts of vampires from Zambia and East and Central Africa contain Western elements (such as firemen and blood transfusions) which are transmuted into images of vampiric menace, thereby implicitly critiquing systems of colonial and neocolonial control (2000: 29). Further to this, Gudeman observes that Geschiere's description of the belief that material well-being is generated by zombie labour (1992) invites us to reconsider Western capitalist economic practices and reflect on their exploitative, non-rational aspects (1992: 288). In this respect, Geschiere's research represents a form of defamiliarisation, as do the other previously cited studies.

Derision

Incidentally, the power of humour may sometimes come to our aid by means of defamiliarisation, albeit this may be a dark kind of humour, given the current nature of the present-day corporatised workplace. Nonetheless, temporarily envisaging the high priests of managerial authority and the powers and principalities that preside over them as those that have become reliant on mystification, fabulation, fetishism and false magic subverts their authority, contributing to the growth of freer, less constrained perceptions. Conditions of this kind are much-needed in the present-day academic context. Burrows observes that many academics run the risk of slumping into a state of "depressive complicity" (2012: 356). Laughter, combined with other strategies, including defamiliarisation and dissent, has the potential to help employees counter the risk of succumbing to the malaise of dejected collusion to which Burrows alludes. Furthermore, some commentators maintain that, in the contemporary restructured higher education milieu, humour may be both subversive and potentially transformative.

For instance, Macdonald and Kam contend that by deriding the norms and procedures of corporatised academia, and emphasising their irrationalities and contradictions, academics may become better equipped to repudiate them. In consequence, subversive mockery may inculcate a spirit of rebelliousness. As Macdonald and Kam remark, the ethos and practices of corporate academia are sustained and perpetuated by "uncritical approbation". They allude to the fairy Tinkerbell in *Peter Pan*, who lives only because the members of the audience declare that they believe in fairies (2007: 650–651). Similarly, they argue, unquestioning approval ensures that the dubious beliefs and practices of managerialised, market-oriented academia will continue to thrive, that the corporate fabulation underpinning them will be reiterated, and that the litany of corporate jargon that imposes and reinforces these will continue to be intoned by many of those who are intellectually equipped to analyse its hollowness (2007: 650–651; see also Harmon, 2006: 241–242).[6] This bears a certain resemblance to the unquestioning belief that has sustained an array of spiritual cults, despite the fact that some of these have questionable aspects and are potentially harmful.

However, a belief in the power of derision might be contested on the grounds that ridicule is unlikely to remove the root cause of a problem. For example, hosts of reactionary world leaders, including George Bush, Tony Blair, Margaret Thatcher and the old South African National Party politicians that implemented apartheid were not unseated by laughter. But nonetheless, satire can disconcert and disturb the authority figures against whom it is directed, while reminding others of the fact that even the most powerful can be belittled by ridicule, and their failings and follies can be exposed and attacked by this means. For instance, in the UK during the Thatcher regime, the satirical TV series *Spitting Images* drew attention to this. Thus, mockery can help preserve a spirit of critique and dissent, especially when other kinds of protest are hindered or suppressed. Political satire fulfilled a function of this nature in South Africa during the apartheid era, for example. Laughter, it is said, never won a war, but it can change the nature of the battlefield in some respects and the terms of engagement. Consequently, both derision and defamiliarisation have the potential to assist many university employees to attain various intellectual, imaginative and psychological freedoms which may – just possibly – help pave the way towards freedoms of other kinds.

There is another factor that might strengthen the resolve of those engaged in a struggle of this kind: the nature of the market university itself. The mysterious, magical aura surrounding the market has been depicted, as has its shifting, elusive nature and the ways in which it is bound up with the workings of the imagination and the influence of the wealthy and powerful. The market university has been constructed on these unstable foundations. Subject to unpredictable outside forms of power and control, be they state-related or products of the machinations and instabilities of the corporate domain, and local and global economic vagaries, it is not as not as fixed and unshakable as it may appear. In other words, it is not built to last. An awareness of this might lend force to staff and student organisations' struggle against corporatisation and market-oriented managerialism and the political and economic authority systems underpinning them. Moreover, envisaging alternatives to free-market capitalism may begin to seem less like a visionary, but overly idealistic endeavour and more like a matter of necessity: indeed, a rational, practical choice in this era of uncertainty.

In conclusion then, we return to the role that could be played by this exploration of the occult aspects of corporate academia. By defamiliarising and destabilising that which may sometimes have come to seem customary, established and inevitable, we can begin to "un-mask the way power is disguised and the mechanisms through which it can be made effective" (Shore and Wright, 1999: 571). Certainly, by opening up the monologic discourses and practices of corporatisation and managerialism to new interpretative possibilities, we can resist their "verbal-ideological centralization and unification" (Bakhtin, 1981: 272). By viewing them on our terms, not theirs, we perceive them anew, subjecting them to ways of seeing that expose their fallacies and flaws. As we revisit and re-appraise the power systems in our societies and our workplaces that control and constrain our lives – and also the way their ascendancy depends in part on our own acquiescence – we may begin to free ourselves from their grasp.[7]

As Giroux maintains, we need to "develop multiple strategies for taking back the universities from the corporations" (2007: 205). By means of a variety of tactics, including recourse to metaphorical comparisons with the occult; methods informed by our own academic disciplines; alliances between staff, student and worker associations; organised resistance to broader socio-economic inequities; and various other strategies at our disposal, we can resist those neoliberal economic forces (and the internal and external managerial systems that act as their agents) that would reduce us to the status of zombies, corporate acolytes, rule-bound managerial minions and symbolic sacrifices to the divinities of the marketplace.

Notes

1 Points adapted from the following sources investigating other occult aspects of higher education have been included in p. 188 and pp. 192–195 of this chapter: Wood (2015b: 54–55), Wood (2010a: 236) and Wood (2010b: 12–13).
2 This was evident, for instance at a plenary session at the 2016 Association for Commonwealth Literary and Languages Studies (ACLALS) Conference at the University of Stellenbosch, South Africa. The speaker, who had played a leading role in the Open Stellenbosch movement opposing racism on campus, observed that it was difficult to envisage alternatives to the neoliberal economic order.
3 The idea of *désexcellence* has been employed especially by universities in Belgium, particularly the Free University of Brussels, and universities in France. This term tends to be translated as "disexcellence", so *désexcellence* is employed here instead.
4 Maggie Berg's and Barbara K. Seeber's critique of the focus on swift, short-term research productivity in *The Slow Professor: Changing the Culture of Speed in the Academy* (2016) is worth considering in this regard.
5 J. R. R. Tolkien's concept of Recovery resembles this. Tolkien contends that Recovery can take place by means of fantasy, which situates the timeworn and mundane in a new or unfamiliar context, thus making them seem original and striking. In this way, Recovery bestows new dimensions or depths of meaning on the familiar and the everyday (1966: 56).
6 For instance, Macdonald and Kam make reference to one feature of contemporary academia that is highly esteemed but deserving of derision: "the cult of publication" in high-ranking journals (2007: 651). Ridicule (and, more worthwhile,

potentially fewer research outputs) is an appropriate response, US academic Michael M. Harmon argues, for competition for prestige, profit and individual and institutional security has eradicated any clear connection between the quantity of research outputs and intellectual significance and social relevance (2006: 241–242).
7 Bakhtin's description of the "centripetal" forces of language, with their monologic qualities, seems an appropriate phrase to deploy when alluding to the closed, centralised nature of the discourse and procedure at corporatised, managerially governed universities (1981: 272).

Bibliography

Abélès, Marc. 1988. Modern Political Ritual. *Current Anthropology* 29 (3): 391–404.
Aitchison, John. 2015. Unscrupulous Academics Buy Into "University 419 Scam". *Mail & Guardian*. December 11–17: 31.
Alexander, Jeffrey C. 2004. Cultural Pragmatics: Social Performance Between Ritual and Strategy. *Sociological Theory* 22 (4) December: 527–573.
Alexiadou, Nafsika. 1999. Management Identities in Transition: A Case Study From Further Education. *The Sociological Review* 49 (3): 412–435.
Amsler, Sarah. 2013. University Ranking: A Dialogue on Turning Towards Alternatives. *Ethics in Science and Environmental Politics* 13: 3–14.
Andrews, Geoff. 2016. Technocrats or Intellectuals? www.signof thetimes.org.uk/pamphlet1/techno.html. Accessed on 22 March 2016.
Anthony, Peter. 1994. *Managing Culture*. Buckingham and Philadelphia: Open University Press.
Appadurai, Arjun. 1986. *The Social Life of Things: Commodities in Cultural Perspective*. Cambridge: Cambridge University Press.
Apple, Michael W. 1999. Rhetorical Reforms: Markets, Standards and Inequality. *Current Issues in Comparative Education* 1 (2): 1–13.
Asad, Talal. 1993. Anthropological Conceptions of Religion: Reflections on Geertz. *Man* 14: 607–627.
Ashforth, Adam. 2001. On Living in a World with Witches: Everyday Epistemology and Spiritual Insecurity in a Modern African City (Soweto). In Moore, Henrietta L. and Todd Sanders (eds). *Magical Interpretations, Material Realities: Modernity, Witchcraft and the Occult in Postcolonial Africa*. London: Routledge: 206–225.
––––– 1998. Witchcraft, Violence and Democracy in the New South Africa. *Cahiers d'Etudes Africaines* 150–152 (2–4): 505–532.
Auslander, Mark. 1993. "Open the Wombs!" The Symbolic Politics of Modern Ngoni Witchfinding. In Comaroff, Jean and John (eds). *Modernity and Its Malcontents: Ritual and Power in Postcolonial Africa*. Chicago and London: University of Chicago Press: 67–192.
Austen, Ralph A. 1993. The Moral Economy of Witchcraft: An Essay in Comparative History. In Comaroff (eds): 89–110.
Baatjies, Ivor G. 2005. The Neoliberal Fantasy and the Corporatisation of Higher Education in South Africa. *Quarterly Review of Education and Training in South Africa* 1 (12): 25–33.
Baatjies, Ivor G. and Carol Spreen and Salim Vally. 2013. The Broken Promises of Neoliberal Restructuring of South African Higher Education. In Pusser, Brian and Ken Kempner, Simon Marginson and Imanol Ordorika (eds). *Universities and the*

Public Sphere: Knowledge Creation and State Building in the Era of Globalization. New York and London: Routledge: 139–158.

Badat, Saleem. 2008. The Trajectory, Dynamics, Determinants and Nature of Institutional Change in Post-1994 South African Higher Education. Paper presented at Higher Education CloseUp 4, 26–28 June, University of Cape Town. http://eprints.ru.ac.za/1391/1/badat_trajectory.pdf. Accessed on 24 January 2010.

Baker, Bruce. 2004. Uneasy Partners: Democratisation and New Public Management in Developing Countries. In Dibben, Pauline and Geoffrey Wood and Ian Roper (eds). *Contesting Public Sector Reforms: Critical Perspectives; International Debates.* Basingstoke, Hampshire and New York: Palgrave Macmillan: 38–53.

Bakhtin, Mikhail. 1981. *The Dialogic Imagination.* Austin: University of Texas Press.

Ball, Stephen J. 2000. Performance and Fabrications in the Education Economy: Towards the Performative Society? *Australian Educational Researcher* 27 (2): 1–23.

——— 1998. Performativity and Fragmentation in "Postmodern Schooling". In Carter, J. (ed). *Postmodernity and the Fragmentation of Welfare.* London: Routledge: 187–203.

Barry, Jim, John Chandler and Heather Clark. 2001. Between the Ivory Tower and the Academic Assembly Line. *Journal of Managerial Studies* 38 January: 87–101.

Bastian, Misty L. 1997. Married in the Water: Spirit Kin and Other Afflictions of Modernity in Southeastern Nigeria. *Journal of Religion in Africa* 27 (2) May: 116–134.

——— 1993. "Bloodhounds Who Have No Friends": Witchcraft and Locality in the Nigerian Popular Press. In Comaroff (eds): 129–166.

Bayart, Jean-François. 1996. *L'Illusion identitaire.* Fayard: Paris.

Beckmann, Andrea and Charlie Cooper. 2004. "Globalisation", the New Managerialism and Education: Rethinking the Purpose of Education in Britain. *Journal for Critical Education Studies* 2 (2). www.jceps.com/?pageID=article&articleID=31. Accessed on 16 April 2010.

Berg, Maggie and Barbara K. Seeber. 2016. *The Slow Professor: Changing the Culture of Speed in the Academy.* Toronto: University of Toronto Press.

Bertelsen, Eve. 1998. The Real Transformation: The Marketisation of Higher Education. *Social Dynamics* 24 (2): 130–158.

Blumenstyk, Goldie. 2014. *American Higher Education in Crisis? What Everyone Needs to Know.* Oxford: Oxford University Press.

Bocock, Robert J. 1970. Ritual: Civic and Religious. *The British Journal of Sociology* 21 (3) September: 285–297.

Boisguillebert, Pierre le Pesant. 1843. Dissertation sur la nature des richesses, de l'argent, et des tributs. In Daire, E. (ed). *Économistes financiers du XVIIIe siècle.* Paris.

Bok, Derek. 2003. *Universities in the Marketplace: The Commercialization of Higher Education.* Princeton and Oxford: Princeton University Press.

Bond, Patrick. 2004. Contradictions Confronting New Public Management in Johannesburg: The Rise and Fall of Municipal Water Commercialisation. In Dibben, Wood and Roper (eds): 192–209.

Boulton, Marjorie. 1960. *The Anatomy of Drama.* London: Routledge and Kegan Paul.

Brooke, Heather. 2010. *The Silent State: Secrets, Surveillance and the Myth of British Democracy.* London: Heinemann.

Buchbinder, Howard. 1993. The Market Oriented University and the Changing Role of Knowledge. *Higher Education* 26 (3): 331–347.
Burrows, Roger. 2012. Living With the H-index? Metric Assemblages in the Contemporary Academy. *The Sociological Review* 60 (2): 355–372.
Case, Peter and Jonathon Gosling. 2010. The Spiritual Organisation: Critical Reflections on the Instrumentality of Workplace Spirituality. *Journal of Management, Spirituality & Religion* 7 (4): 257–282.
Chakrabortty, Aditya and Sally Weale. 2016. Universities Accused of "Importing Sports Direct Model" for Lecturers' Pay. *The Guardian*. 16 November. www.theguardian.com/uk-news/2016/nov/16/universities-accused-of-importin . . . Accessed on 26 May 2017.
Chapman, David. 2013. Abusing Power for Private Gain – Corruption in Academe. *University World News* 290. 1 October. www.universityworldnews.com/article.php?story=2013100110401544. Accessed on 17 October 2013.
Chang, Ha-Joon. 2007. *Bad Samaritans: The Guilty Secrets of Rich Nations and the Threat to Global Prosperity*. London: Random House.
——— 2010. *23 Things They Didn't Tell You About Capitalism*. London: Penguin.
Charlton, Bruce G and Peter Andras. 2002. A System Poisoned by Deceit. *Times Higher Education Supplement* 4 October: 14.
Chartre de Désexcellence. Version 1.1. January 2014. www.lac.ulb.ac.be. Accessed on 2 November 2015. English version translated by Marie-Jeanne Boisacq.
Cherry, Michael. 2014. Sorry Tale of a Post-Merger Mess. *Mail & Guardian*. December 5–11: 39.
Chetty, Nithaya. 2008. In Favour of Free Minds. *Mail & Guardian*. November 21–27: 17.
Chetty, Nithaya and Christopher Merrett. 2014. *The Struggle for the Soul of a South African University*. Available from: soul-of-ukzn.co.za. Accessed on 25 September 2015.
Chevalier, Arnaud and Xiaxuan Jia. 2013. Improved Rankings Boost University Income. *University World News* 269. 27 April 2013. www.universityworldnews.com/article.php?story=20130423155932815. Accessed on 29 April 2013.
Cohen, David William. 2001. In a Nation of Cars . . . One White Car, or "A White Car" Becomes a Truth. In White, Luise and Stephan F. Miescher and David William Cohen (eds). *African Words, African Voices*. Bloomington: Indiana University Press: 264–280.
Cohn, Bernard S. 1987. *An Anthropologist Among Historians and Other Essays*. New Delhi: Oxford University Press.
Coldwell, David. 2008. Defending Our Freedom to Think. *Mail & Guardian Higher Learning Supplement*. November: 2–3.
Collini, Stefan. 2012. *What Are Universities For?* London: Penguin.
Columbia University in the City of New York: Mission Statement. www.columbia.edu/content/mission-statement.html. Accessed on 12 July 2017.
Colson, Elizabeth. 2000. The Father as Witch. *Africa* 70 (3): 333–358.
Comaroff, Jean. 1985. *Body of Power, Spirit of Resistance: The Culture and History of a South African People*. Chicago: University of Chicago Press.
Comaroff, Jean and John. 1999. Occult Economies and the Violence of Abstraction: Notes From the South African Postcolony. *American Ethnologist* 26 (2): 279–303.
——— 1993. Introduction. In Comaroff (eds): xi–xxxvii.

Cooper, Dave. 1997. Introduction: Comments on the "Market" and/or "Development" University With Respect to UCT Discussions on Changing Research Cultures. *Social Dynamics* 23 (1): 23–41.

Corrupt Varsity Officials to Face Charges. 1999. *Mail & Guardian*. June 12. https://mg.co.za/article/1999-03-19-corrupt-varsity-officials-to-face-charges. Accessed on 14 June 2017.

Cowen, Robert. 1996. Performativity, Post-Modernity and the University. *Comparative Education* 32 (2): 245–258.

Crosby, Philip B. 1979. *Quality Is Free*. London: McGraw-Hill.

Crow, Michael. 2014. What Is the Role of Universities in Global Development? http://blogs.worldbank.org/education/what-role-universities-global-evelopment Accessed on 17 May 2017.

Curl, James Stevens. 1991. *The Art and Architecture of Freemasonry: An Introductory Study*. London: Batsford.

Dalton, Doug. 2004. Cargo and Cult: The Mimetic Critique of Capitalist Culture. In Jebens, Holger (ed). *Cargo, Cult, and Culture Critique*. Honolulu: University of Hawai'i Press: 187–208.

Deal with the Problem. 2006. *Daily Dispatch*. 18 November: 12.

Debord, Guy. 1983. *Society of the Spectacle*. Detroit: Black and Red.

Deem, Rosemary. 2001. Globalisation, New Managerialism, Academic Capitalism and Entrepreneurialism in Universities: Is the Local Dimension Still Important? *Comparative Education* 37 (1) February: 7–20.

——— 1998. "New Managerialism" and Higher Education: The Management of Performances and Cultures in Universities in the United Kingdom. *International Studies in Sociology of Education* 8 (1): 47–70.

Deem, Rosemary and Ken Brehony. 2005. Management as Ideology: The Case of New Managerialism in Higher Education. *Oxford Review of Education* 31 (2) June: 217–235.

Deem, Rosemary, Sam Hillyard and Mike Reed. 2007. *Knowledge, Higher Education, and the New Managerialism: The Changing Management of UK Universities*. Oxford: Oxford University Press.

De Frijters, Paul. 2013. In the Courts of Academia. *University World News* 285. 31 August. www.universityworldnews.com/article.php?story=20130828121452103. Accessed on 11 September 2013.

Deming, W. Edwards. 1986. *Out of the Crisis*. Cambridge: Cambridge University Press.

De Rosny, Éric. 1992. *L'Afrique des guérisons*. Paris: Karthala.

Desjeux, Dominique. 1987. *Stratégies paysannes en Afrique noire: Le Congo – Essai sur la gestion de l'incertitude*. Editions L'Harmattan.

De Villiers, W. 2015. SU Management Responds to "Luister" Video. www.sun.ac.za/english/Lists/news/DispForm.aspx?ID=2833. Accessed on 13 October 2015.

Dibben, Pauline and Paul Higgins. 2004. New Public Management: Marketisation, Managerialism and Consumerism. In Dibben, Wood and Roper (eds): 26–37.

Dibben, Pauline and Phil James. 2007. Introduction: Is "Modern" Necessarily Better? In Dibben, Pauline, Phil James, Ian Roper and Geoffrey Wood (eds). *Modernising Work in Public Services: Redefining Roles and Relationships in Britain's Changing Workplace*. Hampshire and New York: Palgrave Macmillan: 1–8.

Dilley, Roy. 1992. Contesting Markets: A General Introduction to Market Ideology, Imagery and Discourse. In Dilley, Roy (ed). *Contesting Markets: Analyses of Ideology, Discourse and Practice*. Edinburgh: Edinburgh University Press: 1–37.

Dorling, Danny. 2011. *Injustice: Why Social Inequality Persists.* London: Policy Press.
Duncan, Jane. 2007. *The Rise of the Disciplinary University.* Howard Wolpe Lecture. University of KwaZulu-Natal. 17 May. http://74.125.77.132/search?q=cache:6SeUQnWmd8sJ:www.ukzn.ac.za/ccs/default.as. Accessed on 26 January 2014: 1–21.
Edmonson, Munro S. 1971. *Lore: An Introduction to the Science of Folklore and Literature.* New York. Holt.
Elliott, Larry and Dan Atkinson. 2007. *Fantasy Island: Waking up to the Incredible Economic, Political and Social Illusions of the Blair Legacy.* London: Constable.
Etzioni, Amitai. 2010. Rain-making in Afghanistan. www.huffingtonpost.com/ . . . etzioni/rain-making in afghanista_6_78268. Accessed on 18 November 2010.
Evans-Pritchard, E. E. 1976. *Witchcraft, Oracles and Magic Among the Azande.* Oxford: Clarendon.
Fernandes, Christina. 2011. Performance Appraisal – A Key Business Tool or an Annual Ritual? www.shrmindia.org/hr-buzz/blogs/shrm-india/performance-appraisal-%E2%80%93-key-business-tool. Accessed on 17 December 2012.
Feynman, Richard P. 1992. *"Surely You're Joking, Mr Feynman!" Adventures of a Curious Character as Told to Ralph Leighton.* London: Vintage.
Fisiy, Cyprian F. and Peter Geschiere. 2001. Witchcraft, Development and Paranoia in Cameroon: Interactions Between Popular, Academic and State Discourse. In Moore, Henrietta L. and Todd Sanders (eds): 226–246.
Foucault, Michel. 1991. *Remarks on Marx: Conversations With Duccio Trombardori.* New York: Semiotext(e).
——— 1977. *Discipline and Punish: The Birth of the Prison.* Harmondsworth: Penguin.
Frank, Barbara. 1995. Permitted and Prohibited Wealth: Commodity-Possessing Spirits, Economic Morals, and the Goddess Mami Wata in West Africa. *Ethnology* 34 (1): 331–346.
Frank, Thomas. 2008. *The Wrecking Crew: The American Right and the Lust for Power.* London: Harvill and Secker.
Funding Pressure on Universities Grows. 2015. *Universities South Africa: Mail & Guardian.* 24–30 July: 4.
Fury at Salary Gap among Varsity Chiefs. 2013. *The Times.* 16 April. www.thetimes.co.uk/tto/news/uk/scotland/article3740258.ece. Accessed on 5 August 2016.
Gaita, Raimond. 1998. Academics Must Fight: Management Jargon is Destroying Our Universities. *The Age* 24 August: 139.
Galbraith, Kenneth. 1975. *The Great Crash 1929.* Harmondsworth: Penguin.
Geertz, Clifford. 1973. *The Interpretation of Cultures.* London: Hutchinson.
George, Z. 2006. University Hunts for Campus Spy. *Daily Dispatch.* 15 November: 1.
Genetzky, Karl and Penelope Mashego and Anton Hyman. 2015. University Funding Grossly Inadequate. *Daily Dispatch.* 20 October: 5.
Geschiere, Peter. 2003. On Witch Doctors and Spin Doctors: The Role of "Experts" in African and American Politics. In Meyer, Birgit and Peter Pels (eds). *Magic and Modernity: Interfaces of Revelation and Concealment.* Stanford, CA: Stanford University Press: 159–182.
——— 1997. *The Modernity of Witchcraft: Politics and the Occult in Postcolonial Africa.* Charlottesville: University of Virginia Press.
——— 1992. Kinship, Witchcraft and "the Market": Hybrid Patterns in Cameroonian Societies. In Dilley (ed): 159–179.

Ginsberg, Benjamin. 2011. *The Fall of the Faculty: The Rise of the All-Administrative University and Why It Matters.* Oxford: Oxford University Press.
Giroux, Henry A. 2007. *The University in Chains: Confronting the Military-Industrial-Academic Complex.* Boulder and London: Paradigm.
Godelier, Maurice. 1996. *L'énigme du don.* Paris: Fayard.
Goldacre, Ben. 2012. *Bad Pharma.* London: Fourth Estate.
Goltz, Sonia M. 2010. Spiritual Power: The Internal, Renewable Social Power Source. *Journal of Management, Spirituality & Religion* 8 (4): 341–363.
Goodsell, Charles T. 1997. Administration as Ritual. *International Journal of Public Administration* 20 (4–5): 939–961.
Govender, Prega. 2016. Bonus for UniZulu's VC "Unjust". *Mail & Guardian.* 16–22 September: 5.
——— 2015. Debt Rockets to R3.9 bn – and Rising. *Sunday Times.* 20 September: 10.
——— 2011. Wits Ready to Spend Big to First Place. *Sunday Times.* 6 October: 13.
Gray, John. 1984. *Hayek on Liberty.* Oxford: Blackwell.
Greene, Francis, Brendan Loughridge and Tom Wilson. 1996. Models of University Organisation: From the Platonic Academy to the Commercial Mall. Extract from *The Management Information Needs of Academic Heads of Departments in Universities: A Critical Success Factors Approach.* British Library Research and Development Report 6252 1996. http://informationr.net/tdw/publ/hodsin/Chap02.html. Accessed on 12 December 2009.
Grossman, Jonathon. 2006. World Bank Thinking, World-Class Institution, Denigrated Workers. In Pithouse, Richard (ed). *Asinamali: University Struggles in Post-Apartheid South Africa.* Trenton and Asmara: Africa World Press: 93–105.
Gudeman, Stephen. 1992. Markets, Models and Morality: The Power of Practices. In Dilley (ed): 279–294.
——— 1998. The New Captains of Information. *Anthropology Today* 14 (1) February: 1–3.
Habib, Adam, Seán Morrow and Kristina Bentley. 2008. Academic Freedom, Institutional Autonomy and the Corporatised University in Contemporary South Africa. *Social Dynamics* 34 (2): 140–155.
Hall, Stuart. 2011. The Neo-Liberal Revolution. *Cultural Studies* 25 (6): 705–728.
Hare, Julie. 2013. Funding Cuts Play Out in Rankings. *The Australian.* 3 October. www.theaustralian.com.au/higher-education/funding-cuts-play-out-in-rankings/ . . . Accessed on 31 October 2013.
Harmon, Michael M. 2006. Business Research and Chinese Patriotic Poetry: How Competition for Status Distorts the Priority Between Research and Teaching in U.S. Business Schools. *Academy of Management Learning & Education* 5 (2): 234–243.
Hedges, Chris. 2009. Higher Education Gone Wrong: Universities Are Turning Into Corporate Drone Factories. http://www.alternet.org/story/133446/higher_education_gone_wrong%3A_universitie. Accessed on 23 July 2015.
Hedley, Steve. 2010. Managerialism in Irish Universities. *Irish Journal of Legal Studies* 1 (1): 117–141.
Hobsbawm, Eric. 1994. *The Age of Extremes: The Short Twentieth Century: 1914–1991.* London: Abacus.
Hochschild, Arlie Russell. 1983. *The Managed Heart: Commercialization of Human Feeling.* Berkeley and Los Angeles: University of California Press.

Howe, Leo. 2000. Risk, Ritual and Performance. *Journal of the Royal Anthropological Institute* 6: 63–79.

Hsu, Shih-Wei. 2003. Beyond Managerialism: Towards an Ethical Approach. Paper presented at Critical Management Studies (CMS) Conference, University of Lancaster. www.mngt.waikoto.ac.nz/ejrot/cmsconference/2003/proceedings/managementgoodness/Hsu.pdf.mi. Accessed on 14 May 2009.

Huge University Salaries Condemned. 2013. icScotland 20 April, 2013; cited in *University World News* 268. 22 April 2013. http://universityworldnews.com/article.php?story=20130419164241803. Accessed on 22 April 2013.

Ite, Uwem E. 2004. Return to Sender: Using the African Diaspora to Establish Academic Links. In Zeleza, Paul Tiyambe and Adebayo Olukoshi (eds). 2004a. *African Universities in the Twenty-First Century: Volume 1: Liberalisation and Internationalisation*. Dakar: CODESRIA: 1–18.

Jebens, Holger. 2004. Introduction: Cargo, Cult and Culture Critique. In Jebens, (ed): 1–13.

Jenvey, Nicola. 2013. Guy Standing – Higher Education and the Precariat Class. Keynote Address: Annual Learning and Teaching Higher Education Conference, Durban. *University World News* 290. 5 October 2013: 1. http://universityworldnews.com/article.php?story=20131002164809137. Accessed on 22 April 2013.

Johnson, Nevil. 1994. Dons in Decline. *20th Century British History* 5: 370–385.

Juran, Joseph M. 1990. *Juran on Planning for Quality*. London: Collier Macmillan.

Kaplan, David. 1997. Universities and the Business Sector: Strengthening the Links. *Social Dynamics* 23 (1): 68–70.

Kaplan, Martha. 2004. Neither Traditional nor Foreign: Dialogics of Power and Agency in Fijian History. In Jebens (ed): 59–78.

——— 2003. The Magical Power of the (Printed) Word. In Meyer and Pels (eds): 183–199.

Kettling of the Voices. 2015. Directed by Chester Yang. CY Films.

Klein, Naomi. 2000. *No Logo*. London: Harper Collins.

Kohl, Karl-Heinz. 2004. Mutual Hopes: German Money and the Tree of Wealth in East Flores. In Jebens (ed): 79–91.

Kron, Josh. 2013. Mahmood Mamdani – an Intellectual Leader in African Higher Education. *University World News* 264. 18 April 2013. http://universityworldnews.com/article.php?story=20130322131149861. Accessed on 18 April 2013.

Langer, Suzanne K. 1951. *Philosophy in a New Key*. New York: New American Library.

Leavitt, Stephen C. 2004. From "Cult" to Religious Conversion: The Case for Making Cargo Personal. In Jebens (ed): 170–186.

Le Mazier, J. 2012. *Luttes étudiantes en France. A bas l'excellence!* [Student Struggles in France. Down with Excellence!] *Vacarme* 61. 22 October. www.vacarme.org/article2194.html. Accessed on 10 November 2015.

Levi-Strauss, Claude. 1963. The Sorcerer and His Magic. In Levi-Strauss, Claude (ed). *Structural Anthropology*. New York: Basic Books: 167–185.

Lindstrom, Lamont. 2004. Cargo Cult at the Third Millennium. In Jebens (ed): 15–35.

——— 1993. *Cargo Cults: Strange Stories of Desire from Melanesia and Beyond*. Honolulu: University of Hawai'i Press.

Lipp, Doug. 2013. Inside Disney U. *Training*. 29 July. https://trainingmag.com/content/inside-disney-u. Accessed on 19 June 2017.

Lodge, David. 2008. *Deaf Sentence*. London: Harvill Secker.

London Metropolitan University: Strategic Plan 2015-2020. www.londonmet.ac.uk/about/our-university/strategic-plan-2015-2020. Accessed on 19 June 2017.

Louw, Alwyn. 2017. From Outputs to Impacts: The Changing Role of Institutions of Higher Education in Africa. *Mail & Guardian.* 4–10 August: 27.

——— 2010. Universities Ready for a Sea Change. *Mail & Guardian Higher Learning.* February: 2.

Lyotard, Jean-Francois. 1984. *The Postmodern Condition: A Report on Knowledge.* Manchester: Manchester University Press.

Luister [Listen]. 2015. www.youtube.com/watch?v=SF3rTBQTQk4. Accessed on 1 October 2015.

Macdonald, Stuart and Jacqueline Kam. 2007. Ring a Ring o' Roses: Quality Journals and Gamemanship in Management Studies. *Journal of Management Studies* 44 June: 641–654.

Macfarlane, David. 2013. Damning CHE Report Into University Performance. http://mg.co.za/article/2013-08-20-damning-che-report-into-university-performance. Accessed on 1 June 2016.

MacGregor, Karen. 2013. More University Inequality = More Academic Inequality. *University World News* 2490. 5 October. http://universityworldnews.com/article.php?story=20131005093204355. Accessed on 10 October 2013.

Macupe, Bongekile and Mogomotsi Magome. 2013. Universities Cannot Live on Fees Alone. *IOL News. Sunday Independent.* 1 September. www.iol.co.za/news/south-africa/universities-cannot-live-on-fees-alone-1.1571 . . . Accessed on 30 October 2013.

Makoni, Munyaradzi. 2016. Higher Education Struggles in an Emerging Democracy. *University World News* 435. 1 November. www.universityworldnews.com/article.php?story=20161101121837308. Accessed on 16 November 2016.

Maluleke, Tinyiko Sam. 2011. Lacklustre Means, Miniscule Output. *Mail & Guardian.* 29 April–5 May: 29.

Mamdani, Mahmood. 2007. *Scholars in the Marketplace: The Dilemmas of Neo-Liberal Reform at Makerere University, 1989–2005.* Dakar: CODESRIA.

Manifesto for Universities That Live Up to Their Missions. 2012. *Université en Débat.* www.univendebat.eu/manifeste/manifesto-for-universities-to-stand-up-for-their-missions. Accessed on 4 November 2015.

Marlowe, Christopher. 1928. *The Tragical History of Doctor Faustus.* Cambridge: Cambridge University Press.

Marseilles, Makki. 2013. Eight Major Universities Suspend Operations Over Cuts. *University World News* 290. 5 October. www.universityworldnews.com/article.php?story=20131004142134786. Accessed on 7 October 2013.

Martin, William G. 2005. Manufacturing the Homeland Security Campus and Cadre. *ACAS Bulletin* 70 (Spring): 1–7.

Marx, Karl. 1976. *Capital: Volume 1.* Harmondsworth: Penguin.

——— 1973. *Grundrisse.* Harmondsworth: Penguin.

——— 1852. The Eighteenth Brumaire of Louis Bonaparte. *Marx/ Engels Internet Archive.* www.marxists.org/archive/marx/works/1852/18th-brumaire/. Accessed on 17 March 2016.

Masien, Geoff. 2013. Higher Education Alarmed by A$2.3 Billion Cut. *University World News* 268. 16 April. http://universityworldnews.com/article.php?story=20130416090623139. Accessed on 29 April 2013.

Mbembe, Achille. 1997. The "Thing" & Its Doubles in Cameroonian Cartoons. In Barber, Karin (ed). *Readings in African Popular Culture*. Bloomington and Indianapolis: Indiana University Press; Oxford: James Currey: 151–163.
McDowell, Nancy. 1988. A Note on Cargo and Cultural Constructions of Change. *Pacific Studies* 11: 121–134.
McKenna, Sioux. 2011. Excellence Is Excellent. Isn't It? *Mail & Guardian: Getting Ahead*. 28 January–3 February: 3.
McKune, Craig. 2009. Tip-Toeing Around Vice-Chancellor Makgoba. *South African Journal of Science* 105 May–June: 163–164.
McPortland, Ben. 2015. French Students March Over Universities in Crisis. *The Local*. 16 October. www.thelocal.fr>french-students . . . Accessed on 12 October 2017.
Mentor, I. and P. Muschamp, P. Nicholls, J. Ozga and A. Pollard. 1997. *Work and Identity in the Primary School*. Philadelphia, PA: Open University Press.
Merton, Robert K. 1988. The Matthew Effect in Science, II: Cumulative Advantage and the Symbolism of Intellectual Property. *Isis* 79: 606–623.
Meyer, Birgit. 1998. The Power of Money: Politics, Occult Forces and Pentecostalism in Ghana. *African Studies Review* 14 (2): 15–37.
——— 1995: Translating the Devil: An African Appropriation of Pietist Protestantism: the Case of the Peki Ewe in Southeastern Ghana, 1847 – 1992. PhD dissertation, University of Amsterdam.
Mills, Nicolaus. 2012. The Corporatization of Higher Education. *Dissent*. Fall. www.dissentmagazine.org/article/the-corporatization-of-higher-education. Accessed on 16 May 2017.
Ministerial Statement on University Funding: 2012/3 and 2013/4. September 2011. South Africa. www.dhet.gov.za/LinkClick.aspx?fileticket=m6n/Mnw6zRg%3D. Accessed on 31 October 2013.
Ministry of Education. February 2004. South Africa. A New Funding Framework: How Government Grants Are Allocated to Public Higher Education Institutions. www.docstoc.com>Art & Literature>Childrens Literature. Accessed on 31 October 2013.
Moja, Teboho. 2004. Policy Responses to Global Transformation by African Higher Education Systems. In Zeleza and Olukoshi (eds). 2004a: 21–41.
Moore, Henrietta and Todd Sanders. 2001. Magical Interpretations and Material Realities: An Introduction. In Moore and Sanders (eds): 1–27.
Moore, Sally F. and Barbara Myerhoff. 1977. Introduction: Secular Ritual: Forms and Meanings. In Moore and Myerhoff (eds). *Secular Ritual*. Assen/Amsterdam: Van Gorken: 3–24.
Morris, Andrew J. and Daniel C Feldman. 1996. The Dimensions, Antecedents and Consequences of Emotional Labor. *The Academy of Management Review* 21 (4): 986–1010.
Morrow, Seán and Nwabisa Vokwana. 2004. "Oh Hurry to the River": The Meaning of uMamlambo Models in the Tyumie Valley, Eastern Cape. *Kronos* 30. November: 184–199.
Muswaka, Wendy, 2010. Interview with Sekuru, Harare.[1]
——— 2010. Interview with anonymous respondent, Alice, South Africa.
——— 2009. Interview with Ruvimbo Masango.

Mwinzi, Dinah. 2004. The Impact of Cost-Sharing Policy on the Living Conditions of Students in Kenyan Public Universities. In Zeleza and Olukoshi (eds). 2004a: 140–156.

Nafukho, Frederick Muyia. 2004. The Market Model of Financing State Universities in Kenya: Some Innovative Lessons. In Zeleza and Olukoshi (eds). 2004a: 126–139.

Nakkazi, Esther. 2016. President Orders Indefinite Shutdown of Top University. *University World News* 436. 4 November. www.universityworldnews.com/article.php?story=20161104143813146. Accessed on 20 November 2016.

Nash, Andrew. 2006. Restructuring South African Universities. In Pithouse (ed): 1–10.

Neave, Guy. 1990. On Preparing for Markets: Trends in Higher Education in Western Europe, 1988–1990. *European Journal of Education* 25 (2): 195–222.

Neave, Guy and Frans A. Van Vught 1991. *Prometheus Bound: The Changing Relationship Between Government and Higher Education in Western Europe.* Oxford: Pergamon Press.

Newbrook, Carl. 2005. *Ducks in a Row: An A-Z of Offlish.* London: Short Books.

Niane, D. T. 1965. *Sundiata: An Epic of Old Mali.* Harlow: Longman.

Niehaus, Isak. 2001a. *Witchcraft, Power and Politics: Exploring the Occult in the South African Lowveld.* Cape Town: David Philip; London: Pluto.

——— 2001b. Witchcraft in the New South Africa: From Colonial Superstition to Postcolonial Reality? In Moore and Sanders (eds): 184–205.

Nilsen, Rodney, 2004. Don't Do What Australia Has Done. *Quadrant.* November. https://scholars.uow.edu.au.display>p. Accessed 9 December 2017.

No Funds for Swazi University. 2012. *Sunday Independent.* 1 January: 2.

Nóvoa, Antonio. 2014. What Is Educational Research For? Paper presented at ECER (European Conference on Educational Research) Porto.

Nyaigotti-Chacha, Chacha. 2004. Public Universities, Private Funding: The Challenges in East Africa. In Zeleza and Olukoshi (eds). 2004a: 94–107.

Nyamnjoh, Francis B. 2001. Delusions of Development and the Enrichment of Witchcraft Discourses in the Cameroon. In Moore and Sanders (eds): 28–49.

O'Day, Rory. 1974. Intimidation Rituals. *Reactions to Reform.* www.intimidationrituals.org/OriginalArticle.html. Accessed on 5 August 2015.

Obasi, Isaac N. and Eboh, Eric C. 2004. The Cost-Sharing Dilemma in Nigerian Universities: Empirical Lessons for Policy Adjustment. In Zeleza and Olukoshi (eds). 2004a: 157–186.

"Obscene" Pay of Varsity Heads under Scrutiny. 2015. *Sunday Times.* 8 November: 10.

Okri, Ben. 1992. *The Famished Road.* Claremont: David Philip.

Olssen, Mark and Michael A. Peters. 2005. Neoliberalism, Higher Education and the Knowledge Economy: From the Free Market to Knowledge Capitalism. *Journal of Education Policy* 20 (3): 313–345.

Orr, Liesl. 1997. Globalisation and Universities: Towards "the Market University"? *Social Dynamics* 23: 42–67.

Otto, Ton. 2004. Work, Wealth and Knowledge: Enigmas of Cargoist Identifications. In Jebens (ed): 209–226.

Ozga, Jenny. 2011. The Entrepreneurial Researcher: Re-formations of Identity in the Research Marketplace. *International Studies in Sociology of Education* 8 (2): 143–153.

Parish, Jane. 2001. Black Market, Free Market: Anti-Witchcraft Shrines and Fetishes Among the Akan. In Moore and Sanders (eds): 118–135.
Parker, Martin. 2014. University, Ltd: Changing a Business School. *Organization* 21: 281–292.
Parker, Martin and David Jary. 1995. The McUniversity: Organization, Management and Academic Subjectivity. *Organization* 2: 319–338.
Peck, Jamie and Adam Tickell. 2007. Conceptualizing Neoliberalism, Thinking Thatcherism. In Leitner, Helga and Jamie Peck and Eric S. Sheppard (eds). *Contesting Neoliberalism: Urban Frontiers*. New York and London: Guilford: 26–50.
Pels, Peter. 2003. Introduction. In Meyer and Pels (eds): 1–38.
Pendlebury, James and Lucien van der Walt. 2006. Neoliberalism, Bureaucracy and Resistance at Wits University. In Pithouse (ed): 79–92.
Peters, Michael A. 1992. Performance and Accountability in "Post-Industrial Society": the Crisis of British Universities. *Studies in Higher Education* 17 (2): 123–139.
Peters, Tom and Robert J. Waterman. 2006. *In Search of Excellence: Lessons from America's Best-Run Companies*. London: Bloomsbury.
Pithouse, Richard. 2006. Introduction. In Pithouse (ed.): xv–xxviii.
Poole, Steven. 2006. *Unspeak: Words Are Weapons*. Great Britain: Abacus.
Power, Michael. 1997. *The Audit Society: Rituals of Verification*. Oxford: Oxford University Press.
——— 1994. *The Audit Explosion*. London: Demos.
Preston, Peter. 1992. Modes of Economic-Theoretical Engagement. In Dilley (ed): 57–78.
Price, David H. 2011. *Weaponizing Anthropology*. Petrolia: Counterpunch.
Quirk, Tom, Tim Duncan and Richard De Latour. 1990. The Clever Country as Cargo Cult: National Needs and Higher Education. *Quadrant* 34 (10): 45–50.
Ramphele, Mamphela. 2008. *Laying Ghosts to Rest: Dilemmas of the Transformation in South Africa*. Tafelberg: Cape Town.
——— 1998. SA Must Invest in Intellectual Capital. *Sunday Times*. May 24.
Readings, Bill. 1996. *The University in Ruins*. Cambridge and London: Harvard University Press.
Rensburg, Ihron. 2010. Reflections on the New Generation University. *Mail & Guardian*. May 3.
Ritzer, George. 2015. *The McDonaldization of Society*. Los Angeles, London, New Delhi, Singapore, Washington, DC: Sage.
——— 1999. *Enchanting a Disenchanted World: Revolutionising the Means of Consumption*. London and New Delhi: Pine Forge Press.
——— 1996. McUniversity in the Postmodern Consumer Society. *Quality in Higher Education* 2 (3): 185–199.
——— 1983. The "McDonaldization" of Society. *Journal of American Culture* 6 (1): 100–107. www.researchgate.net/. . . /227981832_The_McDonaldization_of_Society. Accessed on 28 August 2017.
The Role of the University in a Changing World. 2010. Office of the President, Harvard: Address to Royal Irish Academy. Trinity College, Dublin. www.harvard.edu/president/speech/2010/role-university-changing-world. Accessed on 17 May 2017.
Roper, Ian. 2004. Managing Quality in Public Services: Some Distinct Implications for the Re-organisation of Work. In Dibben, Wood and Roper (eds): 120–136.

Ruth, Damian. 2001. Academic Workload, Performance Appraisal and Staff Development: Issues of Quantification, Criteria, Perception and Affect. *Acta Academica* 33 (1): 194–216.

Ryan, Desmond. 1998. The Thatcher Government's Attack on Higher Education in Historical Perspective. *New Left Review* 27: 3–32.

Saccarelli, Emanuele, 2011. The Intellectual in Question. *Cultural Studies* 25 (6): 757–782.

Sahlins, Marshall. 1972. *Stone Age Economics*. Aldine: Chicago.

Sanders, Todd. 2001. Save Our Skins: Structural Adjustment, Morality and the Occult in Tanzania. In Moore and Sanders (eds): 160–184.

Saul, John S. 1999. Magical Market Realism. *Transformation* 38: 49–67.

Saunders, Malcom. 2006. The Madness and Malady of Managerialism. *Quadrant* 50 (3) March: 9–17. https:www.uow.edu.au>Saunders_article. Accessed 9 April 2010.

Schieffelin, Edward L. 1985. Performance and the Cultural Construction of Reality. *American Ethnologist* 12 (4): 707–724.

Schklovsky, Viktor. 1965. Art as Technique. In Paul Olsen (ed). *Russian Formalist Criticism: Four Essays*. Lincoln: University of Nebraska Press: 3–24.

Schmoll, Pamela G. 1993. Black Stomachs, Beautiful Stones: Soul-Eating Among Hausa in Niger. In Comaroffs (eds): 193–220.

Seddon, Terry. 1996. The Principle of Choice in Policy Research. *Journal of Education Policy* 11 (2).

Sennett, Richard. 1998. *The Corrosion of Character: The Personal Consequences of Work in the New Capitalism*. New York and London: Norton.

Sharp, Lesley A. 2000. The Commodification of the Body and Its Parts. *Annual Review of Anthropology* 29: 287–328.

Shattock, Michael. 2008. The Change From Public to Private Governance of British Higher Education: Its Consequences for Higher Education Policy Making 1980–2006. *Higher Education Quarterly* 62 (3). http://onlinelibrary.wiley.com/doi/10.1111/j.1468-2273.2008.00392.x/full. Accessed on 11 April 2011.

Shaw, Rosalind. 2001. Cannibal Transformations: Colonialism and Commodification in the Sierra Leone Hinterland. In Moore and Sanders (eds): 50–70.

Shivji, Issa G. 2005. Wither University: Education as Market Fantasy or Education as Public Good? *Quarterly Review of Education and Training in South Africa* 1 (12): 34–37.

Shore, Chris and Susan Wright. 1999. Audit Culture and Anthropology: Neoliberalism in British Higher Education. *Journal of the Royal Anthropological Institute* 5: 557–573.

Sikhakhane, Jabulani. 2016. Higher Education, Low Returns. *Sunday Times: Business Times*. 21 February: 11.

Simmel, Georg. 1978. *The Philosophy of Money*. London: Routledge.

Slaughter, Sheila. 1990. *The Higher Learning and High Technology: Dynamics of Higher Education Policy Formulation*. Albany: State University of New York Press.

Slow Science Manifesto. 2010. Slow Science Academy. Berlin. www.http://slow-science.org. Accessed on 11 November 2015.

So "Browned-Out" by Work That You Look Forward to a Heart Attack. 2015. *Sunday Times*. 20 September: 19.

Southall, Roger and Julian Cobbing. 2001. From Racial Liberalism to Corporate Authoritarianism: The Shell Affair and the Assault on Academic Freedom in South Africa. *Social Dynamics* 27 (2): 1–42.

Speckman, Asha. 2016. Call to Almost Double Funds Spent on Higher Education. *Sunday Times: Business Times.* 21 February: 3.
Standing, Guy. 2011. *The Precariat: The New Dangerous Class.* Huntingdon: Bloomsbury.
——— 1999. *Global Labour Flexibility: Seeking Distributive Justice.* London: Macmillan.
Stewart, Peter. 2007. Re-Envisioning the Academic Profession in the Shadow of Corporate Managerialism. *CODESRIA: Journal of Higher Education in Africa* 5 (4): 131–147.
Steyn, Lisa. 2016. Varsities Plagued by "Cost Disease". *Mail & Guardian Business.* 9–15 September: 1.
Stiglitz, Joseph. 2004. *The Roaring Nineties.* Harmondsworth: Penguin.
SU Management Responds to *Luister* video. 2015. August 22. www.sun.ac.za/english/Lists/news.DispForm.aspx?ID=2833. Accessed on 13 October 2015.
Tambiah, Stanley Jeyaraja. 1985. *Culture, Thought and Social Action: An Anthropological Perspective.* Cambridge, MA and London: Harvard University Press.
Taussig, Michael. 2003. Viscerality, Faith and Skepticism: Another Theory of Magic. In Meyer and Pels (eds): 272–306.
——— 1997. *The Magic of the State.* London: Routledge.
Taylor, Paul. 2003. Humboldt's Rift: Managerialism in Education and Complicit Intellectuals. *European Political Science* Autumn 3: 1–7.
Thomas, Adèle. 2009. Ethics and Morals Suffer. *Mail & Guardian: Higher Learning.* February: 4.
Thornton, Margaret. 2004. Corrosive Leadership (Or Bullying by Another Name): A Corollary of the Corporatised Academy? *Australian Journal of Labour Law* 1 (2): 161–184.
Thornton, Robert James. 2007. Marginal Utilities, Time and the "Hidden Hand" of Zombies. Paper delivered at European Conference on African Studies. African Studies Centre, University of Leiden. (Subsequently published as Marginal Utilities, Time and Zombies. *African Ethnologist* 34 (3): 437–439.)
Tolkien, J. R. R. 1966. *The Tolkien Reader.* New York: Ballantine.
Transformation at UCT. University of Cape Town. www.uct.ac.za/about/transformation/. Accessed on 17 June 2017.
Trice, Harrison M. and Janice M. Beyer. 1984. Studying Organisational Cultures Through Rites and Ceremonials. *Academy of Management Review* 9 (4): 653–669.
UJ's Winning Brand Breeds Brand Champions. 2010. *Mail & Guardian.* 4–10 June: 41.
University of Chicago: The Office of the President. https://president.uchicago.edu. Accessed on 12 July 2017.
University of Michigan: Mission Statement. https://president.umich.edu/about/mission. Accessed on 12 July 2017.
University of Stellenbosch. 2010. Performance Management Policy and Strategy. www0sun.ac.za/ . . . /PM0301-Performance-Management-Policy-And-Strategy. Accessed on 23 December 2010.
Vale, Peter. 2011. Higher Education's Lessons Go Unlearned. *Mail & Guardian: Getting Ahead.* November–December: 3.
——— 2009. Servants or Savants. *Mail & Guardian: Getting Ahead.* February: 1, 4.
——— 2004. Transformation in Higher Education Is Long Overdue. *Mail & Guardian Lessons from the Field: A Decade of Democracy.* November: 11.

Vally, Salim. 2007. Higher Education in South Africa: Market Mill or Public Good? *Council for the Development of Social Science Research in South Africa* 5 (1): 17–28.

Van Gunsteren, H. R. 1976. *The Quest for Control: A Critique of the Rational-Central-Rule Approach in Public Affairs*. Chichester: John Wiley.

Vision and Mission Statement. University of the Witwatersrand. www.wits.ac.za/about-wits/governance/strategic-leadership/. Accessed on 16 May 2017.

Warnier, Jean-Pierre. 1993. The King as a Container in the Cameroonian Grassfields. *Paideuma* 39: 303–319.

Wallis, Malcolm. 2004. Public Administration and the Management of Socio-Economic Development in Developing Countries: Some Trends and Comparisons. In Dibben, Wood and Roper (eds): 220–236.

Waruru, Maina. 2013. Thriving Universities Compete for Students. *University World News* 290. 31 August: 3. www.universityworldnews.com/article.php?story=20131002162621160. Accessed on 11 September 2013.

Weber, Max. 1968. *Economy and Society*. Totowa, NJ: Bedminster.

—— 1965. *The Sociology of Religion*. London: Metheun.

—— 1948. Science as a Vocation, In Gerth, H.H. and C. Wright Mills (eds). *From Marx to Weber: Essays in Sociology*. Routledge: London: 129 – 156.

—— 1921. *The Rational and Social Foundations of Music*. Carbondale: Southern Illinois University Press.

Webster, Eddie and Sarah Mosoetsa. 2001. At the Chalk Face: Managerialism and the Changing Academic Workplace 1995–2001. http://chet.org.za/webfm_send/318. Accessed on 14 April 2009. (A later version of this article was published in 2002 in *Transformation* 48: 59–82.)

Weick, Karl E. 1979. Cognitive Processes in Organizations. In Shaw, B.M. (ed). *Research in Organizations* (Vol. 1). Greenwich, CT: JAI Press: 41–73.

Weissmann, Jordan. 2015. Is It Time to Tax Harvard's Endowment? www.slate.com/articles/business/moneybox/2015/09/harvard_yale_stanford_en . . . Accessed on 6 June 2017.

White, Luise. 2000. *Speaking With Vampires: Rumor and History in Colonial Africa*. Berkeley, Los Angeles and London: University of California Press.

Wild, Sarah. 2015. Presenteeism Is the New Office Plague. *Mail & Guardian*. 13–19 November: 19.

Wilson, Monica Hunter. 1936. *Reaction to Conquest*. London: Oxford.

Wilson, Tom. 1991. The Proletarianisation of Academic Labour. *Industrial Relations Journal* 22 (4): 250–262.

Wood, Felicity with Michael Lewis. 2007. *The Extraordinary Khotso: Millionaire Medicine Man of Lusikisiki*. Johannesburg: Jacana.

—— 2004. Interview with Lala Yako.

Wood, Felicity. 2015a. Spirits in the Marketplace: The Market as a Site of the Occult in the South and West African Supernatural and Contemporary Capitalist Cosmologies. *Folklore* 126 (3): 283–300.

—— 2015b. Secrecy, Publicity and Power: Strategies of Occult Practitioners and University Managers. *Southern African Journal for Folklore Studies* 25: 46–57.

—— 2014a. Wealth-giving Mermaid Women and the Malign Magic of the Market: Contemporary Oral Accounts of the South African Mamlambo. In Stephanos Stephanides and Stavros Karayanni (eds). *Vernacular Worlds, Cosmopolitan Imagination*. Amsterdam: Brill Cross/Cultures Series: 59–85.

——— 2014b. Kinship, Collegiality and Witchcraft: South African Oral Accounts of the Supernatural and the Occult Aspects of Contemporary Academia. *Tydskrif* 51 (1): 150–162.

——— 2013. Faustian Pacts and False Promises: The Mamlambo and the Market University. *Southern African Journal for Folklore Studies* 23 (1): 156–172.

——— 2010a. Occult Innovations in Higher Education: Corporate Magic and the Mysteries of Managerialism. *Prometheus: Critical Studies in Innovation* 28 (3): 227–244.

——— 2010b. Sorcery in the Academy. *Southern African Journal for Folklore Studies* 1: 4–28.

——— 2002. Interview with Anele Mabongo.

Wood, R. J. 2014. Business, State and Society in the Western Cape: 1960–1990. PhD Dissertation. Nelson Mandela Metropolitan University.

Zeleza, Paul Tiyambe and Olukoshi Adebayo. 2004a. Introduction: The Struggle for African Universities and Knowledges. In Zeleza and Olukoshi (eds). 2004a: 1–18.

——— 2004b. *Conclusion: The African University in the Twenty-first Century. African Universities in the Twenty-first Century. Volume II: Knowledge and Society.* Dakar: CODESRIA. 2004b: 595–618.

Zwane, Nokuthula and Mkwananzi, Masabata. 2017. Students Protest Against Residence Conditions. *Cape Times.* 21 April: 4.

Note

1 Not the respondent's real name. The respondent is a Harare-based n'anga (medicine man). Many n'angas are called "Sekuru". This is a term of respect, comparable to "father".

Index

academic capitalism 58, 156
academic collegiality, notion of 95, 163
accountability 1, 51, 52, 67, 69, 71, 81, 82, 98, 99, 108, 111, 112, 113, 121, 128, 149, 150, 178, 179, 182; mercantile nature of 68
agents of redemption 5, 97, 139–140
alibis 181–182
Amsler, Sarah 52, 82, 103, 132, 136, 168, 192
apartheid 17, 50, 52, 88, 91n10, 141n3, 176n4, 183, 185, 187n8, 189, 194
Appadurai, Arjun 27, 66
Ashforth, Adam 53, 129
Atkinson, Dan 63, 64, 65
audit/audits 46, 68, 79, 81–83, 85, 90, 94, 98, 106, 108, 110, 111, 112, 114, 119, 121, 128, 131, 137, 140, 157, 168, 169, 184, 192; culture 80, 81, 83, 108, 110, 111, 157; fear 79–81; and harm 137; *see also* fear; performance, audits and; performance indicators; surveillance; zombies

Baatjies, Ivor G. 44, 62, 72n2, 159
Bakhtin, Mikhail 195, 196n7
balanced scorecard 82, 102
Ball, Stephen J. 82, 108
Barry, Jim 47, 75, 78, 83
Beckmann, Andrea 62, 63, 77, 82, 123, 156
benchmark, term 98
Bentley, Kristina 46, 54n5, 85, 91n11, 154, 167, 169, 171
Bertelsen, Eve 8, 17, 32, 36, 37, 43, 45, 46, 60, 61, 62, 72n2, 98, 99, 104, 167, 168, 179, 183
Beyer, Janice M. 57, 59, 87, 88, 93–95, 110, 117, 118, 120, 128

Blair, Tony 63, 65, 194
Bok, Derek 18, 23, 42, 47, 130, 164, 165
brand: Disney 10; protecting the 85–87; universities and corporate brand names 10, 23–24, 42, 104, 135, 188
Brehony, Ken 75
Buchbinder, Howard 18, 21, 22, 39n2, 45, 46
bullying 75–77, 138, 175

calculability 23, 103; fetishism of numbers 135
capitalism 2; and occult 4, 28–35; power of- 38–39; and higher education 42–45; *see also* commodity fetishism; consumerism; free market; hidden hand; mamlambo, seductive aspects and capitalism; market; money
cargo cults 69–70, 73n7; cargo 70–71, 73n8; corporate universities 5, 68–72; knowledge as 71; label 69; performance 111; term 69, 73n7
Chandler, John 47, 75, 78, 83
Chang, Ha-Joon 25, 43, 54n1, 61, 63–65
Chetty, Nithaya 48, 72n2, 85–87, 91n5, 95, 117, 144, 146, 176n8
chikwambo 30, 143, 161–162
CIA (Central Intelligence Agency) 18, 166
Clark, Heather 47, 75, 78, 83
Cobbing, Julian 20n7, 60, 75, 78, 85, 102, 103, 138, 145, 146, 167, 169
collegiality, notion of 57, 95, 163
Collini, Stefan 8, 40n3, 47, 52, 60, 132–133
colonisation 96, 105, 111, 122, 153, 160n3, 171, 181, 184–185, 193; silent 184

Comaroff, Jean 2, 6–7, 14, 26, 30, 31, 53, 92, 96, 106, 133, 153, 161, 171–172, 181–182
Comaroff, John 6–7, 14, 26, 30, 53, 92, 96, 106, 133, 153, 161, 171–172, 181–182
commodification 29, 102, 135; creeping 172, 192; of higher education 4, 23–25, 44–45; of human bodies 153; of human spirit 158; of knowledge 38, 65–66, 180; of labour 153, 158–159; of magic 27; model of 173; neoliberal approach 2, 25, 50, 184; occult and 160n2; in occult economies 153; of public services 102
commodity fetishism 66, 135
community involvement 16–17
competition 2, 35, 129–134, 138, 196n6; *see also* league tables; Merton's Matthew effect; performance indicators; rankings; ratings
consultants 5, 48, 66, 69, 79, 80, 87, 94, 125–126, 139, 140, 165
consumerism: higher education and 44–45, 138, 171; *see also* consumption
consumption 138, 171–172; contracts 91n12, 165, 170 (*see also* fear; precariat); non-renewal of 153, 163, 170; and NPM 68; short-term/temporary 89, 169; *see also* consumerism; neocolonialism
Cooper, Charlie 62, 63, 77, 82, 123, 156
corporate authoritarianism 87, 190
corporate drones 125
corporate loyalty, notion of 86
corporate power words 97–105, 177–181; *see also* excellence; mantras; mission, term; quality; ritual/rituals
corporate social responsibility 16
corporate university 19n2; term 1–2; corporate "universities": Disney University and Hamburger University 10
Corrosion of Character, The 164
Cowen, Robert 44, 109, 124n2
Crow, Michael 15, 17–18

Dalton, Doug 70, 122–123
Deaf Sentence 147, 170
Deem, Rosemary 40n3, 60, 68, 81, 109, 127, 130, 136, 169, 170, 171, 179
defamiliarisation 192–193; Recovery 195n5

Delphic oracle 147–148
depression 49, 167–172, 193; brown-out 159
derision: corporatised universities and 193–195; cult of publication 195–196n6
de Rosny, Éric 53, 128
désexcellence 191, 195n3
Desjeux, Dominique 53, 93
development 172–173, 181, 183, 187n5, 187n7
Dibben, Pauline 22, 72n6, 77, 91n3, 169
Dilley, Roy 26, 28, 53
Discipline and Punish 140
disillusion 172–174
dissent: corporatised universities and 189–192; *see also* protests staff
Duncan, Jane 54n3, 85, 86, 91n5, 91n11, 145, 146, 147

efficiency, term 99, 111, 178, 192
ekong 30, 160n3
Elliott, Larry 63, 64, 65
emotional labour 113, 158–159, 171
ethics 98, 100, 182; Ethical Clearance Certificate 164; *see also* sacrifices, ethical
excellence 82; concept of 191; term 98, 100, 101, 102, 103, 180

familiars 188; corporate 103–107; managerial 105; state 105; witchcraft 163
Famished Road, The 26
Faustus 14, 167, 174; Faustian pact: corporatised universities and managerial staff 166–167, 174–175
FBI (Federal Bureau of Investigation) 166
fear: audits 79–81, 90, 128, 169; contracts 89, 169; disciplinary measures 76–79; -of future 90; humiliation 87–88; insecurity 52–53; -of managerialism 74–76; protecting the brand 85–87; scrutiny 81–85; the uncanny 89–91; *see also* brand, protecting the; corporate loyalty, notion of; depression; surveillance
fees 46–47, 54n4, 55, 86, 183, 187n6, 190
Fees Must Fall 49, 160n7, 187n6, 190
Fisiy, Cyprian F. 31, 35, 53, 139, 153, 154

214 Index

flagship 98
Foucault, Michel 63, 83, 140, 173
Frank, Barbara 29, 53, 162, 163
free enterprise: concept of 32; notion of 54n1
free market 172; capitalist ethos 61, 91; capitalist pressure 3, 4, 7, 31, 189; capitalist principles 180, 185; commodification and vulnerability 172; constraints of 32; deceptive discourse of 32; hidden hand of 34; higher education and 42–44; phrase 32; setting rules of game 185; *see also* capitalism; hidden hand
funding: budget cuts 22, 47, 80, 163; euphemism 177; funding cuts 39n2, 45–50, 54n3, 170; third-stream 44

Galbraith, Kenneth 100–101
Geertz, Clifford 90–91, 93, 94, 105, 114, 115, 188
Geschiere, Peter 6, 7, 12, 19n4, 26, 27, 29, 30, 31, 35, 40n8, 53, 66, 84, 89, 93, 125, 127–129, 136, 138, 139, 141n3, 142, 143, 144, 153, 154, 160n2, 178, 188, 193
Ginsberg, Benjamin 48, 55n9, 72n2, 135, 144, 146
Giroux, Henry A. 18, 21, 24, 64, 72n2, 74, 85, 156, 157, 165, 166, 168, 189, 190, 192, 195
globalisation 130, 185; of academic workplace 167; and neoliberalism 50, 54n1; process of 53–54n1
Goodsell, Charles T. 76, 92, 93, 94, 96, 98, 100, 105, 106, 110, 112, 115–116, 118–120, 149
Greene, Francis 1, 54n3, 55n8, 79, 127, 130
griot (oral poet) 12
Grossman, Jonathon 24, 89–90
Gudeman, Stephen 18, 124n2, 134, 141n5, 146, 157, 193

Habib, Adam 46, 54n4, 85, 91n11, 154, 167, 169, 171
HAIs (historically advantaged institutions) 9, 16, 46, 51, 52, 131, 133, 189
Hard Times 158
HBIs (historically black institutions) 9, 46
HDIs (historically disadvantaged institutions) 9, 46, 49, 51–52, 131, 133, 136, 183, 189

HEFCE (Higher Education Funding Council for England) 78, 147
HEIs (Higher Education Institutions) 79
hidden hand 34
Hillyard, Sam 40n3, 60, 68, 81, 127, 130, 136, 169, 170, 171, 179
Hobsbawm, Eric 34, 49
Hochschild, Arlie Russell 113, 158
Howe, Leo 59, 120–122, 124n5
human resources 153–155; human capital 58, 159; term 153–154
Human Sciences Research Council (HSRC) 85
Human Terrain Teams 166
HWIs (historically white institutions) 9, 46

illness: concealed 170; physical, emotional and psychological 167–172; *see also* depression; disillusion; emotional labour; presenteeism; spiritual resources
immiseration 170
incentive 165; competitiveness and greed 133, 134, 136, 137; as euphemism 177; and market university 39n2; negative 77, 136, 178; paradoxical 178; productivity 40n2
Individual Performance Assessments (IPAs) 82, 112, 134
innovation 2, 180–181
Intelligence Community Scholars Programme 166
International Monetary Fund (IMF) 28, 32, 35, 50, 62, 184; Unholy Trinity 43, 54n1; *see also* International Monetary Fund; World Trade Organisation
intimidation 52, 74–80, 91, 149, 175
inyanga 20n9, 26, 40n9, 126, 137, 141n3, 143, 144
Ivory Tower 187n6

Jary, David 34, 44, 47
jealousy, term 14, 129
Jebens, Holger 70, 73n7
Journal of Management, Spirituality and Religion 158
Jude the Obscure 15

Kafka, Franz 107n3, 148, 149, 175
Kam, Jacqueline 133, 141n4, 183, 193, 195n6

Kaplan, Martha 28, 69, 73n7, 103, 105, 111, 188
Kettling of the Voices 86, 187n6
key performance areas 82, 108
Khan, Fazel 85, 145, 146
Khotso 20n9, 26, 40n9, 137, 141n3, 143, 144, 151, 152, 176n6, 187n10
kinship, hazards of 127–129
Klein, Naomi 23, 24, 165
knowledge: commodification casualty 45; economy, myth of 61–66
knowledge economy cargo cults 71; commodification 45; competitiveness 129; consumerism 138; and corporate "universities" 10; and market 18, 25, 183; and neoliberalism 49; *see also* mythologies, myth of knowledge economy

league tables 132; obsession with 135; *see also* competition; rankings
Le Mazier, Julie 91n12, 191
Lodge, David 15, 147, 170
Lord of the Rings, The 84
Loughridge, Brendan 1, 54n3, 55n8, 79, 127, 130, 171
Louw, Alwyn 8, 15, 59, 62, 183, 187n3
Luister [Listen] 40n6, 86, 91n6, 91n7, 142

Macdonald, Stuart 133, 141n4, 183, 193, 195n6
Mamdani, Mahmood 18, 54n5, 62, 72n2, 168, 176n5, 185, 187n7, 187n9
Mami Wata 26, 29, 40n7, 162, 163
mamlambo 7, 138, 176n2, 186; blood sacrifices 138, 161–162; insatiable desires 162–163; in marketplace 26; occult economies 7; ownership of 27, 40n90, 161–163, 166–167, 175; pact with 171–172, 174, 187n10; and restructured universities 161–176; seductive aspects and capitalism 26; suffering 167–174; temporary wealth 186, 187n10; ultimate disaster 174; *see also* Khotso; sacrifices; ukuthwala
managerialism 2, 5, 19n3; dark side 89, 175; delays and deferments 150; discourse of 97–104, 177–181; management by stress 169; manipulation and deception 150–152; maze of 148–150, 188; mystery and publicity 142–146; *see also* Faustus, Faustian pact; fear

Manifesto for Universities That Live Up to Their Missions 191
mantras: corporate jargon 99; managerial 97; neoliberal 59
market: apotheosis of 35–37; magic of the 21–41, 68, 97, 123, 151, 186; market reputation 86; market university 21–25; nouveau market fetishism 21; occult aspects of 26–39; and the spirit world 25–26, 29; *see also* capitalism; commodification; free market, higher education and; neoliberalism
Marketing and Communication 57, 144
Marlowe, Christopher 14, 167, 174
Marx, Karl 33, 37, 38, 58, 66, 101, 142, 155–156, 185, 186
massification 23, 46, 48, 54n4, 170; cost-cutting and 48; rationalisation and 54n4; *see also* McUniversity
Massive Open Online Courses (MOOCs) 45
Matthew Effect 183, 189
Mbeki, Thabo 35, 41n13
McDonaldisation 23
McDonald's 10, 23, 43, 165
McDonald's Hamburger University 10
McUniversity 23–24
Merrett, Christopher 48, 85–87, 91n5, 95, 117, 144–146, 176n8
Merton's Matthew Effect 183, 189
Meyer, Birgit 26, 31, 188
mission, term 98, 103–104
mission statements 15–17, 103–107, 191; *see also* community involvement; corporate social responsibility; mission, term; Manifesto for Universities That Live up to Their Missions
modernisation 97; process of 61; of public sector 20n6, 67; term 180; UK academia 179; *see also* New Public Management (NPM)
Moloch and Mammon 35–39; pursuit of Mammon 104
money: mystical, magical aspects of 33, 37–38; power of 33; rain money 151–152; religion and 37–38; restructured universities and cash-nexus 182; transitory 185–186; universities and lack of 46, 48–49; US dollar 33; value for 80, 99, 104, 192; wind money 186; *see also* capitalism; mamlambo; Moloch and Mammon; occult economies; wealth-giving magic

Moore, Barbara G. 92, 93, 100, 119
Moore, Henrietta L. 2, 7, 26, 29, 30, 133
Morrow, Seán 46, 54n5, 85, 91n11, 154, 167, 169, 171
Morrow, Seán and Nwabisa Vokwana 161
Mosoetsa, Sarah 8, 75, 91n3, 158, 167–171, 176n3
muti trade 7, 158
Myerhoff, Sally S. 92, 93, 100, 119
mythologies: corporate fabulation 57–61; myth of commodity fetishism 66; myth of knowledge economy 5, 61–66; old myths and new traditions 57–59; real-world 59–61

n'angas 126, 143, 144, 211n1
National Commission on Higher Education (NCHE) 133
National Party 50, 55–56n15, 194; see also apartheid
National Plan for Higher Education 145
National Security Education Program 166
National Tertiary Education Staff Union 145
neocolonialism 34, 181, 184, 193; activities associated with 111, 117, 128, 136, 169, 182; as consumption 171–172
neoliberalism 2, 3, 7–9, 18, 21, 22, 24–25, 31, 36, 39, 42, 45, 183–185; deceptive, flawed nature of 25, 36–37, 49, 57; and globalization 50, 54n1; and higher education 42–44; inequality and 184; myths of – 57–61; opposition and alternatives 190–195; and political and economic power 42, 43; preoccupation with 109; rise of, growth of, influence of 7, 34, 43–46, 49, 50, 54n1, 56n15, 68; in South Africa 50–53; and status quo 96
Newbrook, Carl 57, 177
new-generation universities 59, 139, 180, 181, 187n3
New Labour 64, 68
New Public Management (NPM) 68, 69, 72–73n6, 102, 180; and universities 46, 69, 130, 179
ngangas 12, 84, 126
Niehaus, Isak 19n4, 20n5, 40n9, 127, 136, 153, 163, 176n6
njoka 161, 162
normalization 140, 173

Nyamnjoh, Francis B. 25, 29, 30, 172–173
nyangas 126

occult economies 6–7, 20n5, 26, 39n1, 40n7, 181, 193; belief in 65, 72n5; commodification of human beings 153, 162; universities as 7
Olssen, Mark 18, 40n3, 43, 44, 55n12, 62, 63, 68, 77, 82, 86–87, 108, 124n2, 130, 153
Olukoshi, Abedayo 54n5, 62, 168, 184
Open Stellenbosch movement 86, 195n2
Organisation for Economic Co-operation and Development (OECD) 44, 62
organogram 94, 96, 117, 118, 150
Orr, Liesl 21, 22, 54n1, 81, 116, 130, 133, 167, 180, 184
outcomes 68, 81, 108, 149–150, 166
outputs 54n5, 68, 77, 82, 103, 132, 133, 134, 170, 183, 185, 196n6; measurable 77, 169–170; research 54n4, 132–134, 183, 185, 196n6; term 82
outsourcing 22, 159, 160n7
#Outsourcing Must Fall 160n7, 190
Ozga, Jenny 2, 28, 40n2, 60, 95, 108, 113, 115, 128, 134

panopticon 83, 123, 178
Parker, Martin 34, 44, 47, 72n2, 75, 77, 79, 84, 85, 91n11, 135, 144, 146, 147, 186n2
Pat Roberts Intelligence Scholars Program 166
Pels, Peter 1, 3, 26, 39, 100, 104, 144, 147, 178, 188
Pendlebury, James 54n4, 78, 167, 179
performance 103, 108, 109, 170; audits and 108, 110–112; managerial performances 118–120; neoliberal ethos 109; obsession with 106; performance and ritual: relationship 109–111; performativity, terror of 108; power and control 113–116; proper procedure 106, 116; risks of 120–122; role-playing 76, 110, 113, 120; settings 118; subversion and contradictions 122–123; symbolic items and iconography 118; symbolic performances 67, 111–112; term 98, 99; theatrical aspects 117–120; see also panopticon; ritual

performance indicators 22, 40n2, 82, 103, 108–109, 147; competitive 131; obscure political and ideological agendas 116
performance management 5, 78, 81, 82, 108–109, 112, 115–116, 123, 152
performance measurement 68, 77, 81, 82, 85, 108, 109, 112, 115, 123n2, 124n4, 125, 135, 152, 169
performance monitoring 68, 75, 78, 81, 82, 108, 110–112, 128
perks 33, 48, 135, 139, 145
Personal Development Plans 82, 112
Peters, Michael A. 18, 40n3, 43, 44, 55n12, 62, 63, 68, 77, 82, 86–87, 108, 116, 124n2, 130, 153
Peters, Tom 22, 24, 44, 47, 99, 126, 147
Poverty Reduction Strategy Papers 184; *see also* structural adjustment
Power, Michael 68, 72n6, 80–81, 91n3, 110, 111, 112
PowerPoint 118, 125
precariat: academics as 168–169; and neoliberalism 168
presenteeism 170
Preston, Peter 36
private-for-profit universities 10–11
protests staff 49, 89; student 48, 54n4, 86, 89, 160n7; unemployed graduates 64; *see also* #Fees Must Fall; #Outsourcing Must Fall
punishment 75, 77–78, 84, 85, 126, 136, 175, 178, 184

quality 82, 98, 99, 100, 101, 103, 108, 113; assessments 22, 46, 110; Assurance 5, 57, 82, 83, 102, 112, 115, 123, 139; and audit culture 110; mystical aspects of 102–103, 126; neoliberalism and 99, 102; pressures of 52, 182; quality management boom 126; and quantity 103; symbolic 101–102; weasel-word 102; *see also* calculability; corporate power words; *désexcellence;* mantras; Slow Science Manifesto

Ramphele, Mamphela 8, 45, 60
rankings 9, 10, 28, 82, 103, 109, 131, 132, 133, 134, 135, 181, 195n6; fetishism of 135; *see also* competition; league tables; ratings
ratings 103, 109, 131, 132, 134; *see also* competition; league tables; rankings

rationalisation 2, 22, 103, 156, 180; concept of 179; irrationality of 179; massification and 54n4; process of 23; term 177
Readings, Bill 61, 99–101, 182, 192
Reconstruction and Development Programme (RDP) 55n13
Recovery, concept of 195n5
Reed, Mike 40n3, 60, 68, 81, 127, 130, 136, 169, 170, 171, 179
Research Assessment Exercises (RAEs) 119, 178
Research Excellence Frameworks (REFs) 119
retrenchment 72, 74, 78, 80, 87, 90, 155; and corporate loyalty 86, 147; as euphemism 177; staff as expendable 153; terror of 169; threats of 52, 78, 87, 157, 167, 169, 174
ritual/rituals: corporate jargon 97–107, 177–181; of degradation 87–89; expressive rituals 111–112; language of 103; managing insecurity 92–94; ordeals 13–14, 80; reform and rites of renewal 94–95; repetition 97, 98, 100, 106; routinisation 106; rules 106, 116–117; status quo and 96–97; of verification 111; *see also* cargo cults; excellence; mantras; mission statements; performance; quality; team-building; templates
Ritzer, George 23–24, 45, 103, 156, 179, 180
Russell Group 9, 89
Ruth, Damian 77, 82, 112, 113, 117, 123n2, 137, 141n6, 167
Ryan, Desmond 20n7, 79, 185

sacrifices: academic collegiality 163–164; academic ethos 166–167; blood 138, 160n3, 161–163; ethical 164, 167; *see also* Faustus, Faustian pact; Mami Wata; mamlambo
salaries: disparity 48, 55n10, 135, 139, 154, 160n5, 169; low 47, 49, 136, 169, 170; secrecy 78, 145
Sanders, Todd 2, 7, 26, 29, 30, 133
Saunders, Malcolm 72n2, 168, 171
Schieffelin, Edward L. 96, 103, 105, 111
Scholars in the Marketplace 18
In Search of Excellence 99, 126, 147
secrecy 5, 84, 142–145; concealment and 142; publicity and 144, 147; revelation and 178; self-promotion and 144–145

Index

Shattock, Michael 22, 40n3, 47, 54n4
Shaw, Rosalind 6, 153, 160n3
Shore, Chris 68, 80–81, 86, 99, 108, 110, 112, 124n2, 128, 131, 136, 140, 142, 147–148, 157, 177–178, 184, 192
Slow Science Academy 191
Slow Science Manifesto 191
South Africa, universities in 17–18, 50–53
South African Defence Force 88, 91n10
Southall, Roger 20n7, 60, 75, 78, 85, 102–103, 138, 145, 146, 167, 169
spin doctors 66, 85, 110, 126
spinning: fantasy associations 66–67
spiritual resources 158
Spitting Images 194
Standing, Guy 45, 60, 79, 156, 168–169, 190, 192
Starving the Beast 47, 187n6
Stewart, Peter 8, 107n3, 113, 115, 123n2, 131, 155, 167, 169
Stiglitz, Joseph 33, 40n10–11, 160n5
structural adjustment 32, 47, 65, 184
Sundiata 12
surveillance 75, 81–85, 115, 166, 169; *see also* performance monitoring

Tambiah, Stanley Jeyaraja 71, 106, 113, 114
targets 75, 81, 102, 109, 123; failure to meet 76, 78; mercantile nature of 68
Taussig, Michael 35, 37, 93, 142, 155
Teaching and Learning Centres 5, 139–140
Teaching Quality Assessments 184
team-building 57–58, 95, 98, 128
templates 5, 105–108, 111, 113, 116–117, 140
Thatcher, Margaret 20n6–7, 47, 60, 65, 68, 79, 107n2, 182, 194
Thornton, Margaret 19n2, 67, 76, 77, 81, 83, 138, 168
Tolkien, J. R. R. 84, 195n5
transparency 83, 99, 108, 145, 149, 178
Trice, Harrison M. 57, 59, 87, 88, 93–95, 110, 117, 118, 120, 128

ukuthwala 26, 40n9, 144, 161, 162, 167, 172, 174, 176n6, 186, 187n10
Unholy Trinity, Chang's 43, 54n1
United Nations Sustainable Development goals 183

Universities in the Marketplace 18
university/universities: academic limitations and transformation 14–19; disparities 9–11, 52, 131, 133, 183; occult aspects of traditional 11–14, 93; private 10–11; self-styled corporate 10; South African universities 50–53; term 1–2; types of 9–11; *see also* corporate university; market, market university
utilitarianism: Ure 155, 177

Vale, Peter 20n7, 36
Vally, Salim 25, 129, 130
value for money (VFM) 80, 99, 104, 192
van den Berg, John 85, 145
van der Walt, Lucien 54n4, 78, 167, 179

Wallis, Malcolm 68, 72n6
Waterman, Robert H. 99, 126, 147
wealth-giving magic *see chikwambo*; Khotso; Mami Wata; *mamlambo*; *njoka*; occult economies; *ukuthwala*
Weber, Max 39, 98
Webster, Eddie 8, 75, 91n3, 158, 167–171, 176n3
White, Luise 40n8, 59, 160n3
Wilson, Monica Hunter 161
Wilson, Tom 1, 54n3, 55n8, 79, 127, 130
wind money 186; *see also* money
witchcraft: accumulation and deprivation 135–136; belief in 53; consumption 138, 171; jealousy 129, 133, 139; kinship and 127–129; of labour 154; malevolence of 136–139; practices 163; rumours of 31; selfishness and greed 133–135; term 6–7; of wealth 6, 30–31, 154; witchfinding 126–127; *see also* competition; consumption; familiars; mamlambo
Wits Enterprise 36, 61
Wood, R. J. 50, 56n15
World Bank 18, 28, 32, 35, 45, 50, 62, 64, 80, 181, 184, 185, 187n7; Unholy Trinity 43, 54n1; World Bank thinking 89; *see also* International Monetary Fund (IMF); World Trade Organisation (WTO)

world class 98, 99, 100, 130, 180
World Trade Organisation (WTO) 28, 35, 50, 62; Unholy Trinity 43, 54n1; *see also* International Monetary Fund (IMF); World Bank
Wright, Susan 68, 80–81, 86, 99, 108, 110, 112, 124n2, 128, 131, 136, 140, 142, 147–148, 157, 177–178, 184, 192

Zeleza, Paul Tiyambe 54n5, 62, 75, 168, 184
zombies 6, 7, 161; academia 153–160; auditable bodies 157; as human resources 153–155; instruments of labour 155–158; outsourcing 159; as western-related witchcraft 160n4; zombification 173, 192; *see also* emotional labour; spiritual resources